I0110325

Sanctuary Making

Sanctuary Making

IMMIGRANT FAMILIES RESHAPING
GEOGRAPHIES OF DEPORTABILITY

Carolina Valdivia

UNIVERSITY OF CALIFORNIA PRESS

University of California Press
Oakland, California

© 2026 by Carolina Valdivia

All rights reserved.

Library of Congress Cataloging-in-Publication Data

Names: Valdivia, Carolina author
Title: Sanctuary making : immigrant families reshaping geographies of
    deportability / Carolina Valdivia.
Description: Oakland, California : University of California Press, [2026] |
    Includes bibliographical references and index.
Identifiers: LCCN 2025042769 (print) | LCCN 2025042770 (ebook)
    | ISBN 9780520426511 cloth | ISBN 9780520426528 paperback |
    ISBN 9780520426535 epub
Subjects: LCSH: Noncitizens—United States—Social conditions |
    Immigration enforcement—United States | Adult children of
    immigrants—United States—Social conditions | Immigrant youth—
    United States—Social conditions | Immigrant families—United States—
    Social conditions
Classification: LCC JV6475.V53 2026 (print) | LCC JV6475 (ebook)
LC record available at https://lccn.loc.gov/2025042769
LC ebook record available at https://lccn.loc.gov/2025042770

GPSR Authorized Representative: Easy Access System Europe,
Mustamäe tee 50, 10621 Tallinn, Estonia, gpsr.requests@easproject.com

35   34   33   32   31   30   29   28   27   26
10   9   8   7   6   5   4   3   2   1

Para mi papá y mamá,
por todo lo que sacrificaron

CONTENTS

ILLUSTRATIONS

FIGURES

TABLE

ACKNOWLEDGMENTS

I am first and foremost grateful to the young adults and families I spoke to over the course of this research. Thank you for trusting me. I am grateful for the opportunity to learn about and share your stories, which are above all a testament of your sacrifice, care, and perseverance.

A very special thank you to Marisol Clark-Ibañez for your mentorship, encouragement, advocacy, and contagious sense of hope. Over the years you have poured in much of your time and energy to guide so many of us through our educational trajectories and professional endeavors. I am in both awe and gratitude for the type of mentor, collaborator, educator, and person that you are.

I began this project as a doctoral student at Harvard and am deeply grateful to my dissertation committee for their expertise and mentorship. Roberto Gonzales, thank you for the many doors you have opened and for your guidance at each step of the way. I appreciate your invaluable advice and unwavering support through the ups and downs of graduate school and beyond. Natasha Warikoo, thank you for your in-depth feedback during various stages—reviewing outlines, interview materials, and drafts of my dissertation—I appreciate the time and care with which you provided guidance. David Carrasco, you always encouraged me to dig deeper into the data and my experiences. Your guidance made this project both more meaningful and empowering. Tanya Golash-Boza, your insights on U.S. enforcement practices and the consequences of deportation helped shape the kinds of questions I asked, informed my approach to recruitment and interviews, and encouraged me to broaden the scope of my analysis.

To Shannon Gleeson, Walter Nicholls, and Monica Varsanyi, thank you for reviewing a full draft of the manuscript. Your encouragement and feedback were crucial for deepening the analysis and moving the project forward. To Cecilia Menjívar, thank you for serving as my mentor for the UC President's Postdoctoral Fellowship. I am grateful for the time you devoted to reviewing multiple outlines and an earlier draft of the manuscript, including the new chapters I would send you almost every month. I benefited tremendously from your expertise and guidance.

To David S. FitzGerald and Lisa Garcia Bedolla, thank you both for serving as my mentors for the Center of U.S.-Mexican Studies fellowship at UC San Diego and the UCHRI Scholars Program, respectively. I am grateful for your insights on my work and for your mentorship during the final stages of my doctoral studies and my transition into my first faculty job. Thank you to Tom K. Wong, Jill Esbenshade, and Jung Choi for providing invaluable research and teaching opportunities at an early stage, which further solidified my interest in academia.

To Leisy J. Abrego and Genevieve Negrón-Gonzales, thank you for the opportunity to contribute a chapter to *We Are Not Dreamers* (Duke University Press, 2020). Both of you carved out a unique space where fellow contributors and I could deepen our analysis and communicate key findings from our work—all the while allowing us to build community with one another and find joy through the writing process. Relatedly, I am grateful to have built a sense of community with Lucy León and Katy Maldonado Dominguez through our collaborations, conversations, and reflections about navigating academia.

Thank you to Kevin Escudero, Edelina Burciaga, Andrea Flores, Joanna Perez, and Lisa M. Martinez for your guidance and mentorship during earlier stages of this work. Our collaborations and discussions helped me solidify much of my earlier thinking about the geographies of deportability.

Thank you to my colleagues at UCI, including Susan Coutin, Val Jenness, Sora Han, Lee Cabatingan, Irene Vega, Kristin Turney, and Gustavo Carlo for your mentorship. To Ana Muñiz and Naomi Sugie, thank you both for your unwavering support and guidance. Thank you to my chair, Emily Owens, and Dean Jon Gould for your steady encouragement and for providing key resources.

To the students I have had the opportunity to work closely with at UC Irvine—Josefina Espino, Danielle Puretz, Angie Monreal, Isabel Patten, Evelyn Jimenez, Luis Gutierrez, Elliott Alvarado, Maria Calva, and Angel Parra—thank you for reading parts of the book, meeting to discuss related work, and reviewing some of the transcripts. I am also grateful to Jairo

León, Deysi Merino, Jose Ruiz, and Gladys Guzman for your research assistance during early stages of this work, including reading select chapters and quotes.

A very special thank you to Eva D. Leon for your friendship over the years and the care with which you create meaningful art for the immigrant community. To Yera, Gina, Deysi, Esther, Naza, Liz, Flor, Maria, and Vivi, thank you for not only cheering me on and supporting my work, but also reminding me to pause and enjoy every stage of life. I am grateful for your friendship. To Rita Guerra, Mike Castro, Alberto Ribas-Casasayas, Roberto, and Olga, thank you for believing in my potential, supporting me through critical moments, and imparting lifelong lessons along the way.

I am also thankful to the many friends, colleagues, students, educators, counselors, staff, and organizers whom I have gotten to know over the years through this book and related work with the UndocuResearch and UndocuBasic Needs projects, and the My Undocumented Life online platform I founded in 2011. This includes Amie Scully, Luke Lara, Susan Miller, Angela Garcia, Caitlin Patler, Silvia Rodriguez Vega, Stephanie Canizales, Diana Camilo, Keisha Goosby, Samantha Prado, Caroline Theiss, Nydia Ramirez, Fredi Garcia, Maribel Solache, Angela Chen, Alberto Ledesma, Milena Melo, Daysi Diaz-Strong, Rafael Martinez, Ireri Rivas, Marisa Salinas, Xuan Santos, Iliana Perez, Denisse Rojas, Angie Bautista-Chavez, Renata Mauriz, Cynthia Carvajal, Ben Roth, Elizabeth Kennedy, Norma Torres, Diana Giron, Alfredo Garcia, Alejandra, Ana, Angelica, Angie, April, Armando, Brenda, Carlos, Carolina, Celeste, Christina, Daniela, Dahana, Daphne, David, Diana, Diya, Dulce, Gloria, Kenia, Jonathan, Jorge, Juan, Juana, Ismael, Laura, Lilibeth, Lucas, Maira, Marilyn, Nery, Norma, Oswaldo, Patricia, Paulina, Perla, Ramon, Robert, Rocio, Rossana, Salvador, Sarai, Selina, Sonia, Sussana, Xiomara, and Yazmin. Many of you helped spread the word about my work (including recruitment flyers), invited me to speak at events, shared your experiences and advice, and supported my trajectory in other ways; thank you.

I am grateful for the funding I received for this work from the UC President's Fellowship program, UC Humanities Research Institute, Ford Foundation, Chancellor's Inclusive Excellence office at UC Irvine, Society for the Study of Social Problems, Weatherhead Center for International Affairs at Harvard, National Research Center in Hispanic Children & Families, and the Center for U.S.-Mexican Studies at UC San Diego. Some of the participants' quotes and descriptions featured in this book previously appeared in articles published in *Law & Policy* (2019), *Harvard Educational Review* (2021), the *Journal of Ethnic and Migration Studies* (2022), and a book chapter on *We Are Not Dreamers* (Duke University Press, 2020).

To Naomi Schneider, alongside the editorial and production teams, at UC Press, thank you for believing in and supporting this work through the multiple stages of peer review and production. I am grateful to have found a great press and editorial team.

Megan Pugh, Shanon Fitzpatrick, and Greta Alquist, thank you for reviewing earlier chapters. I appreciate your insights and feedback, which were particularly helpful whenever I felt stuck in the writing process.

To my parents, Javier and Guadalupe, thank you for the many sacrifices you made—from making the difficult decision to immigrate, raising us, and dedicating long working days and nights to provide for us. *Sus sacrificios no fueron en vano.* To my siblings, Diana and Daniel, thank you for your unconditional love and support.

To my husband, Roberto, words cannot possibly capture my gratitude. You have been patient, encouraging, and comforting at each stage of this work—long before I even conceptualized my dissertation topic, through data collection and writing. You wore many hats during this long process and eagerly continued to support me; thank you. To my son, you kept me company during the dissertation and book writing process, always patient and eager to help as you grew older. I cannot wait to read your books. To my daughter, you not only reminded me to keep working steadily to meet my book deadlines, but most importantly, you made us so excited for your arrival. Both of you fill me with pride, joy, and inspiration each day.

ONE

Enforcement in the Shadows

"THEY TOOK DAD" were the only words that Damián Aguilar could hear through the phone when his younger brother, Julián, called him in tears.[1] As he rushed home from work, Damián immediately thought of the worst-case scenario: their father, Gabriel, had been either kidnapped or taken by Immigration and Customs Enforcement (ICE) officers.

Earlier that morning, Gabriel's phone rang. It was his employer, asking if he could come in to clean the restaurant because an inspection was scheduled for later that day. It was supposed to be his day off, but without hesitation, Gabriel agreed. Before leaving, he gently woke up his wife, Monica, to let her know about the sudden change of plans. Usually she would wake up with him to prepare his lunch, then go back to sleep for a little longer. But today she decided to start her day once he left. As she got ready, there was a knock at her bedroom door. It was her youngest son, Julián. He said, "Mom, a guy in the front door is looking for you. He said someone stole my dad's car." Monica was confused. Gabriel had just left for work. If something had happened to his car, he would have told her. "Tell him I'll be there in a few minutes," she said. As she finished getting ready, she glanced out the window overlooking the street where Gabriel had parked. His car was still there. A few moments later, Julián returned, his expression more troubled. "This man really wants to talk to you. Now." Monica shook her head, confused. "But the car is outside. I can see it from the window." Julián hesitated, then said, "ICE took my dad."

Later that morning a neighbor came to tell Monica what had happened. Her daughters were driving away from the house when they saw several men surround Gabriel as he was getting into his car. Monica pieced together this information and concluded that the men were undercover immigration officers. She later learned from Gabriel that one of the agents had asked him for his driver's license and proof of legal status. As a father of two who is undocumented and lives in the state of California, Gabriel had a driver's license, but he could not provide the latter.[2] The officers proceeded to hand-cuff Gabriel and placed him in a van with other people who had been arrested that same morning. Gabriel's blue truck remained parked outside his home, with his lunch box and other belongings inside it—a troubling sign of how abruptly he was taken.

Overnight the Aguilar family struggled financially as they grappled with Gabriel's sudden absence. Their household income of $16,000 per year was immediately cut in half now that Gabriel was inside a detention center. Damián, who was 21 years old at the time, began searching for a better-paying job. His mother, Monica, was already busy with her work cleaning homes but now began selling homemade food to neighbors to make up for the lost household income.

Their health also deteriorated. Damián stayed awake most nights as he mentally prepared for a future in which his family might be separated indefinitely. Monica's blood pressure dropped drastically, and she also had trouble sleeping. She was exhausted most nights but was unable to get much rest. Her mind kept racing with memories of the family's last few days together before the arrest, memories that were now painful to recollect. Julián, who was only in high school at the time, was similarly saddened and worried. Inside the detention center, Gabriel struggled to eat and rest. He lost more than 20 pounds within just a few weeks.

I first met the Aguilar family through a mutual acquaintance who knew about my research project on the effects that undocumented and mixed-status families experience under the threat of deportation and when actual deportations take place. (In mixed-status families, at least one member is undocumented, while another has some form of legal status.) After this acquaintance mentioned my project to Monica, and with her permission, she forwarded Monica's contact information to me so that I could reach out to her to schedule an interview. At that point, Monica's husband had spent close to three months inside the detention facility. We planned to meet on Monica's only day off from work to discuss how Gabriel's detention was affecting their family.

When I arrived at their house, Julián answered the door, greeted me, and called his mother. Monica soon came downstairs. We sat on the couch, and within the first few minutes of my visit, Monica said, "*lo deportaron anoche* [they deported him last night]," and broke down in tears. *"Lo siento* [I'm sorry]," were the only words I could muster at the time.

I met with Monica for three and a half hours that afternoon. In the years that followed, I had several conversations with Monica and her sons as they tried to piece together what had led to Gabriel's arrest and subsequent deportation.[3] The Aguilar family knew that ICE had a record of Gabriel's first deportation from more than two decades ago. Back then, U.S. Customs and Border Protection (CBP) officers had arrested him during his initial attempt to cross the U.S.-Mexico border without legal authorization. Many of the family's questions, however, remained unanswered. Why was ICE targeting Gabriel now? Almost two decades had passed since his first deportation. He also did not have any previous encounters with law enforcement that might have flagged him. How did ICE know where he lived and what he looked like? How did they know what time he left for work and what car he drove? If they had spied on him to collect this information, for how long had they done so, and what other private details did they gather? Equally concerning was the now palpable threat that ICE could return to their home to arrest Monica, who was also undocumented. Monica grew fearful in her own home and unsure whom to trust, worried she might be reported to immigration authorities. The Aguilar family was also contending with a difficult decision: Should they attempt to reunite in the U.S. or remain separated? Gabriel was eager to return to the U.S. to reunite with his wife and sons. However, his only option was to return clandestinely. This would put him at risk for immediate deportation, a permanent bar to legal status, and the loss of any chance for family reunification. He also faced the danger of injury or death, as CBP's expanded "prevention through deterrence" strategies push migrants into remote, hazardous terrains.[4]

As the oldest of two children and a participant in the Deferred Action for Childhood Arrivals (DACA) program, Damián dedicated substantial time and energy to supporting his family during this tumultuous period.[5] He was only five days away from moving out on his own when his father's arrest ultimately compelled him to postpone his decision. Instead, Damián increased his financial contributions to cover a greater share of the household's expenses, including rent, utilities, and groceries. He also became especially concerned about his family's well-being. Damián reassured his mother that if she needed to move to Tijuana to live with their father, he would understand. Damián explained: "They fought so hard to be together. His family was not very keen to them being together and they didn't care. There was a lot of family problems because of it, and they managed to get through all that and you know, just this happens." To keep the family united across borders, Damián prepared for a future in which his parents would reunite in Tijuana, while he became the sole caretaker of his younger brother in San Diego.

For more than two decades, I have witnessed firsthand the hardships that young adults like Damián and their families encounter, both through research and personal experience. I have met many families who were forcefully separated by an immigration arrest, detention, or deportation. Others remain haunted by the very specter of deportation. They carry out their daily routines fearing that at any moment a loved one or they themselves could be apprehended by ICE or CBP. Still others are contending with the compounding effects of a family member's detention or deportation and another's vulnerability to being detected.[6] Their stories reflect those of the more than 23.8 million people across the U.S. who are directly affected by immigration policies and enforcement as members of undocumented and mixed-status households.[7] Many of them have lived in the U.S. for more than a decade and as such have formed strong ties in their local communities, schools, work, and homes. They are contributing to the federal, state, and local governments through taxes.[8] They are performing essential labor across industries, often at higher rates than the native born.[9] As such, their stories are about the fabric of the nation, about how communities strive to function and are torn apart.

Scholars of immigration and education have long sought to understand the lived experiences of young adults who migrate to the U.S. before the age of 12 and grow up undocumented (the 1.5 generation) or those who are born in the U.S. to immigrant parents (the 2nd generation).[10] For undocumented young adults, the lack of legal status is thought to function as a type of "master status"—a condition that dominates and overwhelms all other aspects of identity, constraining educational opportunities, career paths, and access to essential resources.[11] However, the central role that immigration enforcement plays—both in the background and foreground—in shaping how people's master status is fully articulated remains undertheorized in existing research. I show how one's master status not only functions as a barrier to securing employment, educational opportunities, and public provisions, but actually plays a much more expansive role that includes the reconfiguration of the structure and dynamics of the family. From an early age, children in undocumented and mixed-status families develop a heightened awareness of the ever-present threat of deportation as they navigate different spaces in their communities. Over time, they adjust their identities and family roles—either to protect their loved ones in a challenging environment or in response to the arrest of a family member. I trace how the destabilizing impact of interior enforcement shifts responsibilities among young adults within their families, particularly in relation to their undocumented parents, leading to overburdened roles, missed opportunities, derailed trajectories, and significant emotional burdens. By tracing how enforcement operates through intimate familial relations across different places, I recenter it as a constitutive axis of young adults' master status, extending its impact relationally and spatially. This conceptualization foregrounds the embodied and emotional labor of living under the constant specter of enforcement.

To capture this reality, I have developed an overarching conceptual framework—the geographies of deportability—that maps the threat of deportation onto evolving social and physical geographies. I demonstrate how changes in interior enforcement practices have implicated a new set of actors such as employers, police officers, and estranged neighbors (social geographies) who extend immigration efforts into public and private places (physical geographies). I trace these evolving geographies of deportability to changes in U.S. immigration policy and practices that have been unfolding since the latter part of the 20th century. I find that enforcement is increasingly expanding beyond traditional sites of enforcement such as the physical U.S.-Mexico border, ports of entry, and federal immigration checkpoints to nontraditional sites such as public roads, worksites, ethnic grocery stores, and even homes. As the geographies of deportability expand and intensify, families are compelled to constantly restructure important aspects of their lives. Their protective efforts exemplify what I refer to as "sanctuary making," which I define as the collective, socioemotional process through which families stake a claim to the spaces that they inhabit by cocreating a sense of safety, protection, and belonging in ways that allow them to better circumvent and contest the geographies of deportability. At the heart of families' sanctuary making efforts is the emotional and material labor of young adults. They must assume parental responsibilities as needed ("backup parents"), act as primary sources of emotional support for family members ("emotional anchors"), and broker legal processes as they pertain to their family's immigration case ("legal brokers").

Families experience and respond to the geographies of deportability in varying ways, depending in large part on what I define as their "enforcement status." This status refers to an individual's position within the spectrum of enforcement, which ranges with increasing vulnerability from being un-documented and living under the threat of deportation at one end, to un-dergoing a detention, deportation, or reentry at the other. The concerns and burdens ascribed to an individual's enforcement status extend to the entire family, affecting its collective standing. I refer to the family's collective sta-tus as simply the "family's enforcement status." A family whose enforcement status falls under the more extreme end tends to face a greater set of cumula-tive challenges and consequences. For example, families who have reunited in the U.S. after deportation have grave concerns about their loved one's de-portation records being accessed by government authorities and other insti-tutional agents. The stakes of navigating the geographies of deportability are especially high, as any encounter with immigration officers can result in in-carceration, deportation, and a permanent bar on status adjustment for un-documented returnees. Under these circumstances, the burden placed on a returnee extends beyond the individual to the entire family, even when some members are U.S. citizens. The fear of exposure makes families hesitant to share personal details about their loved one with others, including school personnel, hospital workers, and landlords. For young adults, the process of creating sanctuary shifts—which once may have involved advocating for their legal rights—becomes an exhausting effort to shield their loved one, requiring not only careful planning for their return but also the painful work of erasing traces of their existence from official and informal records. The decision to erase a loved one's presence from records is more than just a clerical task; it is a painful and often irreversible act driven by fear and ne-cessity. Families are forced not only to remove a returnee's information from documents but also to deny their existence to others across social and legal settings. This is not a choice made lightly; it carries immense regret, guilt, and emotional turmoil. These erasures also carry tangible consequences—for example, a young adult may receive reduced financial aid because their household income accounts for only three people, excluding the parent who returned after deportation. Ultimately, how families perceive and respond to the geographies of deportability tends to evolve over time depending on their enforcement status.

I also find that children in undocumented and mixed-status families—across different individual legal statuses (including U.S.-born citizens and green card holders) and family enforcement statuses—act as mediators be-tween the state and the family as a whole. Through this process of media-tion, children develop a unique legal consciousness that is both relational and spatial. This consciousness is deeply rooted in their awareness of their family's vulnerability within the geographies of deportability and their own sense of responsibility to protect them. The relational aspect reflects the emotional and protective bonds children feel toward their family members, especially as they become acutely aware of the precariousness of their loved ones' circumstances. The spatial dimension of this consciousness emerges from the varied risks posed by different physical and social geographies. For children navigating these spaces, the surrounding context profoundly influences their perceptions of safety and danger. As a result, children become hyperaware of their surroundings, learning to promptly assess and adapt to the risks inherent in the geographies of deportability. Over time, young adults' consciousness crystallizes and manifests in missed opportunities, chronic stress, and sacrifices that significantly change their life course, such as dropping out of school to help their families. Ultimately, I argue that interior enforcement inflicts growing levels of legal-spatial violence on young adults and their families by making unwelcome inroads into their communities and in turn regulating intimate parts of their personal lives.[12]

I believe that my conceptual framework—a matrix defined by geographies of deportability and sanctuary making—organically arises from our current era of enforcement. After all, this period of interior enforcement has been increasingly characterized by a more socially intrusive (a wider range of all sorts of actors have been deputized to play the role of immigration enforcement, from employers to police officers) and physically pervasive (there has been an increase in hot spots, from public roads and schools to grocery stores and people's homes) set of enforcement practices. Due to the increasingly *covert* nature of interior enforcement, I describe our current era as one of enforcement in the shadows. (I discuss this phenomenon in greater detail in the next section.)

The geographies of deportability that stem from this mode of enforcement extend beyond targeted individuals, creating collective and enduring consequences that, although mitigated by sanctuary making efforts, have costs we are only starting to understand. The shift of enforcement practices from the exterior to the interior has resulted in a shift of everyday responsibilities within the family, with young adults taking the lead in providing greater support for the family. I argue that my conceptual framework is uniquely positioned to reveal the full extent of the impact that enforcement in the shadows has had on restructuring the everyday lives of families, particularly from the perspective of young adults.

Changes in U.S. immigration policy and practices, namely through the expansion of immigration enforcement at the local level, the criminalization of immigration, and the increasing use of surveillance and technology, have given rise to what I refer to as the "era of enforcement in the shadows." This is an era that is defined by the expansion of immigration enforcement into everyday spaces and the enlistment of nontraditional actors, coupled with the covert use of surveillance and data exploitation to monitor and control immigrant families beyond traditional sites of enforcement. This context is crucial to understanding how young adults and their families respond to enforcement practices at the local level, which provides key insights into the geographies, costs, and possibilities of families' pursuits of collective safety.

In the era of enforcement in the shadows, immigration officers penetrate spaces of social reproduction: the settings that families must frequent to meet their essential needs, such as specific neighborhoods, ethnic grocery stores, worksites, and their homes. Officers also take cover, for example, by wearing plain clothing, relying on the police, accessing personal identifying information from utility databases, or waiting until dawn to conduct an arrest. This type of enforcement makes it even harder for the public to see and comprehend the true depths of families' suffering.

The era of enforcement in the shadows is characterized by (1) an expansion of enforcement that targets a broad array of places, such as homes, public roads, ethnic grocery stores, and worksites, transforming them into localized sites of control; (2) a wide-reaching approach that integrates a broad range of actors such as employers, social service providers, and police officers into the immigration enforcement apparatus, despite their fundamental roles being distinct from immigration enforcement; (3) an exploitation of nonimmigration databases to monitor families in the service of enforcing immigration law; and (4) an increase in covert surveillance, such as driving in unmarked vehicles and dressing in plain clothes to profile and monitor individuals. These tactics are in concert with long-standing efforts to criminalize and surveil immigrants, as others have documented.[13] Yet they also require a new conceptual framework—enforcement in the shadows—to account for the relatively recent, qualitative shifts in how immigration law is enforced on the ground, marked by growing opacity, expanded discretion, and the diffusion of enforcement into everyday spaces and relationships.

First, the scope of places that are associated with immigration enforcement has significantly expanded, subsequently leading to a heightened threat of apprehension. During the 19th century, a series of U.S. Supreme Court rulings confined immigration policy to the federal government,[14] and they subsequently contained matters of enforcement in federal settings like ports of entry along the U.S.-Mexico physical border, detention centers, and immigration courts. By the mid-1990s, however, the passage of the Illegal Immigration Reform and Immigrant Responsibility Act (IIRIRA), the Antiterrorism and Effective Death Penalty Act (AEDPA), and the Personal Responsibility and Work Opportunity Reconciliation Act (PRWORA) enabled states and cities to play a key role in enforcing matters of immigration. Since then, various state and local laws have been introduced to either expand or restrict undocumented immigrants' access to benefits, services, and opportunities.[15] This is a phenomenon typically referred to as "immigration federalism,"[16] though geographer and political scientist Monica Varsanyi and her colleagues reconceptualized the implementation of these changes at the local level as part of a broader "multilayered jurisdictional patchwork" to capture the often contradictory landscape of enforcement across the federal, state, and local levels.[17] This devolution of immigration law, from the federal to the state and local levels, has significantly altered the geography of enforcement.[18]

Today, immigration enforcement unfolds across police departments, jails, and worksites, among other settings. This is in part because of the introduction of programs such as E-Verify, Secure Communities, and 287(g) agreements. For example, E-Verify facilitates immigration officers' ability to ascertain individuals' legal status in many workplaces, either during the application process or once they are employed.[19] The program has its roots in the passage of the Immigration Reform and Control Act (IRCA) of 1986, which required for the first time that certain employers request evidence of work authorization.[20] Ten years later, IIRIRA introduced the use of three pilot programs: Basic Pilot, the Citizen Attestation Pilot, and the Machine-Readable Document Pilot. The Basic Pilot program compared information from an employee's I-9 form to information stored by the then Immigration and Naturalization Service (INS) and the Social Security Administration (SSA). The Basic Pilot program is the only one of the three that remains in use today by many employers and is more commonly known as E-Verify.[21] To be sure, not every employer uses E-Verify, though more than 800,000 worksites participate in the system nationwide.[22] The growing use of E-Verify shapes the landscape of enforcement by transforming the workplace into a key site of enforcement characterized by increased state presence.[23] As legal scholar Juliet Stumpf notes, the use of E-Verify has also created a new type of private relationship in which many employers now function as immigration law gatekeepers.[24] Although these are federal programs, they are implemented at the local level at worksites (in the case of E-Verify), law enforcement agencies (287g agreements), and state and local jails (Secure Communities) across the country. These practices in turn influence where and how immigration law is enforced at the local level,[25] and they have great implications for immigrants' ability to find work and exercise their legal rights.[26]

In the era of enforcement in the shadows, immigration officers are increasingly expanding their reach into public spaces (such as specific roads, neighborhoods, local parks, and public transportation centers), state government agencies (the Department of Motor Vehicles [DMV], the SSA, the Internal Revenue Service [IRS]), social service agencies (hospitals, community health clinics), worksites, commercial places (ethnic grocery and discount stores, swap meets), and specific apartment complexes in predominantly Latino neighborhoods.[27] This expansion impacts immigrant families' daily routines, well-being, and ability to feel safe. It also shapes the characteristics of those being targeted for deportation. As immigration enforcement penetrates private and intimate settings that are critical to immigrants' ability to meet their essential needs for housing, food, and employment, those who are primarily targeted by the era of enforcement in the shadows are likely to have strong ties in the U.S. with homes, communities, and forms of employment.

Second, and relatedly, immigration officers are increasingly relying on other social actors whose primary role is not to enforce immigration law—people whom I refer to as the "pseudo-migra."[28] They include employers; police officers; government employees; landlords; health-care workers; and at times estranged neighbors, former partners, and acquaintances.[29] Some of these actors may be motivated by discrimination, racism, abuse, and conflict to report to immigration authorities individuals suspected or confirmed to be undocumented.[30] As the landscape of enforcement expands through tactics of deceit, surveillance, and camouflage, it is also possible for individuals to unknowingly become implicated in the enforcement of immigration law.

Initially, the responsibility of enforcing immigration law fell solely to federal immigration officers. Over the years others, such as employers, police officers, county sheriffs, and more recently military officers, have also become implicated in the process of enforcing immigration laws. The passage of IRCA in 1986 marked the beginning of this growing trend toward the distribution of enforcement responsibilities onto other parties within the public and private realms by implicating employers in the enforcement of immigration law.[31] By introducing E-Verify into the workplace, IRCA required many employers to request and verify evidence of work authorization during the hiring process. This system not only mandated certain employers to screen for documentation status but also effectively integrated them into the enforcement apparatus. Whether employers actively utilize the information or not, the data they collect through E-Verify becomes part of a broader infrastructure that immigration officers can access. This connection allows enforcement agencies to use employer-collected data to conduct raids or target specific individuals, thereby significantly extending the reach of immigration enforcement into employment settings and enlisting employers as participants in the enforcement process. Similarly, police officers later became part of the pseudo-migra through initiatives such as 287(g) agreements, which enable state and local law enforcement officers to collaborate with immigration agencies. As of this writing, over 100 law enforcement agencies across 24 different states have some type of 287(g) agreement.[32] In general, police officers working in localities that have an active 287(g) agreement are authorized to interview individuals to ascertain their immigration status, check databases maintained by the Department of Homeland Security (DHS) for information about individuals, issue immigration detainers to hold individuals in jail until ICE takes custody, or enter data into ICE's database, among other powers.[33] This program and initiatives such as Secure Communities, the Criminal Alien Program, and the Priority Enforcement Program disproportionately target individuals with relatively minor criminal offenses or no criminal history.[34] In the process, the relationship between the police and local communities is harmed.[35] Relatedly, some have argued that the growing reliance on "private enforcement," such as when employers or landlords partake in the enforcement of immigration law, has the potential to reach into the realms of education, medical care, charity services, and private citizenship.[36]

While the enforcement of immigration law still largely falls under the purview of federal immigration authorities, the rise of the pseudo-migra is central to the workings of enforcement in the shadows. The range of social actors that immigrant families have come to associate with immigration enforcement has expanded to include other social actors whose primary role is not to enforce immigration law, but who nevertheless may be implicated in the process, such as landlords and social service providers.[37] Family members must not only determine whether a particular setting is safe or dangerous, but they must also decipher whether an individual is (or could become) part of the pseudo-migra. Thus, through the lens of young adults and their families, the landscape of enforcement consists of both the expansion of physical sites where the threat of deportation is heightened and the proliferation of social actors who might initiate the deportation process at a moment's notice.

Third, the infrastructure of today's enforcement apparatus has dramatically grown in ways that expand immigration officers' ability to monitor immigrants at the U.S.-Mexico physical border and beyond.[38] For the first few decades of its existence, the INS grew at a relatively slow rate, and by 2000, the agency had a total of 17,654 officers.[39] Its workforce now spans across three separate federal immigration agencies and consists of about 100,000 employees and contractors. This includes 19,000 workers employed by U.S. Citizenship and Immigration Services (USCIS).[40] It also includes 60,000 individuals working for CBP and 20,000 working for ICE.[41] Funding for these agencies has also grown drastically. ICE's annual budget has nearly tripled, from $3.3 billion in 2003 to $8.3 billion in 2021. In the span of 30 years, the annual budget of the CBP increased more than tenfold, from $299 million in 1991 to nearly $4.9 billion in 2021.[42] Its arsenal has also grown considerably over the years. Under the pretext of the "war on drugs" during the 1980s, the military began to provide immigration agencies with equipment such as infrared scopes and ground sensors, as well as training, ground troops, and aerial surveillance.[43] During Donald Trump's second presidential administration, more than 1,500 active-duty personnel from the U.S. Army and the U.S. Marine Corps were deployed to assist CBP in the enforcement of immigration law at the U.S.-Mexico physical border.[44] President Trump also ordered the expansion of a detention facility in Guantanamo Bay to hold as many as 30,000 migrants.[45]

As the infrastructure of the enforcement apparatus grows, so does its ability to monitor and surveil. Today, immigration officers rely on a complicated web of surveillance that consists of cloud-based services, databases, ankle monitors, and license plate readers, among other tools, to routinely collect, store, screen, and share information on noncitizens and citizens alike.[46] This is on a par with the growing use of surveillance and technology in the law enforcement context.[47] Immigration agencies also make use of data collected by other nonimmigration institutions and private companies to retrieve personal identifying information, such as an individual's home address, telephone number, transactions, and whereabouts. For example, a report by the Center on Privacy and Technology at Georgetown Law revealed that ICE purchased data collected from utility records through private data brokers to locate people for deportation proceedings.[48] What's more, a centralized government system run by DHS, known as the Automated Biometric Identification System (IDENT),[49] collects and stores individuals' biographic and biometric information, such as their photographs, fingerprints, and signatures.[50] Immigration officers also have access to other federal databases (such as GangNET, NCIC, and IAFIS), state government systems (DMV, CalGang), and even databases created by private companies (like CLEAR).[51] As the research of sociologist Ana Muñiz demonstrates, these initiatives have further blurred the lines between the criminal justice and immigration systems, expanded the number of people under surveillance, and created many more opportunities for officers to categorize noncitizens as criminals.[52]

In the era of enforcement in the shadows, immigrant families struggle to grasp the full extent of the information immigration officers have at their disposal. Even families directly impacted by a loved one's arrest are never made aware of the surveillance mechanisms used against them. This lack of transparency creates endless uncertainty about the type, range, and depth of information authorities may have on any given family. By keeping families in the dark, enforcement agencies compel them to navigate their past, present, and future through the lens of hypersurveillance—questioning every past interaction and remaining constantly vigilant in their current and future environments. With no definitive understanding of what might trigger enforcement actions, families must now anticipate and assess an endless array of hypothetical risks, continuously calculating every move and interaction to avoid unseen dangers.

The fourth and last characteristic of the era of enforcement in the shadows entails immigration officers' ability to hide in plain sight in part by dressing in regular clothing; driving unmarked vehicles; waiting until dawn or dusk to conduct arrests; and employing deceitful tactics, such as falsely claiming they are police officers.[53] Such approaches can seem quite distinct from border policing wherein the state's power to exclude is staged and made, as anthropologist Nicholas De Genova puts it, "spectacularly visible."[54] That staging includes the use of physical barriers such as walls, gates, fences, stadium lights, and cameras at ports of entry, as well as relentless images of roving patrols along the U.S.-Mexico physical border.[55] At the same time, CBP and ICE came under increased scrutiny in recent years as images of families forcefully separated or caged inside detention centers, along with troubling accounts of young children who died during increasingly dangerous migration journeys, circulated on traditional news media outlets and social media platforms.[56] Sociologist Irene Vega notes that such information challenges officers' moral authority, which compels them to construct what she refers to as "legitimation narratives" about the supposed criminality of immigrants.[57] In the meantime, away from the spectacle, immigration officers simultaneously adopt a type of camouflaged presence in their routine operations, both in the border region and across the country.

Consequently, enforcement practices can be said to unfold along a spectrum of (in)visibility on which at any given moment immigration officers may opt for maximum exhibition or ultimate disguise. The former has become the norm during presidential election cycles when the topic of immigration is front and center or following inauguration as part of a new administration's attempt to reassure the public that the "failing" immigration system is under "control." Such public displays of failure are necessary insofar as they serve as a pretext for additional enforcement spending—a point emphasized by other scholars who have noted how the spectacle of dysfunction justifies the expansion of punitive state capacities.[58] On most days, however, the routine operations of enforcement in the interior of the country are closer to invisibility. As a prime example, consider the behind-the-scenes manner in which information about noncitizens is collected, sold, and stored en masse by multiple private and public agencies for immigration enforcement purposes.[59] Ultimately, while undocumented immigrants have always "lived in the shadows" or led "shadowed lives" as a means of circumventing enforcement,[60] interior enforcement can be best described as occurring in the shadows, where it is arguably more effective in circumventing public scrutiny.

The era of enforcement in the shadows that these policies have ushered in, which is driving mass deportations today, facilitates immigration officers' ability to conduct arrests in a manner that is left largely unseen by the public. Instead, what the public is largely exposed to are carefully crafted narratives by the state about the presumed criminality of immigrants.[61] Covert enforcement tactics also allow immigration officers to conduct arrests on the ground relatively undisturbed and subsequently more swiftly. The concentration of enforcement activities in predominantly Latino communities over a sustained period also normalizes the presence of immigration officers in these neighborhoods. Finally, it forces families into a constant state of heightened awareness and risk calculation. The era of enforcement in the shadows communicates to young adults and their families that the threat of deportation is *everywhere* in their neighborhood—one must carefully consider every move and interaction.

EXPANDING GEOGRAPHIES OF DEPORTABILITY AND SANCTUARY MAKING

What happens to our understanding of the lived experiences of young adults when we center enforcement? In other words, what new insights can we gain, and how might these contribute to, complicate, or challenge previous conclusions? These are the questions that I initially set out to answer when working on this book. To address them, I examine how the immediacies and intimacies of young adults' everyday lives—at the level of perceptions, behaviors, routines, roles, aspirations, emotions, relationships, and responsibilities—are shaped by broader historical, structural, social, and legal processes that are embedded in space. This includes examining how deportability, and illegality more broadly, are produced, sustained, contested, and experienced across space and time.

Scholars typically use the term "illegality" to capture the set of policies and practices that create the sociolegal category of the undocumented, as well as to describe an individual's awareness of their lack of legal status and their experiences navigating the wide range of limitations and barriers associated with being undocumented.[62] A core aspect of illegality is what Nicholas De Genova termed "deportability," or the omnipresent threat of deportation.[63] The extent to which individuals experience the effects of illegality and deportability varies by their immigration status, age at migration, racial and ethnic background, gender, city and state of residence, skin color, and perceived (in)visibility to record-keeping institutions, among other factors.[64] The process through which this unfolds is widely believed to occur within shifting "contexts of reception," a term that refers to the policies and practices at the local, state, and federal levels that shape immigrants' trajectories.[65]

Despite great advances in our understanding of illegality and immigrant incorporation, scholars have generally dealt with space as an object that is static and neutral. It is an empty canvas on which policies simply unfold in ways that result in contexts that are either welcoming or hostile. Yet this conceptualization of space is limited and prevents us from fully capturing its dynamic function, including the mechanisms through which space can be both transformed and transformative, as geographers Henri Lefebvre, David Harvey, and others have argued.[66] Space can simultaneously derive its meaning from changes in the law and practices and shape consciousness and influence behavior.[67] Space is inherently relational; its meaning is continually reconstituted through social and political dynamics that encompass diverse interpretations, interactions, memories, and imaginaries.[68] Underlying everyday life is a dynamic process whereby various social actors are contesting the meaning of space in ways that intimately shape the distribution of resources and the consciousness of those who inhabit those spaces.[69] Moreover, space consists of the physical terrain that can be readily observed; the mental (or conceptual) representation of space; and what geographer Edward Soja conceptualized as "thirdspaces," a term that denotes both the material aspects of space and the subjective and emotional in ways that allow for a more nuanced understanding of how people experience and interpret the spaces they inhabit.[70] Understanding how an individual interacts with space—along with the memories, possibilities, emotions, and risks they associate with it—is essential, as these factors can significantly influence the meaning they attribute to particular settings and their experiences within them.[71] At any given moment there are different spatial contexts of sociolegal and emotional practices at work in which certain representations of space are prioritized over others. A dynamic and relational view of space is essential to account for the range of actors, laws, meanings, memories, emotions, possibilities, and interactions involved in the creation and transformative effects of space.

In today's era of enforcement in the shadows, I find that changes in U.S. immigration policies and practices are localizing deportability beyond sites traditionally associated with enforcement (like ports of entry, detention centers, and federal immigration checkpoints) and are instead increasingly permeating nontraditional sites (such as public roads, ethnic grocery stores, neighborhoods, and apartment complexes). This suggests a shift from the public to the private sphere of immigrants' lives. Families refer to these sites of significant enforcement activity as "hot spots." A setting may be transformed into a hot spot because there are sightings of immigration officers, news about an immigration arrest, or information about an immigration raid. Such events, whether rumored or confirmed as facts, alter the meaning that is associated with that particular site and create a ripple effect of fear and worry within immigrant households. The pseudo-migra can also transform an otherwise mundane setting into a hot spot through the enforcement of immigration law by proxy. For example, police officers transform public roads into hot spots when they patrol specific neighborhoods with frequency or when they set up driving under the influence (DUI) checkpoints. Even though these encounters are ostensibly about driving-related violations, such as driving under the influence, without a license, or over the speed limit, they nevertheless function as forms of immigration enforcement, as police officers can inquire about an individual's immigration status either at the time of the encounter or during processing (if the person is taken to jail).

The growing number of hot spots become coordinates across a shifting terrain of enforcement, or what I have been referring to as the geographies of deportability—the social, political, and physical sites produced by the law in which immigration enforcement is localized, thereby heightening undocumented immigrants' vulnerability to deportation.[72] In the era of enforcement in the shadows, we are seeing the expansion and intensification of the geographies of deportability such that families are becoming fearful not only of sites traditionally associated with enforcement (like the federal immigration checkpoints), but also of nontraditional sites like the surrounding public roads and neighborhoods. They are also becoming distrustful not only of immigration officers, but also of police officers, their neighbors, and their coworkers. As the threat of deportation increasingly permeates the most private and intimate settings of daily life, the geographies of deportability limit immigrants' physical mobility and undermine their ability to feel safe, create trusting relationships, and even rest.

By employing a sociological and geographical imagination,[73] we can render often invisible and seemingly random enforcement activities into an assessment that is more legible and subject to change. It can also help us gain a deeper understanding of young adults' everyday practices and their modes of relating to the social world around them, including the ways these reflect the dynamics underlying the geographies of deportability they (and their families) are embedded in and transforming. Indeed, families' responses to enforcement in the shadows and the geographies of deportability manifest in complex efforts to reclaim space and create sanctuary by reshaping family dynamics.

To make sanctuary, family members constantly shift their roles, responsibilities, and routines. It is a process of collective action whereby families define their relationship with the environments they live in and cocreate a sense of safety, protection, and belonging through intimate ties of trust, care, and mutual commitment. In the process, families are also charting new terrains away from hot spots through alternative living arrangements, routes, and routines where enforcement is seemingly out of reach. To some extent then, families are constructing their own geographies of sanctuary where they can cultivate a sense of safety and stability in the face of enforcement.

The idea of "sanctuary" in the immigration context can be traced back to the 1980s, when a network of religious organizations mobilized to aid migrants from El Salvador and Guatemala who were seeking asylum in the U.S.[74] At a time of growing anti-immigrant sentiment, churches played an important role in welcoming and providing shelter to those migrating and seeking asylum. Today, the term is often used to distinguish jurisdictions that limit cooperation between immigration and law enforcement. Generally, states like California are thought of as sanctuaries because of their efforts to be more inclusive of immigrants and limit the ability of law enforcement to assist immigration officers.[75] The term has also been extended to discussions about the role of schools in protecting and supporting undocumented students.[76] Sanctuary then is typically conceptualized as a form of protection, relief, safety, or support that is given—whether by the state, churches, or schools—to immigrant families. But I argue that people also work, as individuals and as families, to make sanctuary, via socioemotional and relational processes to stake a claim in the spaces they inhabit by creating a buffer against deportation, mitigating its effects, and nurturing a sense of security and belonging in the face of tremendous vulnerability.

Scholars of immigration have long documented the range of efforts that parents and children alike undertake to endure conditions of vulnerability and insecurity.[77] In the context of the threat of deportation, undocumented parents adopt strategies such as selective disclosure and engagement with institutions, whereby they are extra careful about the type of information they share with others.[78] Undocumented young adults are also strategic about the people they disclose their immigration status to when applying to college or for jobs.[79] A similar pattern emerges among parents and children following detention, deportation, or incarceration, whereby families more intently avoid record-keeping institutions.[80] Yet the experiences of families as they navigate the geographies of deportability reveal a deeper process: they are not merely managing risks but are actively shaping their spatial realities through their sanctuary making efforts, demonstrating agency in navigating and transforming the spaces they inhabit. Unlike conventional assessments of families' risk management and coping strategies, which focus on mitigating external threats, sanctuary making foregrounds the socioemotional process through which individuals actively shape their relationship to their environment through collective efforts. Central to this process are young adults, who not only navigate these challenges but also play pivotal roles—both materially and emotionally—in leading and sustaining their families' sanctuary making efforts.

As this book illustrates, many young adults are at the forefront of sanctuary making within their households. Young adults become "backup parents" by gradually assuming parental roles and responsibilities. This includes performing an increased number of household tasks such as cooking and cleaning, while also making greater financial contributions, caretaking, driving, and providing emotional support to younger siblings. Young adults also partake in "emotional anchoring" by learning how their family members are feeling and coping, then adopting responsibilities to support them.[81] For example, young adults may observe changes in their loved one's demeanor and proceed to dedicate more time to them to reduce their stress levels. Young adults also engage in "legal brokering" by mediating information related to the law between their parents and legal institutions (and actors).[82] By examining these changes, this book highlights young adults' attempts to chart new geographies of sanctuary for their families.

Sanctuary, then, is not solely determined by the state and is not just an outcome or a goalpost: it is also a process undertaken by young adults and their families as they exercise what agency they have, or can make, amid the changing geographies of deportability. At a time when those geographies are expanding and deepening, even within so-called sanctuary states like California, families are figuring out how to live with conditions of vulnerability. In this context, it becomes imperative to consider how families nurture their own sense of safety and protection through intimate ties of trust, sacrifice, shared responsibility, and mutual commitment. While sanctuary making primarily unfolds within the family—requiring ongoing adjustments to familial roles and responsibilities—external support from social service providers, school personnel, and immigrant rights organizers can play a crucial role in reinforcing these efforts and easing the burden on young adults. For example, organizers could set up alert systems to notify community members about confirmed sightings of immigration officers. Young adults could use these alerts to inform their parents about potential checkpoints or raids. This would allow them to quickly share verified information, saving significant time and effort. To this end, it is imperative to look at the core of families' sanctuary making efforts through the lens of young adults.

Because of their legal and social positionality, young adults are often not the official main targets of enforcement. Yet through the expanding geographies of deportability, enforcement in the shadows permeates the everyday rhythms of family life in ways that compel young adults to lead their families' sanctuary making efforts. Within the geographies of deportability, young adults are much more likely than their parents to have access to some type of legal protection, as DACA recipients, legal permanent residents, or U.S. citizens, which allows them to feel relatively safe from deportation when compared to their parents who are entirely undocumented. (Although not all young adults have some type of legal protection.) Young adults also perceive that immigration officers or the pseudo-migra are more likely to racially profile their parents and target them based on characteristics such as the type of car their parents drive, the language they speak in public, their skin color, and their occupation. As the geographies of deportability deepen and expand, their parents are also more frequently exposed across a greater number of spaces and durations. This includes during their commutes to and from work, while at work or running errands, and increasingly even at home where they live and strive to raise their children. Moreover, young adults with access to resources and networks both in and outside of the school setting are uniquely positioned to stay up to date with information about changes in U.S. immigration policy and enforcement practices. Such insights can be vital for knowing how to navigate the geographies of deportability, including whom to trust, which locations are relatively safe, when the risk of detection is most pronounced, and what type of services or forms of relief are available. Taken together, these circumstances compel young adults to familiarize themselves with the geographies of deportability and to lead their families' sanctuary making efforts.

Legal scholars have long examined how individuals' everyday encounters with the law shape their understanding of it, or what is known as their "legal consciousness."[83] Within the context of immigration law, prevailing discourse and legal restrictions cultivate a consciousness among undocumented young adults that is shaped by the stigma of realizing that, unlike their documented peers, they are legally barred from driving, working, or accessing federal financial aid, among other restricted rights and privileges.[84] Responsibility and privilege further inform this consciousness, particularly among documented young adults raised in mixed-status families, who often assume caregiving roles and act as translators on behalf of their undocumented parents.[85] Beyond stigma and responsibility, I find that fear and heightened vigilance also play a crucial role in shaping how young adults interpret the law, navigate their surroundings, form their identities, engage with social institutions, and assume roles within the household. As the threat of deportation increasingly permeates the most private and intimate dimensions of family life, young adults cultivate a heightened awareness of the spaces, social actors, processes, and symbols associated with enforcement. This awareness emerges in moments such as encountering police officers or orange cones at DUI checkpoints, responding to intrusive questions about their family's country of origin, or being asked to provide identification or a Social Security number in routine situations, such as applying for housing or employment. Within this environment, young adults internalize a sense of being "different," "excluded," and vulnerable, learning to remain perpetually alert to the conditions that might precipitate the most feared outcome: the deportation of their parents or themselves.

This point merits close attention, as young adults learn not only to identify immediate and overt threats—such as the presence of immigration officers or a DUI checkpoint—but also to cultivate a heightened sensitivity to the broader conditions that may give rise to worst-case scenarios. Within this context, they remain attuned to both tangible and imagined risks. For example, young adults may hesitate to pursue improved housing opportunities not because of definitive knowledge that a prospective landlord collaborates with immigration enforcement or that the apartment complex is a known hot spot, but because of an acute awareness of the structural vulnerabilities embedded in the housing process itself. Requirements such as having to provide identification, a Social Security number, or a credit score, or submitting to a background check, can potentially expose undocumented status and, in certain circumstances, prompt a landlord to alert authorities. These calculations reflect the realities of navigating the geographies of deportability, where the mundane becomes a site of risk.

Young adults also grapple with what a deportation represents in ways that challenge conventional understandings of it as merely a physical removal—the ultimate form of exclusion from their family, their community, and the nation-state. From their perspective, a deportation signifies a social loss: the absence of a loved one; the disruption of roles, responsibilities, and relationships within the family; prolonged separation; and the inability to benefit from their family's collective sacrifices. Taken together, these nuanced understandings of enforcement, along with the emotions and states of being that arise from the geographies of deportability and the restructuring of family life, reveal that the impact of deportation extends beyond its direct consequences. For young people, it entails profound socioemotional transformations they must navigate from an early age. Over time, these transformations can amount to a form of legal-spatial violence that threatens to derail young adults' trajectories.

THE REPRODUCTION OF LEGAL VIOLENCE THROUGH SPACE

The concept of legal violence draws attention to the harmful effects of the law, legal institutions, and legal practices. Sociologists Cecilia Menjívar and Leisy Abrego first introduced the concept to capture the often normalized but injurious effects of the law that have the potential to derail immigrants' incorporation trajectories in the U.S.[86] In their study of Central American immigrants living with tenuous legal statuses, Menjívar and Abrego observed that the immigration regime generates various forms of violence, particularly in light of the growing mergence between the immigration and criminal justice systems. This includes lengthy family separations and periods in which information about a loved one's whereabouts is scant both during the migration journey and in the aftermath of an immigration arrest. It also includes the fear and insecurity that families experience during their daily routines. Menjívar and Abrego contend that while not always physically harmful, the conditions that families must endure nevertheless generate suffering. Other immigration scholars have found the term useful for understanding immigrant women's exposure to sexual harassment in the workplace and undocumented workers' occupational injuries,[87] as well as the consequences of detention and deportation on entire families.[88]

Notably, scholars have largely conceptualized legal violence as a product of the law that is otherwise nonspatial.[89] That is, while scholars acknowledge that legal violence unfolds across different scenarios and settings, it is ultimately the product of the law, legal institutions, and legal practices. There has been very little mention of the central role that space plays in the production and reproduction of legal violence. Relatedly, the relationship between legal violence, space, and consciousness has remained undertheorized.

The experiences of young adults leading their families' sanctuary making efforts in the context of the geographies of deportability demonstrate that legal violence can be generated in and through space, shaping not only material conditions but also consciousness. It is through the strategic use of space that immigration officers create a hostile landscape of enforcement that compels young adults to prioritize their family's well-being and safety over their own in ways that can be detrimental to their mental health and trajectories. In the era of enforcement in the shadows, the state reappropriates the use of space to produce a palpable threat of deportation. For example, immigration officers may turn specific public roads or grocery stores into sites of enforcement by conducting a raid or a checkpoint. To do this, officers in part utilize objects that are typically associated with other meanings (such as orange cones or temporary traffic control signs, which are commonly used in construction) or that are otherwise deemed ordinary (such as white vans and SUVs with tinted windows) to blend the unordinary with the ordinary.

In this environment, young adults develop a heightened sensitivity to the dynamics that produce these sites of enforcement and the vast scope of tangible and hypothetical risks that exist out of these conditions. They become alert to their surroundings, recognizing that any place could turn into a hot spot. They also grow cautious of strangers and authority figures, aware that anyone could potentially be part of the pseudo-migra. They are mindful of the information they share, knowing it could be used to monitor and track their families. This heightened sensitivity is often a matter of survival, as family members need to be acutely cognizant of their surroundings and interactions to be able to circumvent direct encounters with immigration enforcement at a moment's notice. This way of relating to one's social world comes with profound psychosocial costs. Any resemblance to a site of enforcement, whether real or imagined, can often trigger young adults, limit their movement or opportunities, and engender a wide range of distressing emotional responses: anxiety, fear, and pain.

Young adults' experiences reveal the process through which the state generates legal forms of violence by transforming settings, actors, and objects into representations of immigration enforcement. It injects anguish and insecurity into the everyday lives of young adults and their family members in ways that intimately shape their perceptions, routines, behaviors, emotions, relationships, and aspirations. People continue to endure these transformations even after acquiring some type of legal protection (such as DACA or legal permanent residency) or in their countries of birth post-deportation. U.S.-born citizens also develop a consciousness like their undocumented relatives'. When we center space in our understanding of legal violence, we come to recognize that this landscape of enforcement facilitates the erosion of protections that are otherwise associated with DACA, legal permanent residency, or U.S. citizenship, such that it becomes possible for members of undocumented and mixed-status households to experience shared forms of legal-spatial violence in the short and long term, regardless of their individual immigration status.

Ultimately, the era of enforcement in the shadows facilitates exclusion and suffering that is both subtly undertaken and wide reaching. Immigration officers leave intact the obscene and grandiose border spectacle,[90] simultaneously transforming otherwise mundane settings, objects, processes, and actors into symbols of immigration enforcement in ways that become normalized yet remain injurious to young adults and their families. While this type of enforcement is widespread, its reach is most acutely visible and profoundly felt by those directly affected by illegality, including undocumented immigrants, deportees, formerly undocumented individuals, and their families. By this I do not mean that the public never sees or feels the consequences of enforcement; they occasionally do, through news media reports or books on immigration that reach mainstream culture. Rather, I make a distinction between seeing and feeling almost at a superficial level versus more sensitized ways of knowing and being that are keenly attuned to and influenced by the geographies of deportability.

THEORIZING UNDOCUMENTED LIFE THROUGH THE LENS OF THOSE DIRECTLY AFFECTED

This book is based on research and personal insights that span the course of more than two decades. Some of them stem from my own experiences: I had to navigate life while undocumented between 2001 and 2016.[91] Between 2017 and 2019, I conducted interviews with 103 members of undocumented and mixed-status families in California, most of them young adults who

TABLE 1 Summary of Participant Demographics

	All Participants	Alert Phase	Confinement Phase	Expulsion Phase	Reentry Phase
Number of respondents	103	29	22	24	28
Number of households	75	22	15	19	19
Number of family members					
Range	2–11	2–9	2–11	2–9	3–10
Mean	5.1	5	5.3	5.2	5.3
Immigration status					
Undocumented	19	6	1	3	9
DACA, TPS, U-Visa, or political asylum	44	19	11	6	8
Legal permanent resident	4	1	2	0	1
U.S. citizen	34	3	8	14	9
In Mexico postdeportation	2	–	–	1	1
Age					
Range	18–55	18–55	18–54	19–51	18–55
Median	25	23	25.5	28.5	23.5
Sex					
Female	79	25	18	17	19
Male	24	4	4	7	9

grew up in San Diego County. (See table 1 for a summary of participant demographics.) Throughout this book, all individuals' names have been replaced with pseudonyms to protect their confidentiality and privacy.[92] In cases where I interviewed multiple family members, I have assigned the same last name to participants from the same family. For all other individuals, only first names are used as pseudonyms. I have also replaced the names of participants' relatives, friends, and schools with pseudonyms. I spent additional time with some participants in their homes, churches, and schools and attended events geared toward supporting undocumented students or informing immigrants about their rights. I also conducted follow-up interviews with some participants. As someone who is deeply embedded in the networks I write about and study, I left the "field" but not the community, and my connections with some of the families are ongoing.

I interviewed undocumented immigrants, DACA recipients, legal permanent residents (some of whom identified as formerly undocumented), and U.S. citizens from mixed-status families. During this research, some respondents transitioned from being DACAmented to becoming legal permanent residents. Others became naturalized U.S. citizens. Most participants who were undocumented or DACAmented at the time of the interview, however, remained in those statuses even with the passage of time and new presidential administrations. The reality is that for many undocumented immigrants in the U.S., their status has become a fixed condition that they must endure for decades.[93] This is a direct consequence of immigration policies that have curtailed pathways to citizenship. Although politicians from the Democratic Party traditionally positioned themselves as advocates of immigration reform, it has been close to four decades since Congress last enacted legislation that provides a pathway to U.S. citizenship for undocumented immigrants.[94] Instead, we are witnessing a shift toward greater enforcement and a diminishing sense of protection among undocumented immigrants, green card holders, and U.S. citizens from racial minority backgrounds.[95]

I also interviewed individuals whose families occupy one of four different phases along the spectrum of enforcement. First is the alert phase, in which a member is aware of the threat of deportation but has never been arrested. Second is the confinement phase, in which a member is arrested and detained by immigration officers. During this phase, an individual may be released on bond or adjust their immigration status through marriage to a U.S. citizen or by other means. Alternatively, their case may be temporarily closed. In many cases, individuals who enter the confinement phase go on to the third phase, which is expulsion. During this phase, a member is deported and is forced to live outside of the U.S. The means through which the deportation occurred can vary; it may be through a "voluntary departure," wherein an individual signs a form waiving their rights to legal counsel or a formal deportation. Finally, the fourth phase is reentry, in which a member returns to the U.S. after deportation, either legally or clandestinely. Given the hardships associated with legal reentries, the latter is most often the case.[96]

Upon direct contact with the enforcement apparatus, an individual's immigration status may or may not change, but their position along the spectrum of enforcement drastically changes. For example, an individual may spend years living under the threat of deportation only to suddenly be taken into a detention center following an encounter with immigration officers. During this time, the individual is still undocumented, but their position along the spectrum has abruptly changed as their family transitions from the alert to the confinement phase. Such transitions are often marked by severe financial hardship, acute anxiety and depression, and increased avoidance of record-keeping institutions.[97]

As individuals move along the spectrum of enforcement, each phase carries a unique set of challenges.[98] This is because progression along the spectrum is typically characterized by greater precarity and legal ramifications. For example, when an individual enters the expulsion phase following a deportation, they often encounter extreme housing and employment instability. This is in part because of the stigma that is associated with being deported.[99] After being forcefully removed from their families, homes, and communities, deportees also struggle with a sense of isolation, depression, and alienation.[100] From afar, their spouses and children similarly struggle with depression, stress, and mounting responsibilities.[101] During the reentry phase, individuals must contend with the set of laws that regulate inadmissibility to the U.S., including the 3- and 10-year bars, or the permanent bar.[102] These conditions prevent many deportees from legally reuniting with their families in the U.S.[103] For those who manage to return postdeportation without legal authorization, life as a returnee entails an added layer of fear and stigma. These circumstances impact their family members, too, who often internalize a sense of criminality and subsequently conceal information about their loved one's immigration status *and* deportation history (including their reentry attempts) as a precautionary measure.[104] Movement along the spectrum—from the alert phase to reentry—tends to heighten the degree to which deportability is experienced by all members of the family and subsequently reshapes how individuals perceive and respond to enforcement.

An individual's movement within the spectrum of enforcement also has spillover effects. For example, when a member is deported, the entire family endures a period of separation and acute uncertainty over the possibility of reunification (whether in the U.S. or in the member's country of birth).[105] Many families experience the spectrum as a pipeline by virtue of having a member who progresses through all four phases. Others also experience it as a continuum after a family member occupies any given phase more than once. Consequently, it is possible for families to move in and out of phases along the spectrum of enforcement while members' individual immigration statuses remain constant.

A central point to remember is that a family's position corresponds with and is dictated by the individual member who is the furthest along the spectrum. For example, a young adult may be a U.S. citizen in a mixed-status family most of whose members occupy the alert phase, except for a parent who has been deported. In this case, the family's position would be that which corresponds to the most advanced phase (of expulsion), and the

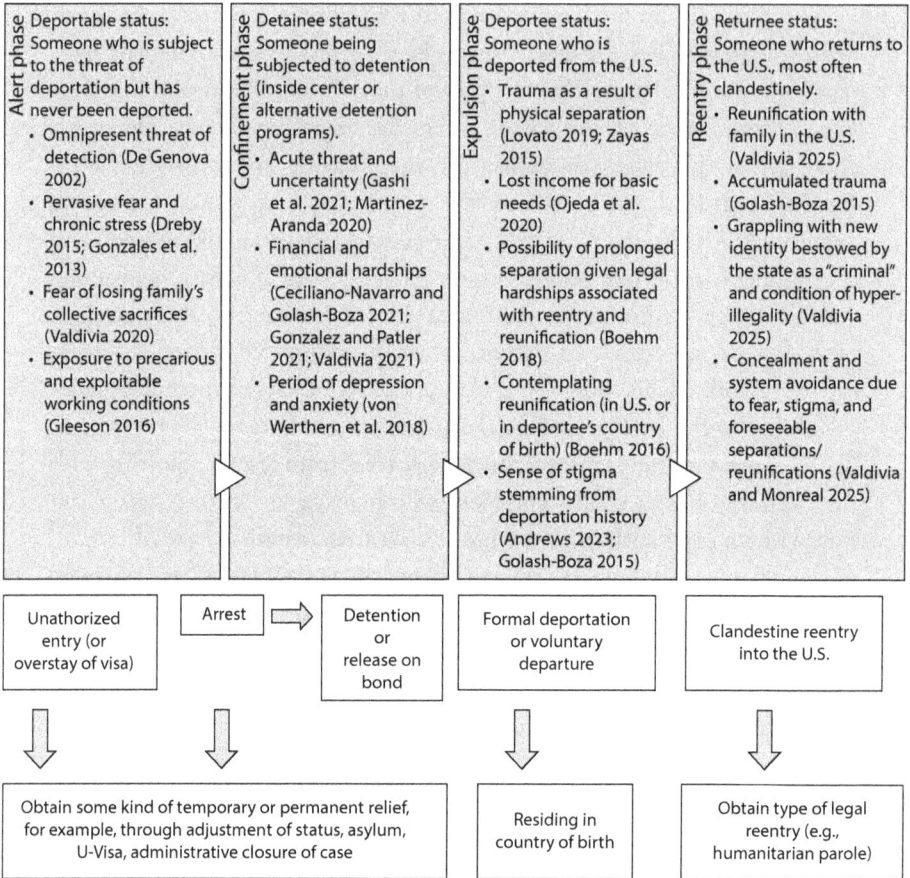

Alert phase	Confinement phase	Expulsion phase	Reentry phase
Deportable status: Someone who is subject to the threat of deportation but has never been deported.	**Detainee status:** Someone being subjected to detention (inside center or alternative detention programs).	**Deportee status:** Someone who is deported from the U.S.	**Returnee status:** Someone who returns to the U.S., most often clandestinely.
• Omnipresent threat of detection (De Genova 2002)	• Acute threat and uncertainty (Gashi et al. 2021; Martinez-Aranda 2020)	• Trauma as a result of physical separation (Lovato 2019; Zayas 2015)	• Reunification with family in the U.S. (Valdivia 2025)
• Pervasive fear and chronic stress (Dreby 2015; Gonzales et al. 2013)	• Financial and emotional hardships (Ceciliano-Navarro and Golash-Boza 2021; Gonzalez and Patler 2021; Valdivia 2021)	• Lost income for basic needs (Ojeda et al. 2020)	• Accumulated trauma (Golash-Boza 2015)
• Fear of losing family's collective sacrifices (Valdivia 2020)	• Period of depression and anxiety (von Werthern et al. 2018)	• Possibility of prolonged separation given legal hardships associated with reentry and reunification (Boehm 2018)	• Grappling with new identity bestowed by the state as a "criminal" and condition of hyper-illegality (Valdivia 2025)
• Exposure to precarious and exploitable working conditions (Gleeson 2016)		• Contemplating reunification (in U.S. or in deportee's country of birth) (Boehm 2016)	• Concealment and system avoidance due to fear, stigma, and foreseeable separations/ reunifications (Valdivia and Monreal 2025)
		• Sense of stigma stemming from deportation history (Andrews 2023; Golash-Boza 2015)	

Unathorized entry (or overstay of visa)	Arrest ⟹	Detention or release on bond	Formal deportation or voluntary departure	Clandestine reentry into the U.S.

Obtain some kind of temporary or permanent relief, for example, through adjustment of status, asylum, U-Visa, administrative closure of case	Residing in country of birth	Obtain type of legal reentry (e.g., humanitarian parole)

FIGURE 1. The spectrum of enforcement. Figure by author.

degree to which the family experiences deportability tends to heighten (following their loved one's deportation).

Rather than viewing immigration arrests, detentions, deportations, and reentries as discrete administrative events, I view them as part of a spectrum such that it is possible for individuals to come into direct or indirect contact with the enforcement apparatus in ways that significantly impact the entire family (see figure 1 for an illustration).[106] This broader conceptualization of enforcement is crucial because it captures the wide range of transformations that families endure long before or after an arrest. It reveals that there is a type of enforcement status that family members share and are subjected to based on their position along the spectrum of enforcement as a unit.

In mixed-status families, it is often the case that there are at least two individuals whose legal status may be in jeopardy, thereby further compounding the effects on the family's enforcement status as a whole. A family's enforcement status will therefore have a bearing on how they experience and respond to the geographies of deportability they encounter. While it is imperative to assess the impact of an individual's immigration status, the concept of legal status itself does not fully capture the nuanced ways in which families experience both direct and indirect encounters with enforcement. Therefore, I discuss the meaning and implications of both an individual's immigration status *and* their family's enforcement status throughout this book.

The experiences of members of undocumented and mixed-status families are shaped by various factors including legal status, gender, and generation.[107] By employing the spectrum of enforcement concept, we come to see that there is also great heterogeneity across households depending on an individual's immigration status and their family's enforcement status.[108] By capturing both types of status that span the individual and family levels, we can better understand the effects of enforcement on young adults and their families and its dynamic and cumulative nature.

In 2022 and 2023 I supervised an additional set of interviews with immigrant rights organizers and volunteers.[109] This includes individuals who facilitate "Know Your Rights" workshops, in which families learn what to do if they encounter an immigration officer or strategies to confirm rumors of enforcement activities. These participants were active members of grassroots and nonprofit organizations throughout San Diego County, often for many years. Some of them identified as currently or formerly undocumented (or as U.S. citizens with undocumented family members). This was an important perspective for me to include, given that there is a long history of immigrant rights organizing in San Diego.[110] In many ways, organizers and volunteers are uniquely positioned to expose the inner workings of the enforcement apparatus from the ground up by nature of their collective and long-standing efforts to support immigrant families. Taken together, these conversations and experiences allowed me to gain a rich portrait of how interior enforcement impacts young adults and their families in ways that are mediated in and through the geographies of deportability.

The county where much of my research is based consists of Carlsbad, Chula Vista, Coronado, Del Mar, El Cajon, Encinitas, Escondido, Imperial Beach, La Mesa, Lemon Grove, National City, Oceanside, Poway, San Diego, San Marcos, Santee, Solana Beach, and Vista (see figure 2). It is home

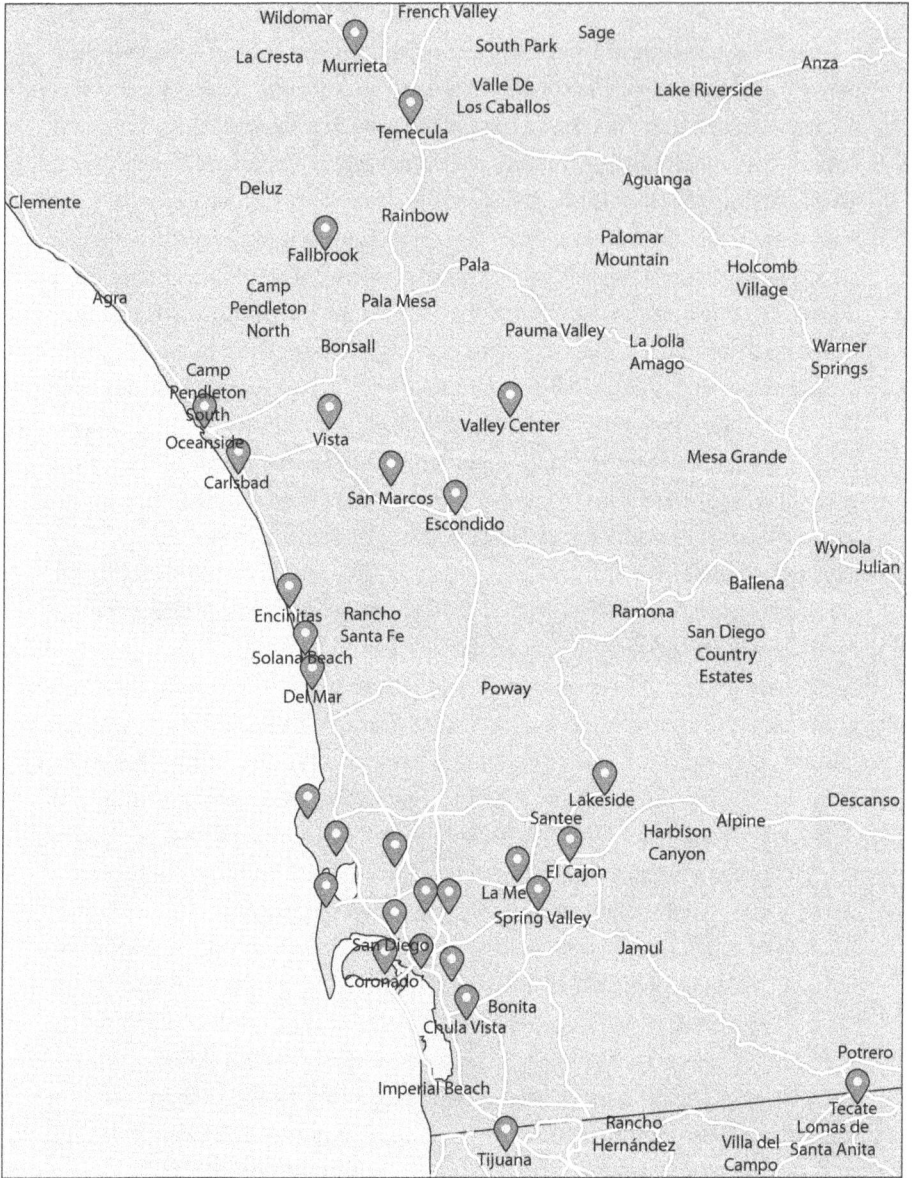

FIGURE 2. Map of where participants lived, worked, and went to school. Figure created by author using Google Maps.

to approximately 169,000 undocumented immigrants, most of whom were born in Mexico and have lived in the U.S. for more than a decade.[111] The county sits between the U.S.-Mexico physical border and two federal immigration checkpoint stations, located on the main Interstate 5 and 15 freeways.

San Diego residents also live within what is considered the "100-mile border zone." A series of federal policies and U.S. Supreme Court decisions have extended CBP officers' authority to stop and search vehicles within 100 miles of any U.S. land or sea border.[112] In this region, CBP officers have incredible power, including the ability to deport individuals through expediated removal if they have been in the U.S. for less than two years.[113] An estimated two-thirds of the U.S. population lives within this 100 mile border zone, which includes all San Diegans.[114] For these reasons, undocumented and mixed-status families in the region frequently hear about enforcement activities, which—true to present form—are often in the shadows.

Historically, there has long been real hostility toward undocumented immigrants and their families in San Diego and in the state of California more generally. As anthropologist Leo Chavez documented, some residents organized "Light Up the Border" rallies during the late 1980s, in which they lined up their cars along the U.S.-Mexico physical border and shone their headlights in opposition to "illegal immigration."[115] Part and parcel of San Diego's anti-immigrant history, California voters passed Proposition 187 in 1994, which would have denied undocumented immigrants access to a wide range of services including public education and nonemergency health care. It also would have required school and health workers to report anyone that they suspected of being undocumented to immigration authorities.[116] More than a decade later, in 2006, the city of Escondido, which is in North County San Diego (a region that includes the cities of Escondido, San Marcos, Oceanside, Vista, and Fallbrook), passed an ordinance that would have banned landlords from renting to undocumented immigrants.[117] A battle then ensued between immigrants' rights organizers, legal advocates, landlords, residents, and the city council, until the ban was rescinded.[118]

Over the years there has been an ongoing struggle to create a more welcoming context in California. To this end, numerous policies have expanded undocumented immigrants' access to a wide range of opportunities such as financial aid, driver's licenses, professional licenses, and health insurance.[119] Notably, on January 1, 2014, California passed the Trust Act, which prevents local jails from holding individuals and transferring them to the custody of immigration officers solely because of their immigration status. Four years later, on January 1, 2018, the California Values Act, Senate Bill 54, went into effect. This piece of legislation further limits collaboration between law enforcement and immigration officers.[120] These and other changes in policies distinguished California as a "sanctuary state" for immigrants.

At first glance, one might accept these categorizations at face value, concluding that certain states, such as California and New York, are inclusionary, whereas others, such as Arizona and South Carolina, are exclusionary. A similar binary may be drawn between cities in San Diego and Orange Counties, which appear to represent opposite ends of a spectrum. However, such portrayal risks oversimplifying the complexities involved in the (re)making of space. It obscures the tensions and multiple dimensions at play, including the simultaneous enactment of both inclusionary and exclusionary practices, particularly in the context of enforcement occurring in the shadows. Moreover, it overlooks the interplay between the objective and subjective dimensions of enforcement as experienced and reimagined by young adults and their families within specific spatial contexts.

Rather than viewing the county of San Diego as an exception to California's "welcoming" context, I view it as a microcosm for the study of enforcement in the shadows, which features constantly shifting and fraught physical and social geographies of inclusion and exclusion that defy binary framing. These dynamics are at work in California and in other parts of the country. Take for example the ability of immigration officers to expand the geographies of deportability by patrolling specific neighborhoods and apartment complexes. Just a few days before Trump's second presidential inauguration, there were confirmed reports of immigration officers conducting raids at gas stations, stores, and public roads across the Central Valley in California.[121] On the one hand, this scene does not make sense in a state that prides itself on being a sanctuary.[122] On the other hand, it does make sense because of the political climate following the 2024 U.S. presidential election. Complicating these seemingly contradictory or compatible realities further is the fact that there are reports of immigration officers employing similar tactics in other parts of the state, such as in the city of Santa Barbara, and throughout the country, including New York and Washington.[123] Ultimately, San Diego serves as a case study for a close examination of the era of enforcement in the shadows that is at work across the country.

To be sure, this is not a comparative study, nor is it a study about a border town. My focus is on San Diego County, which undoubtedly includes distinct border towns such as San Ysidro and Otay Mesa. Yet it also consists of inland cities (like San Marcos and Escondido) and coastal cities (such as Del Mar and La Jolla) where young adults and their loved ones are both residents and workers. The county also consists of military activities and landmarks, such as the USS Midway Museum and Camp Pendleton.[124] In San Diego and elsewhere, the era of enforcement in the shadows and its ensuing geographies of deportability are shaping how young adults and their families negotiate and remake their everyday lives together.

CHAPTER OVERVIEW

Chapter 2 dives deeper into the theoretical framework guiding the study by explaining how through changes in U.S. immigration policy and practice, immigration officers and the pseudo-migra transform specific settings throughout San Diego into sites of immigration enforcement and thereby a heightened risk of apprehension. Examples of hot spots include DUI checkpoints, public roads, ethnic grocery stores, and specific apartment complexes in predominantly Latino neighborhoods. The analysis is based on the perspectives of young adults and their families and reveals how the law, space, and social actors reproduce the threat of deportation on the ground. Such dynamics reveal an important shift in the landscape of enforcement from traditional to nontraditional settings, and from the public to the private realms, in ways that permeate the lives of undocumented and mixed-status families. As a wide range of places and social actors are becoming enveloped within the geographies of deportability, there are fewer places and moments of respite for young adults and their loved ones. By documenting these spatial realities, I advance the argument that the geographies of deportability are expanding and deepening in ways that compel entire families to participate in sanctuary making efforts.

In chapter 3 I document how enforcement in the shadows and its resulting geographies of deportability lead families to constantly restructure their daily routines and responsibilities, with young adults taking the lead as backup parents, emotional anchors, and legal brokers. Backup parenting entails the gradual assumption of parental roles and responsibilities. This includes making greater financial and caretaking contributions and doing things like driving younger siblings to school and checking in on parents to ensure their safety when they are out of the house. Young adults also become primary sources of emotional support for their family members by partaking in emotional anchoring. For example, young adults may spend significant time reassuring their loved ones and reducing their stress levels. Young adults also engage in legal brokering by mediating information related to the law between their parents and the state, including legal institutions such as courts and government representatives. This includes instances when young adults search for trustworthy immigration lawyers or inquire about potential options for immigration relief for their parents. By examining young adults' evolving roles within their families, we see that sanctuary making is not just about mitigating external threats. At a deeper level, it is about families actively reshaping their roles and relationships to stake a claim to space—establishing a sense of belonging through ties of care and trust. This analysis highlights the active, relational, and transformative nature of sanctuary making.

Chapter 4 examines the often overlooked emotional and material consequences of enforcement for young adults. As young adults navigate the geographies of deportability and participate in sanctuary making efforts, they make significant personal sacrifices and endure dramatic changes in their health. There are also tensions, traumas, and a sense of grief that young adults must contend with as roles and responsibilities are redistributed based on members' varied determinations of who is most vulnerable or protected within the family. Compounding these effects is the reality that young adults often refrain from seeking emotional support from others, including their family members, and in turn cope in isolation with the toll of enforcement. By specifying the ways that current immigration enforcement regimes harmfully impact young adults in particular, this chapter demonstrates the need for collective support.

Chapter 5 shifts from the level of the household to the community by featuring the experiences of individuals who become politically engaged and strive to equip families with the information, tools, and resources that are essential to contesting the era of enforcement in the shadows and its ensuing geographies of deportability. This includes Know Your Rights workshops for potential encounters with immigration officers, hotlines for reporting hot spots, and anti-deportation campaigns for preventing a loved one's removal. It features the work of immigrant rights organizers and volunteers to demonstrate how their efforts, alongside families', carve out spaces of safety, protection, and trust. In doing so, this chapter advances the argument that social actors such as immigrant rights organizers can bolster families' sanctuary making efforts at the family level through sanctuary making efforts at the community level. By preventing or mitigating some of the burdens and challenges associated with enforcement, the broader community can help to nurture a politicized consciousness among young adults. This is essential for understanding the lives of young adults and their families as part of broader structural and collective struggles, rather than merely as personal ones.

The book concludes with a set of recommendations for deepening our understanding of the experiences of young adults and immigrant families and for supporting them based on the following conclusions drawn from the empirical chapters. First and foremost, physical space, its use, and the meaning that is derived from it are not uniform or static. This book invites readers to grapple with the state's strategic use of physical space. Relatedly, it encourages readers to reimagine landscapes based on communal definitions of resistance and solidarity. Second, the era of enforcement in the shadows is facilitating the expansion of the geographies of deportability. Policymakers at the federal, state, and local levels can hold officers accountable, diminish the role of the pseudo-migra in the enforcement of immigration law, and regulate the use of surveillance and technology that is employed against millions of undocumented immigrants and their families. Third, the expanding geographies of deportability at the local level undermine statewide efforts to support immigrant families. Policymakers can do more at the federal level to ensure the safety and privacy of immigrant families. Fourth, it is not enough to rely solely on solutions aimed at individuals. This book reveals that a family's enforcement status significantly contributes to inequality. Consequently, comprehensive support is necessary for the whole family, which must encompass pathways to U.S. citizenship for family units (not just individuals) and assistance for members who are currently prohibited from legally rejoining their families in the U.S. after deportation. Fifth, many of the existing policies and services do not adequately grapple with the social, physical, and emotional terrain of deportability, and subsequently with the psychosocial toll of enforcement on young adults as they participate in backup parenting, emotional anchoring, and legal brokering. Working with young adults requires us to acknowledge the multiple roles they are adopting from an early age and the costs of remaking sanctuary amid evolving geographies of deportability.

TWO

Geographies of Deportability

ON WEDNESDAY, August 30, 2017, a warning circulated rapidly—via social media, text messages, and emails—across immigrant households in San Diego County about an impending immigration raid: "We have received this from a very reliable source: ICE plans to make a massive raid in North County [San Diego] this Friday, September 1st in the morning. It may last all day. They know where undocumented [immigrants] live and work. DACA [beneficiaries] please beware given 45's recent statements." Donald J. Trump had promised, since his first presidential campaign, to terminate the DACA program that allows eligible undocumented young adults to receive temporary work authorization and relief from deportation. It was difficult to know then if and how the program would end. The authenticity of the source could not be confirmed, and its details were vague, but the promise of imminent danger compelled both DACA beneficiaries and many others in the undocumented community to take immediate action. People forwarded the message to their families and friends as a safety precaution. By the end of the day, there was an even more ominous update on Facebook that read, "You will recall that I posted an alert about a possible ICE raid this Friday in North County San Diego. This is now confirmed. I assume the raids will include the cities of Escondido, San Marcos, Vista, Valley Center, and Oceanside. I cannot confirm that DACA students will remain safe." I personally remember seeing the message from multiple people across my social media accounts and email. I, too, forwarded it to those I knew out of precaution while simultaneously trying to confirm the source, to no avail.

Immigrant families know from experience that although rumors such as these may not be verified, they cannot be fully certain until the day the raids are set to occur. In the meantime, families are stuck in a waiting period that exacerbates their worries about the possibility of detection. Some families may refrain from discussing the subject altogether. This is a common response, as the mere thought of being deported engenders a profound level of fear and anxiety, as well as the need to repress such feelings. Others struggle to take additional steps to avoid being arrested during the day the raids are rumored to occur.

Gabriela Martínez is a 25-year-old DACA beneficiary who was aware of the uncertainties surrounding DACA and rumors about raids. She recalled receiving the same messages late at night on August 31 and forwarding them to her friends with a note: "Yeah it's just a rumor, but they're just asking people to be careful." She was already in bed getting ready to sleep when she also made sure to forward the message to her sister and asked her, "Hey, can you tell the parents just to be careful?" She included a screenshot of the message and added, "I don't know if this is true or not but just tell them to be careful tomorrow." Gabriela and her younger sister, Marisol, decided to take preventative measures to protect their mother, Alejandra, who was undocumented and earned a living by cleaning homes in North County San Diego. Gabriela and Marisol were especially worried that immigration officers could target their mother during her commute to work. As a precaution, Marisol (who is a U.S. citizen) accompanied her mother as she drove around the city on September 1.

At the end of the day, the Martínez family was still safe. They did not see any evidence that raids had taken place. Organizers with Alianza Comunitaria, a grassroots immigrant rights organization in San Diego, drove through the city on the same day to be on the lookout for raids. They, too, did not observe anything that could indicate that the rumors were true. Young adults and their families could breathe again, albeit temporarily.

The following week there were rumors of raids once again as part of a planned nationwide operation called Operation MAGA. This time the rumors were confirmed by NBC News and other news media outlets.[1] The operation was scheduled to unfold across the span of five days and target over 8,000 undocumented immigrants across the country. Although the nationwide operation was ultimately called off, on September 5, 2017, the Trump administration formally announced its plans to terminate DACA.[2]

In the era of enforcement in the shadows, such periods of acute uncertainty are more frequent. They leave young adults grappling, both psychologically and pragmatically, with what-ifs and worst-case scenarios. *If DACA ends, what will I tell my employer? Where will I find work without a permit? Will ICE have access to my personal information?* Most days are also filled with endless concerns about other family members. *Are they safe? Will they make it to work? Will the police profile them while driving? Should they take a different route to avoid a potential encounter with immigration? When are they returning?* These uninvited thoughts and the emotions that ensue pierce through whatever sense of normalcy might be possible otherwise.

In the process, these disruptions in everyday life fundamentally alter the social and physical geographies young adults and their families need to navigate. Young adults like Gabriela and their families identified various settings throughout San Diego County that became associated with immigration enforcement, including the streets and freeways that Alejandra used as she went from one job to another. Families often referred to these localized sites of enforcement as "hot spots." They also used words such as *caliente* (hot) or *activo* (active) to describe them. A particular setting may be transformed into a hot spot following sightings of immigration officers, information about a raid, news about someone's immigration arrest, or the presence of the pseudo-migra such as police officers. These conditions, whether rumored or confirmed as facts, create a ripple effect of fear, stress, and worry within immigrant families, who subsequently learn how to navigate this terrain with extra caution.

Hot spots are part of the geographies of deportability at which enforcement is localized in ways that heighten undocumented immigrants' vulnerability to deportation.[3] Some of these sites are what we might call "traditional," places like detention centers, federal immigration checkpoints, or ports of entry along the U.S.-Mexico physical border.[4] Others are "nontraditional," places like parks, stores, streets, swap meets, or homes, which might have once seemed mundane or even safe but have since become associated with new threats and meanings. In the era of enforcement in the shadows, young adults and their families are keenly observing how the geographies of deportability are expanding from traditional to nontraditional sites. This shift marks a concentration of enforcement beyond the U.S.-Mexico physical border and federal immigration checkpoints into the sphere of social reproduction. In other words, from the perspective of families who are directly impacted, enforcement appears to be increasingly concentrating in the settings that they must frequent and that are necessary for them to fulfill their essential needs. Through their lens, we can see how changes in immigration policy and practices shape the terrain of enforcement on the ground in ways that influence every element of young adults' (and their loved ones') lives.

FROM THE U.S.-MEXICO PHYSICAL BORDER
AND FEDERAL IMMIGRATION CHECKPOINTS
TO SURROUNDING ROADS

A main set of hot spots surrounding San Diego County includes the federal immigration checkpoints (on the north) and the U.S.-Mexico physical border (on the south). Orange County and Riverside County in California have maintained the federal immigration checkpoints just north of San Diego since 1924. The first of these checkpoints was originally established in a remote location in the Temecula Valley, but it has since been relocated and now sits along one of the main interstate freeways (I-15N) in Murrieta.[5] (Among families it is still commonly referred to as the Temecula checkpoint.) There is also a second checkpoint on I-5N in San Clemente. These checkpoints are part of more than 100 stations located within 100 miles of the U.S.-Mexico border and are among the eight that agents of the San Diego Border Patrol Sector oversee.

These settings are state representations of immigration enforcement on public freeways where border patrol officers can create inspection blockades. Within minutes, officers can bring traffic to a halt—signaling the start of a blockade. When the checkpoint is open, officers stand between the lanes and stop traffic to question people about their immigration status and their intended destination. Some cars will be waved through with minimal or no questioning, while others will be subjected to further inspection. This decision is largely discretionary and has been a point of contention between CBP and immigrant rights organizations.

It is difficult for immigrant families to gauge whether or not it is safe to drive through a hot spot at any given moment because the timing of the checkpoints is unpredictable.[6] Officers could open a checkpoint at any time. On occasion, officers may go for weeks (even months) without opening either checkpoint. At other times they may open either checkpoint as frequently as twice a week or more.

Alternate routes that run parallel to the freeway also typically have roving patrols or "mobile checkpoints." The latter refers to spontaneous blockades initiated by CBP agents at a location near the checkpoint that is not fixed. For example, CBP agents might set a mobile checkpoint near freeway exits or in a long stretch of road. These conditions leave immigrant families with few options for travel. Some opt to drive through the roads that run parallel to the freeway to avoid the possibility of encountering the federal immigration checkpoint when it is open. Emilia Villa, a 24-year-old DACA recipient, and her sister (Sandra) both recalled their parents driving frequently north of San Diego as part of their involvement with their church. To avoid going through the checkpoint, their parents would "take the long route. Instead of it taking two hours to get to L.A., it takes four hours, so they go around the I-15 where the mountains are," Emilia explained. However, even this strategy involves risk, and some young adults had family members who were stopped by CBP agents on those alternate routes.

These rhythms of deportability leverage much fear among immigrant communities with the least amount of personnel and public scrutiny. A single roving patrol is generally carried out by one or two CBP agents. At mobile checkpoints, often less than a handful of CBP agents are present. This is in sharp contrast to scenes of an open federal immigration checkpoint where there is at least one CBP agent per lane with several others only a few steps away, questioning drivers who have been sent to "secondary inspection," and still many other agents on standby. Given the sheer amount of personnel and time necessary to question drivers during an open federal immigration checkpoint, traffic is significantly slowed and can easily stretch for miles.

Driving north of San Diego County on both I-15N and I-5N, it is also routine to see CBP agents parked alongside the freeway, overlooking drivers. Sometimes their vehicles are marked with the CBP emblem on the side doors. At other times, however, agents drive unmarked white vans or black SUVs with tinted windows. This makes it difficult for undocumented immigrants to determine whether the vehicle belongs to immigration officers (if unmarked), there is an officer inside the vehicle, and if the officer may decide to follow them. These tactics enlarge the hot spot while simultaneously attempting to blend in with the environment. To the public, these unmarked vehicles become normalized and inconspicuous, part of drivers' daily commutes. Through the lens of drivers who are undocumented, however, the vehicles are troubling and deeply consequential.

Having grown up undocumented for more than a decade in San Diego, Yuridia Cervantes, a 28-year-old with DACA, was familiar with these tactics. She noticed that CBP officers "start sensing or trying to see who's driving up north." She noted that they "are actually screening or seeing what is happening even before" families drive through the checkpoint. A few days before our interview, Yuridia saw "random white cars parked on the freeway and my boyfriend was telling me that those are undercover too, they just don't have the symbol or green stripe, but they're still seeing what's happening." Growing up undocumented in this region, Yuridia and her boyfriend became keenly attuned to the tactics CBP officers employed to monitor, profile, and stop drivers.

The careful orchestration of this hot spot instills in young adults and their families a sensation that they are constantly being monitored and preyed upon, and that they might be followed even when the checkpoint is closed. This is because there are still forms of passive monitoring permeating the surrounding area. This includes the type of vehicles that Yuridia and others recalled seeing alongside the freeway, where it is unclear if there is an immigration officer inside, and the use of other surveillance and technology tools such as license plate readers.[7] Young adults and their families encounter these challenges while commuting for work and during school or family trips. Personally, I have witnessed both clearly marked CBP vehicles and suspicious cars on the side of the freeway at different hours of the day.

A unilateral axis of visibility and power gives hot spots like the checkpoints (and supplementary patrols) the meaning and ability to generate a wide range of emotions among immigrant families. Officers could decide when to open the checkpoint and whom to stop and send to secondary inspection for further questioning. They could also surveil people at any moment without necessarily informing young adults and their families of such monitoring. Families are often unable to confirm whether CBP officers are surveilling them and to what extent. As a result, families are forced to grapple with the distress that is associated with driving through the checkpoints, the anguish of not knowing whether they will make it through safely, the heightened awareness of being monitored, the fear of being stopped, and for those who have been detained there, the despair that follows. Sleepless nights often occur in anticipation of the day that young adults and their families need to drive through the checkpoint. *What if the checkpoint is open? Is it the right decision? Is it worth the risk? Will we be safe? Should we postpone the trip?* A deep sense of powerlessness and guilt arises at the thought that, in their need to cross the checkpoint, the family may be separated.

There are instances when immigration officers follow individuals before or after they drive through a checkpoint heading in either direction. Even if the checkpoint is closed, agents are still active in the area. These circumstances prevent families from knowing whether they are truly safe until they are much farther away from the checkpoint. During these moments, families experience powerful and conflicting emotions. On the one hand, there is an immediate sense of relief upon seeing that the checkpoint is closed.

On the other hand, this type of relief is quickly punctured by dread and distress when families see in their rearview mirrors that immigration officers may be following them—a sign that the threat of detection persists, is imminent, and in some ways is now more difficult to evade. Among families who were tailgated by immigration officers, some were eventually pulled over and questioned about their immigration status. This subsequently led to their arrest, detention, and in some cases their deportation. In other instances, immigration officers tailgated individuals for miles before eventually letting them continue their drive.

Melissa, a 22-year-old who was born in the U.S., was followed by immigration officers on more than one occasion. She lived with her family in Temecula and frequently commuted to North County San Diego for school. Once, while heading south, Melissa was followed by immigration officers who were parked near the checkpoint, which was closed at the time. The officers followed her for more than 30 miles. The officers did not stop following her until she arrived at her destination: the college campus where she was a student. Melissa concluded that officers suspected her of being undocumented based on her darker skin color and the older vehicle she was driving. And those suspicions, Melissa felt, were only removed once she entered the college campus—an action that revealed her identity as a student. Although Melissa, a U.S.-born citizen, was safe, her parents were not. Both had deportation records, making them especially vulnerable to being targeted. Melissa had already been profiled twice while driving her car, reinforcing her understanding that older vehicles, particularly in certain areas, were more likely to attract officers' scrutiny. Aware that her family's enforcement status heightened the risks, she chose to sell the car to protect her parents.

Others like Melissa suspected that immigration officers profile drivers based on appearance—such as skin color, gender, and clothing—as well as the vehicle's type and condition, especially older vans or trucks used for landscaping, construction, or painting. Those enrolled in school often felt relieved by their identity as students. They believed that if questioned, their status as college students would offer them relative safety and protection. To be sure, an officer's decision to follow someone and pull them over varies significantly and is highly unpredictable. Nevertheless, this environment fosters a sense of being subjected to profiling and discrimination for both young adults and their families.

These suspicions are relevant in other contexts as well. Young adults and their families generally felt that immigration officers or the pseudo-migra were more likely to doubt someone's country of birth—and by extension, their immigration status—based on appearance. This may help explain why some undocumented immigrants rely on strategies often described as "legal passing" or "blending in," such as speaking English in public, acting "normal," driving newer vehicles, and wearing mainstream clothing brands.[8] It also highlights why family members perceived as more able to "pass" or "blend in" may take on the responsibility for traveling to high-risk areas alone or accompanying loved ones when necessary.

While research on legal passing provides important insights into these strategies, it is also crucial to critically examine the broader structures that compel immigrants to engage in them in the first place. The geographies of deportability framework helps illuminate how discretionary immigration enforcement decisions actively shape racialized understandings of who is undocumented, creating conditions in which "passing" or "blending in" becomes not just a personal choice but a response to systemic pressures. More specifically, enforcement patterns shape the spatial and social meanings of particular settings, signaling messages about race and ethnicity that young adults and their families internalize. As they witness and hear about officers disproportionately targeting individuals based on racialized assumptions of who is undocumented, they come to understand that certain skin tones, languages, mannerisms, clothing, possessions, and behaviors can attract scrutiny and unwanted attention.

What is particularly challenging for families as they navigate the geographies of deportability is that the boundaries of any given hot spot are constantly in flux, and in the era of enforcement in the shadows, such parameters are continually expanding. For example, the roving patrols are seen on roads and in neighborhoods that are farther away from the checkpoint. In Oceanside (a city located approximately 14 miles away from the San Clemente checkpoint), officers park in gas stations near freeway entrances that lead up to the checkpoint. In Escondido (a city located 40 miles away from the Temecula checkpoint), officers similarly park on freeway on-ramps and exits. Consequently, young adults and their families learn to associate an expansive area with immigration enforcement. This is an area that is miles outside the fixed checkpoints and spreads in all directions. It encompasses the cities of Murrieta, Temecula, San Clemente, Fallbrook, Oceanside, and Escondido.

The presence and ever-growing expansion of these hot spots creates a type of "internal border zone" that is demarcated by the federal immigration checkpoints on the north and the U.S.-Mexico physical border on the south.[9] This notion of an internal border zone hinders young adults' and their families' physical mobility inside and outside of its perimeters. During separate interviews, several young adults spoke about these restrictions. Veronica, a 31-year-old DACA recipient, shared that her family refrained from traveling "past the checkpoint limits" located just north of San Diego. Carlos, a 26-year-old DACA recipient who grew up in North County San Diego, similarly felt "trapped in this little circle in San Diego" because of the checkpoints. He recalled being aware of these spatial conditions and constraints, adding, "I was just extremely aware of that since I was young, and I think my parents were as well. I think even though we didn't go near those more northern areas, I think they knew that we would see the Border Patrol on the freeways in town." Carlos described being fearful of an expanded area that included the checkpoints and the nearby towns: "I think when I was younger, you would see Border Patrol agents at restaurants and trying to pick up people. They were visible in the town." His awareness about deportability as mapped onto space, like that of many other young adults, developed at an early age.

Young adults and their families generally refrain from approaching the southern perimeter of this internal border zone because they associate proximity to the U.S.-Mexico physical border with a stronger presence of immigration officers. This in turn compels them to avoid altogether driving to the cities of Chula Vista, Otay Mesa, San Ysidro, and Eastlake. These strategies, however precautionary, disrupt family travel plans, outings with friends, and work opportunities. This is especially true for those working in occupations such as landscaping, construction, painting, and cleaning, who would sometimes receive work orders in those cities.

For young adults who are active in immigrant rights organizing efforts, these spatial conditions may also limit their ability to participate in events that take place in or near the border. Juana, a 28-year-old community organizer, was eager to join fellow volunteers during a trip to the border to drop off water and canned food for migrants who might be attempting to cross clandestinely. Juana explained, "I always wanted to do it, and I couldn't do it because I don't have legal documentation." Once she got approved for DACA, she asked one of the organizers if she could join. Out of a concern for her safety, however, the organizer told Juana "you don't want to risk it." At this point, Juana felt, "What's the point of being on DACA if I can't go?" She realized that while DACA protected her from deportation, its coverage had geographical limits, and it might not fully shield her at the U.S.-Mexico physical border.

Hot spots throughout San Diego are deeply consequential for young adults and their families. The geographies of deportability severely restrict travel and access to a wide range of opportunities. Families who reside within this region are unable to safely travel outside of it for medical services or work. They are also prevented from participating in school field trips; church events; and other important occasions such as graduations, family vacations, and birthday celebrations. Whether open or closed, the mere threat—of being monitored, followed, or detained—that is localized at and near the checkpoints can be enough to dissuade young adults from joining their friends for outings or events that require them to drive through the checkpoints or close to the U.S.-Mexico physical border. This is true even if the event is located relatively close, such as in the counties of Orange, Riverside, or Los Angeles.

In the case of Yuridia, the checkpoint prevented her mother (who was undocumented) from visiting her once she moved to Temecula. Despite physical proximity, families living on opposite sides of the checkpoint often refrain from visiting each other. Young adults hesitate to even invite their parents for fear of having them risk driving through the checkpoint. Instead, young adults remain connected with their parents through the phone or social media, or schedule trips to visit their parents whenever possible. In the process, relationships and opportunities for bonding are fractured by the unpredictability and enlargement of this traditional hot spot.

FROM BORDERS AND CHECKPOINTS TO PUBLIC SPACES AND WORKSITES

Immigration officers are gradually expanding their enforcement activities beyond the federal immigration checkpoints and the U.S.-Mexico physical border and subsequently penetrating more deeply into the interior of the U.S.[10] DUI checkpoints are a primary example of how the state transforms public roads into nontraditional hot spots in part through the pseudo-migra's use of space. Although a DUI checkpoint is not ostensibly a site of immigration enforcement, police officers working there ask drivers for their license, vehicle registration, and car insurance. These are documents that someone who is undocumented may not be able to furnish.[11] Without them, undocumented drivers are vulnerable to further questioning and inspection from law enforcement, having their cars be towed, or being reported to immigration officers. Notably, DUI checkpoints are typically set up during the morning or evening as parents drive to and from work or their children's school. This reordering of space and time has led young adults and their families to fear the possibility of encountering a DUI checkpoint during their daily commutes.

Veronica has lived undocumented in San Diego since she was 14 years old and has witnessed DUI checkpoints on multiple occasions. Tellingly, when I asked her if she could describe the types of immigration enforcement that occur in her neighborhood, she referenced such checkpoints. She recalled hearing about DUI checkpoints quite often in Oceanside, at times seeing them right in front of her house. She mentioned, "I remember sometimes I would have to go to work, and I would say, 'No, I'm not going to be able to go to work right now because there's a [DUI] checkpoint right in front of my house.' So, I'm not going to put myself in a deportation situation." Young adults like Veronica, and their families, commonly avoid specific roads and neighborhoods where DUI checkpoints are frequent, and sometimes avoid entire cities that are notorious for having DUI checkpoints, such as Escondido, San Marcos, Vista, and Oceanside. Patricia, a 29-year-old undocumented woman, similarly noted, "I avoid Escondido. I avoid Oceanside. [. . .] I just mainly avoid areas where there's DUI checkpoints. That's what I do because they'll ask for a driver's license."[12] As an active member of an undocumented youth-led organization in San Diego, Patricia refrained from attending any of the meetings or events that were held in North County. Consequently, her inability to safely travel to North County San Diego limited her political participation.

Young adults' keen awareness about hot spots also helps to illustrate racial patterns underlying the expansion and intensification of the geographies of deportability. This is not a matter of immigration enforcement taking place in entirely random settings. Rather, enforcement by and large is concentrated in predominantly Mexican, immigrant, and low-income neighborhoods.[13] These are communities where many immigrant families live and work. For example, DUI checkpoints are more frequently set up in North County San Diego, specifically in neighborhoods where the majority of residents are of Mexican descent. Indeed, the two are often related. Studies in other parts of the country reveal that the chances of running into a DUI checkpoint are greater in Latino and low-income neighborhoods.[14]

Ismael, a community organizer who grew up undocumented in San Diego, aptly commented on the differential concentration of enforcement activities along racial and socioeconomic lines. He noted, "Who's living in La Jolla, right? Because it is a predominantly . . . a white community, so ICE isn't there as much. So, the people that live there, that means they're financially stable enough to live there, so they're not targeted as much." In sharp contrast to La Jolla, Ismael described, "It's usually the areas that are predominantly inhabited by minorities or immigrants, and who are economically not as well off that are targeted. Because they know that they don't have access to resources, they don't have access to attorneys, and they feel like they have the jurisdiction and ability to do whatever they want without any impunity." Ismael's reflection serves as a compelling critique of the era of enforcement in the shadows, which facilitates immigration officers' ability to conduct arrests in a manner that is left largely unseen by the public. Without the public to bear witness, "there's no accountability, there's no oversight," in his words. Yet these are the roads and neighborhoods that young adults and their families frequent for work and school. These are the areas where they socialize, shop, and reside. Taken together, these circumstances raise important questions about the right to feel safe in the city, the lack of transparency when it comes enforcement activities, and the possibilities for change and solidarity building that are repressed in the process.

As research on racialized policing practices has long shown, race-based enforcement can have both subjective and objective consequences, such as leading racial and ethnic minorities to experience a form of hypersurveillance in public spaces.[15] A similar pattern emerges in the context of immigration enforcement. Through a careful examination of daily life and enforcement activities from the perspective of young adults and their families, we learn that otherwise mundane activities are distinctly marked by the threat of detection. Each activity corresponds to a specific time frame. This includes the acts of leaving for work (4:00 a.m.–6:00 a.m.), leaving for school (6:00 a.m.–8:00 a.m.), traveling from work to run errands (3:00 p.m.–6:00 p.m.), and returning home (3:00 p.m.–7:00 p.m.). For at least a third of the day, young adults and their families must be on alert.

As young adults and their families navigate the geographies of deportability, they also contend with a sensation of entrapment and persecution. Upon entering a hot spot like a DUI checkpoint, undocumented immigrants and their loved ones experience a sudden and acute fear of being apprehended. In an instant, individuals become hyperaware of their surroundings. Elena

Ruiz, a 47-year-old mother of three children who is undocumented, recalled an instance when she was heading home with her husband and they quickly noticed several orange cones, bright stadium lights, cars lining up, and a heavy police presence. These were all indications that a DUI checkpoint was underway. Elena, who was sitting on the passenger side at the time, vividly described what happened next:

> Right next to it there was a shopping center and a taco shop and some stores where we could have gone in . . . made a right turn, park, go into a restaurant as if we were going to buy some tacos. But the same fear with which we live in this country prevented us from thinking and saying, "what should we do?" So, my husband suddenly started backing up. Backing up! Completely. Let's say two or three cars back. He backed up to go into the other crossing street. If the police officer would have caught up to us, he simply would have said, "Why are you backing up? What do you have in your car? Why? Why are you running?"
> They didn't see us. But we entered the freeway, and we were still scared. I kept turning around and saying, "It was a mistake, it was a mistake! They are following us; they are following us!" Thank God we were probably about a mile away. . . . [W]e exited the freeway. . . . [W]e parked, and we could finally breathe. But we did notice that the fear prevents us from thinking because right there it would have been easy to turn right and enter the taco shop.

Hot spots instill in members of immigrant families a feeling of being held suspect—their very presence, decisions, and actions becoming hypervisible and subject to questioning—in their own neighborhood. Elena recalled feeling as though the police were closely watching and, later, following them. Hot spots also evoke a sense of shared vulnerability. In this instance, the DUI checkpoint reminded both undocumented parents about the possibility of deportation while driving home from work. This level of vulnerability and fear is exacerbated while in the hot spot, which subsequently hinders an individual's ability to think clearly about what to do next. Indeed, moments like these often have a paralyzing effect and trigger a "fight or flight" response.

In this case, Elena and her husband were able to quickly leave the checkpoint by backing up—one of the few exit strategies available in a checkpoint with multiple enclosures. However, Elena was still grappling with the encounter. She wondered why they did not opt for a less suspicious and safer action: to enter the taco shop right before the checkpoint. During our interview, she expressed deep regret: "Why did we back up? It was a mistake that could have cost us our future here. We could have been over there [in a detention center] or even be deported. So yes, we all have to be very careful about each decision that we take." Actual encounters with a hot spot are often relatively brief, lasting only a few seconds or minutes. Yet these episodes leave residual stress. Individuals are tasked with processing information about the hot spot and its dynamics in relation to their individual immigration status, their family's enforcement status, and an endless number of what ifs and worst-case scenarios. These types of intrusive thoughts bring to the forefront questions about their whereabouts, (in)actions, and surroundings.

From an early age, U.S.-born citizen children of undocumented parents learn that being at the wrong place at the wrong time could have disruptive consequences for the entire family. Irene Herrera, a 21-year-old DACA recipient, shared that even her younger sister, Amanda (who is a U.S.-born citizen), was frightened over the possibility of entering a DUI checkpoint. She explained that Amanda "has been in the car with my mom, and my mom has almost fallen into a couple of checkpoints, and so she sees my mom freak out almost to the point where she's crying so I think my sister has carried my mom's trauma with her too because even though my sister is born here, she's a citizen, I think just seeing my mom freak out makes her scared." Irene had witnessed firsthand Amanda's internalized fear of DUI checkpoints. She recalled that "there were a couple of times I was driving, and my sister was in the back seat, and there were some cones, there was a checkpoint right in front of us, but we were going in a different lane, so it wasn't going to affect us. She was like, 'Oh my god, there's a checkpoint, don't turn!' She was freaking out. And I was like, 'Why are you freaking out?' She was like, 'There's a checkpoint. Don't you see it?'" to the point where Amanda started crying. Tellingly, even though Amanda is a U.S.-born citizen, she had a strong reaction at the sight of a police officer and DUI checkpoints. Isabel Quesada's sister (who is a U.S. citizen) has a similar reaction to the police: "She'd see cops and she'd cry." These accounts reveal how the state embeds social actors like police officers into the pseudo-migra, reappropriates the use of space, and in the process generates symbolic forms of violence for both undocumented immigrants and citizens. In this case, otherwise mundane settings such as public roads and objects like orange cones are transformed into symbols of enforcement. These accounts also deepen our understanding of the intergenerational impact that encounters with enforcement—as mediated through the geographies of deportability—have on young adults.[16]

Notably, while San Diego consists of unique border towns like San Ysidro and Otay Mesa, much of the county is made up of inland, coastal, urban, military, and suburban towns. In this terrain, military bases—which are both governmental facilities and worksites—can also function as hot spots. Adrián Guerrero, a 20-year-old U.S. citizen, recalled the day his mother (who was undocumented and worked cleaning offices and homes) was detained at a military base where she was scheduled to work. On that day, his sister accompanied their mother, alongside a friend, to help with work. Upon realizing that they might be asked for an ID to enter the base, Adrián's mother (who was driving) switched seats with her daughter to avoid being questioned. However, "one of the officers actually saw her switching, and asked her why she switched. And then they called the police, and then the police called immigration. And then they apprehended my mom, and they detained her." At the time of my conversation with Adrián and his sisters, their mother had a pending immigration case.

The geographies of deportability framework reveals the interconnected actors and sites that contribute to immigration enforcement, often in ways that might otherwise go unnoticed. These connections span workplaces, government facilities, law enforcement agencies, and ultimately immigration authorities, demonstrating how deportability is produced through multiple, intersecting settings. Military bases, for example, illustrate these entanglements. As government facilities, they serve as both workplaces and enforcement sites where military personnel—who function as both government officials and at times employers—can report undocumented workers to local police, setting off a chain of events that leads to immigration enforcement. Even in the absence of E-Verify requirements, independent contractors working in such spaces may find themselves vulnerable, as the locations where they are called to work can become hot spots. This dynamic underscores that deportability is not confined to any one institution but is instead sustained by a web of relationships across multiple spaces.

As public roads and worksites are transformed into hot spots, the implications are vast and grave for young adults and their families. For instance, otherwise mundane activities such as leaving for work become especially frightening for both parents and their children. A few months before I met Carmen, a 19-year-old DACA recipient, immigration authorities had gone into the local restaurant where both of her parents worked. Officers were there to conduct an audit of all the employees' legal authorization to work in the country. Officers did not arrest anyone but threatened workers and warned they would soon return. This put Carmen and her parents on high alert. The family was not only concerned that immigration officers would return to the restaurant, but they also feared that they could show up at their home. This could happen because officers would soon have access to employee records, which contained personal information such as their full names and home addresses. This severely impacted Carmen's mental health. She explained, "I can tell you for sure that it's affected me emotionally a lot because I'm not able to sleep. Thankfully it's getting better, but I remember. And there's still some nights where I stay up really late until 4 and I hear my dad leave and I start getting really anxious and panicky because I'm scared that something might happen. And I worry; *Is he going to make it to work?*" Even the hours leading to her father's departure were filled with angst over the possibility that he might be apprehended during his commute or at work. Isabel Quesada, whose father was arrested on multiple occasions, felt similarly: "I get so much anxiety, like I'd wake up and I'd hear my dad going to work, and I think, 'oh no!'" Isabel was also experiencing nightmares about her father being detained once again.

As the geographies of deportability expand and intensify—filling the hours leading up to a parent's departure from home with dread—young adults experience noticeable bouts of distress. These emotions sometimes interfere with their sleep schedules and prevent them from either falling or staying asleep. Even while asleep, young adults remain on alert. This was evinced by young adults' hypersensitivity to the sounds and motions that signaled their parents' departure (such as the turning on of lights, opening doors, or preparing food), and the sudden awakenings near their parents' time of departure. Equally concerning is the frequency and duration at which young adults and their families endure these conditions. Months often pass before families experience temporary moments of relief.

Relatedly, while the biological need to sleep may be realized at night, the concerns from the day sometimes replay in the form of nightmares that prevent young adults from getting full rest. It is difficult to say how frequent immigration-related dreams are over the life course, but many young adults remembered at least one with rich detail.[17] What was most striking to me was how many young adults were battling with recurrent immigration nightmares and the striking similarities in the themes that emerged in their dreams. They often dreamed that their parents were suddenly back in Mexico and were unable to safely return to the U.S. Or they dreamed that they were being reported to immigration authorities or outright persecuted by them. Other young adults dreamed that they themselves were in deportation proceedings—in handcuffs outside of their home or waiting to board a plane that would take them to a country they had not been to in years.

While scholars from a range of fields and disciplines, including social work, history, and public health, have documented individuals' immigration-related nightmares,[18] there is a need to develop the conceptual tools to better understand what prompts these nightmares, what they represent, and what their toll is. Through a geographies of deportability lens, nightmares are the product of hot spots and their debris. While the specific details of each nightmare vary, the themes of persecution, entrapment, and imminent loss are prominent.

Young adults often internalize the dynamics of the geographies of deportability in the dream world, remaining vigilant even in their sleep. An element of alertness—the by-product of the day's waking hours—can continue to regulate the minds of young adults. In their sleep, the dreamer is faced with scenarios and environments that animate their unconscious need to be hyperaware of their surroundings and cognizant of danger. Ximena, a 31-year-old DACA beneficiary, recalled a nightmare in which she was suddenly being chased by immigration officers "at a mall, and I was in the car, and somebody was driving the car. I think it was my brother. Suddenly, I'm surrounded by Border Patrol agents and he's like, *I'm going to go the other way.* He tries to go the other way, but that way is blocked. I'm just surrounded and they're coming for me." When Ximena woke up, she was short of breath and experiencing chest pains.

The dynamic of "predator and prey" between immigration officers and undocumented immigrants that characterizes the geographies of deportability can present itself in the form of a fictitious arrest in the dream world. Even if the dreamer has not personally undergone an immigration arrest in the waking world, the by-product of the day can be internalized unconsciously in such a way that they recreate, in intricate detail, the moment of an arrest. In the process, the dreamer contends with the distressing experience of being chased, trapped, tricked, monitored, or ensnared by immigration officers. The dreamer also grapples with the corresponding need to flee and to look for possible exits. By virtue of the state's ability to infuse fear through space and relationships, the geographies of deportability compel people to fear not only for themselves but also for their loved ones, in both the waking and dream worlds.

Nightmares also illustrate the tension that is embedded in space. Even settings that are commonly thought of as mundane, or in some cases as relatively safe, such as stores and shopping centers, may have material features that immigration officers can quickly manipulate for enforcement. For example, officers may block lanes to channel vehicles in a particular direction. They might block exits or make them difficult to reach. Given the frequency with which immigration-related nightmares seem to occur among young adults and their toll, this represents an important area of future research through which we could gain a deeper understanding of the meanings associated with space in the context of the era of enforcement in the shadows.

OFFICERS ON THE GROUND IN ETHNIC GROCERY AND DISCOUNT STORES

Young adults and their families also learn to associate ethnic and discount stores with enforcement because they have heard rumors about immigration officers being at these locations, either inside the premises or in the parking lot. This includes Food 4 Less, Vallarta, Northgate (commonly known as El Tigre), Wal-Mart, and 99 Cents Only stores. Some families may limit their time spent at these stores or decide to only visit them occasionally while relying on other stores for most of their groceries. In other families, young adults with access to some type of legal protection volunteer to get groceries. Some avoid a particular store only on days when there are active rumors about a raid. Others avoid the store for a week, a few months, or even permanently out of an abundance of caution.

The fear that is associated with specific grocery and discount stores varies in intensity across time and place. Some young adults associate a very specific location with immigration enforcement, such as the Food 4 Less in Escondido, where there have been rumors about raids in the past. Alternatively, their fear may be more encompassing and include *all* Food 4 Less stores throughout San Diego County.

When I asked Natalia Cervantes, a 24-year-old DACA beneficiary who grew up in Escondido for more than a decade, if there were certain settings her family avoided because of the threat of deportation, she noted that "it's mostly supermarkets." She explained her reasoning: "I don't think I'm going to find an ICE officer if I go to Sprouts or if I go to Trader Joe's, whereas if

I go to Vallarta or I go to Northgate [Mexican grocery stores], most likely I'm going to see an ICE officer or a border patrol in those places." Zulema Molina, a mother of three who is undocumented, similarly remarked that immigration officers would not go to a Starbucks, but they would be more likely to target stores such as Home Depot, Lowes, Northgate, and 99 Cents Only. Therefore, Zulema avoided shopping there whenever possible, especially when rumors about raids resurfaced. Yet while shopping at a Trader Joe's might be a safer option, as Natalia noted, these stores tend to be more expensive and are located farther away. In the city of Escondido, for example, ethnic and discount stores are more prominent at the center of the city, where Latinos make up more than 90 percent of residents.[19] Alternative stores like Trader Joe's and Sprouts are on the outskirts of Escondido, while more expensive stores like Whole Foods are even farther away, in La Jolla and Del Mar.

These conditions impact families' access to affordable food and other items, and subsequently the range of efforts required of families to navigate such geographies of deportability. Fatima, an 18-year-old who was unable to apply for DACA, explained how her family went through a period of staying at home to avoid being arrested: "[W]hen I was small, my parents would not leave the house, not even for groceries. We would ask someone to help us by bringing groceries for us because it was like a year or two that it was really hot and there would be raids." Families like Fatima's—in which both parents are undocumented, and the children are either too young to drive or undocumented themselves—may rely on extended relatives or friends for help navigating hot spots. This support is crucial during periods when there are rumors about raids.

These spatial and temporal conditions intimately shape young adults' and their families' sense of safety and belonging. For example, the swap meet in Escondido is known for offering a variety of goods at a discounted rate, including clothing, prepared meals and desserts, books, toys, and plants, among many other items. It is also a place where many immigrants, regardless of their immigration status, may "feel at home because they go there every Friday, have lunch there, listen to bands, and spend time with their families and friends," as Arumi Fernandez (a 23-year-old DACA recipient) explained. Throughout the years, however, immigration officers have transformed this place of cultural significance into a hot spot of immigration enforcement by conducting arrests both inside and near the premises.

Tellingly, the swap meet has remained a hot spot even as the years pass. On May 12, 2004, the *San Diego Union Tribune* reported immigration enforcement activities taking place at bus stops, supermarkets, and swap meets (including the swap meet in Escondido).[20] Matías Herrera, who grew up in Escondido for over two decades, recalled during one of our conversations in 2019 that "a while back . . . I don't know if it was a raid that ICE did or a lot of people getting deported around that area." A couple of years later, someone uploaded a video to an online group in social media, showing what appeared to be two undercover immigration officers questioning a person less than a three-minute drive from the swap meet.[21] As reports circulate about these sightings and arrests, young adults and their families have learned to associate this site with immigration enforcement, even to this day. As Arumi explained, "The swap meet has a really bad reputation saying that the *migra* [immigration] goes in and could take you out. . . . When Trump went into office [during his first presidential term], the swap meet died." These conditions prevent undocumented immigrants from going to the local swap meet temporarily or altogether and subsequently block their access to an important source of income, socialization, cultural connection, and respite.

Young adults' insights (and their families') also reveal the expansive nature of the geographies of deportability. If we take the city of Escondido as an example, there have been dozens of hot spots reported over the years (see figure 3). The map represents sites that became nontraditional hot spots at some point between January 2017 and October 2020. It consists of more than 45 pins demarcating unique locations where immigration officers have been spotted or have carried out an arrest, and where police officers have conducted a DUI checkpoint.[22] This includes locations such as the street in front of the Escondido Police Department, where law enforcement frequently conducts DUI checkpoints; the swap meet; residential areas where there have been sightings of immigration officers; and parking lots in shopping centers where immigration officers have conducted arrests.

This map does not represent every nontraditional hot spot, nor is it static. While some traditional hot spots like federal immigration checkpoints have remained relatively stable over time due to their fixed infrastructure, many nontraditional hot spots fluctuate. Nonetheless, this map provides a visual portrait of the precarious terrain that young adults and their families must navigate daily, highlighting the risk of deportation that is mapped onto the city.

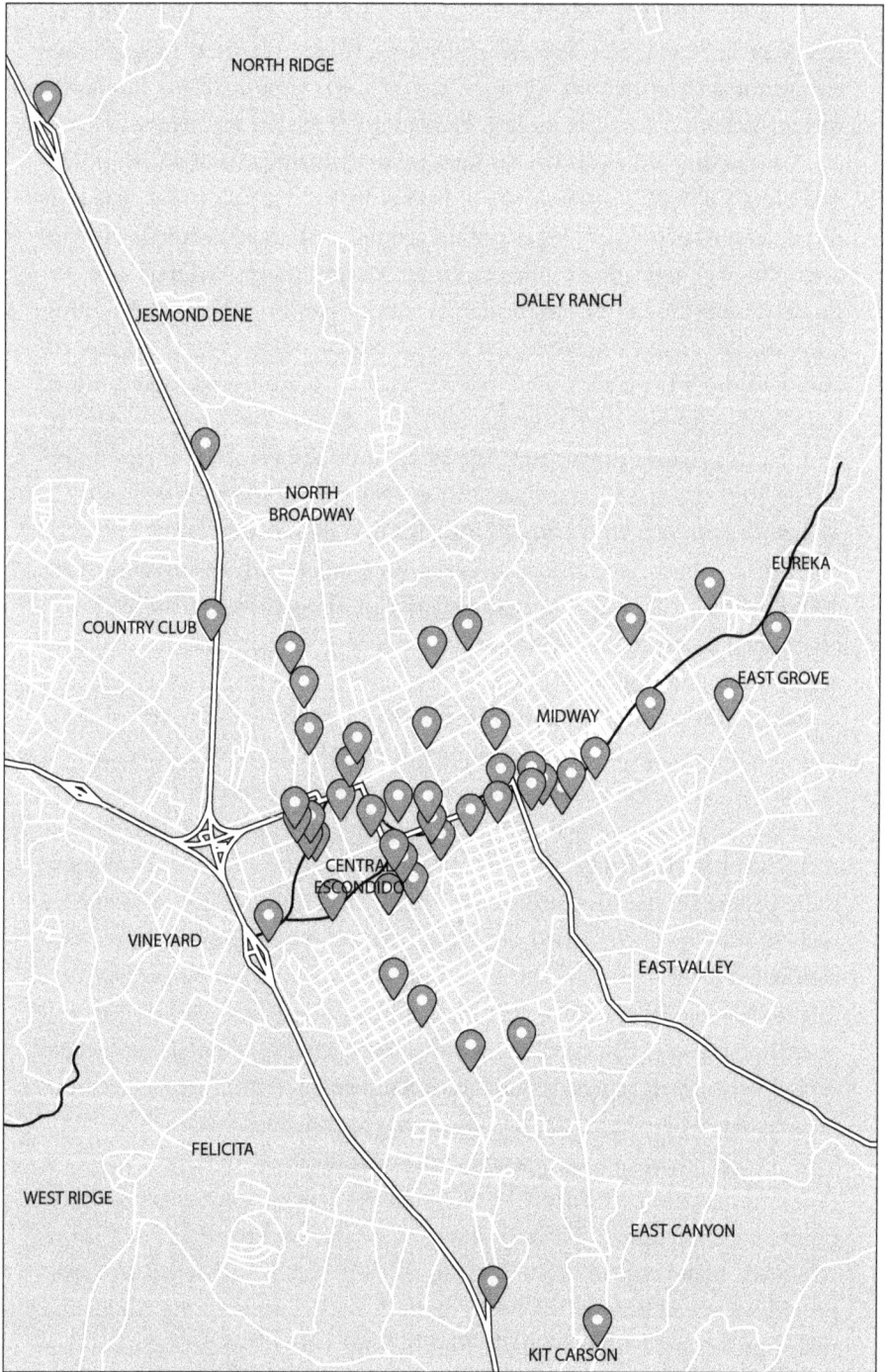

FIGURE 3. Nontraditional hot spots in Escondido, CA, in recent years. This includes areas where immigrant rights organizers have seen immigration officers. Figure created by author using Google Maps.

PENETRATING PRIVATE SPACES: ENFORCEMENT
IN APARTMENT COMPLEXES AND HOMES

One of the most troubling aspects of the expanding geographies of deportability is the state's ability to transform settings typically associated with safety and privacy into hot spots. This includes specific apartment complexes and homes. The home of Maribel, a 21-year-old DACA beneficiary, was turned into a hot spot. During the summer of 2017, Maribel's world drastically changed when her neighbors reported her family to immigration authorities following a dispute. After arresting her father, the officers also threatened Maribel, her mother, and her aunt with deportation. Although Maribel had DACA, she worried that immigration agents might still be able to arrest her because of the anti-immigrant political climate fostered under the Trump administration.[23]

Notably, during various points in the development of a hot spot, immigration officers may attempt to exploit the fragility of loose ties between residents who share the same spaces (as is the case in apartment complexes). Maribel recalled that after her neighbors provided immigration officers with information about her family's immigration status and home address, officers approached people who lived in the neighboring units to see if they would help them identify Maribel's father and his precise whereabouts on the day of the arrest.[24]

When officers ruptured Maribel's sense of safety with respect to her own home and those close to her, it was difficult for her not to internalize the feeling that she was constantly being watched. In her own words, Maribel felt, "It was scary to know that [immigration officers] knew how my car looked. I just became so paranoid ... thinking that anyone that would be staring at me was them, and then not being able to leave my house without looking ... like literally over my shoulder every second." At the time, her mother was living in a separate location so that if immigration officers returned to their home, which they had threatened to do, they would not find her. Maribel was helping her mom with rides during this time, and such routines were marked with an acute sense of vigilance. Maribel added, "Dropping my mom off where she was staying at, just like going in alleys making sure I'm not followed." The hostile conditions that transform a family's home into a hot spot reshape how young adults like Maribel interpret the social world around them, not just within their household but beyond their home, and the emotions and states of being that course through their lives. Once associated with relative safety and protection, the home is now both where the initial arrest took place and where new vulnerabilities exist. Their residence, routines, whereabouts, and travel routes become ripe for suspicion over the possibility that immigration officers could be monitoring them and may subsequently return to conduct additional arrests.

Of the families I spoke with who had directly experienced a loved one's deportation, more than a dozen indicated that the initial arrest took place in or near their homes, including in the parking lot. By targeting individuals in their own homes, immigration officers do more than just conduct an administrative arrest. In the process, officers also reproduce individuals' estrangement from a previous self that felt safe and secure at home to a new alienated self that becomes hyperaware and suspicious of their surroundings. This is evinced by the thoughts and emotions that are now associated with being in or near one's home. Even when immigration officers are not present, young adults whose home has been turned into a hot spot are primed to be on edge, and their senses are heightened. Maribel powerfully remarked: "I don't feel safe. I hear a knock on the door, and I get scared. I don't want to admit it to myself, but that's what it is." For Maribel and many others, something as simple as an unexpected knock on the door now triggered painful memories and powerful emotional reactions filled with fright. Home no longer served as a refuge from the world—a space for restoration and renewal. These revelations are evidence of the harms that young adults and their families sustain as a direct consequence of the expanding geographies of deportability.

Once planted, the seeds of vigilance and distrust inform how families construct their own geographies of sanctuary. Maribel, her mother, and her aunt significantly altered their living arrangements and daily routines after the arrest. Maribel's mother temporarily relocated to a small room she was renting from a friend—charting new terrains outside of the scope of the geographies of deportability. Maribel explained the depths to which all three family members went to enact a form of protection at a time of tremendous uncertainty and vulnerability. Her aunt "had to completely change her appearance like dye her hair, cut her hair." Maribel cut her hair too, adding, "The guy, the immigration officer told me, he's like, 'I'm going to be looking for someone in a bun.' So, I even had to do that. It took me to that extremity that I had to cut my hair, and I have not had my hair this short since I was like in third grade." When Maribel continued explaining that her mom also had to significantly alter her appearance, she became too emotional to continue. "My mom did too. My mom had long luscious hair and she had to do away with it because of . . . ," Maribel began to cry. I could sense the depth of Maribel's fear during the interview. She paused every time she saw a black SUV enter the parking lot. At one point Maribel painfully shared, "I don't know how I can sit here and tell you this without just freaking out because it's just. . . . I hate going home. I'm constantly being watched. It's just the worst feeling ever." She lowered her voice when strangers walked near us and frequently looked over her shoulder. Her demeanor vividly reflected her response to the era of enforcement in the shadows and its ensuing geographies of deportability, in which immigration officers are often undercover and drive unmarked vehicles while patrolling the neighborhood.

Maribel was not only coping with the aftermath of her father's detention and fighting tirelessly to prevent his deportation, but she was also the subject of hypersurveillance. Now that agents knew exactly where the family lived, Maribel feared that they could come any day, unannounced, for any reason. Moreover, the neighbors were no longer friends and now might in fact call immigration officers. By acting as part of the pseudo-migra, her neighbors broke the trust the two households had established over the years. Their proximity and complicity meant that they could passively monitor the family and their whereabouts, even when immigration officers were not present. Now, it also felt as though there was nothing preventing those around Maribel from using her immigration status against her in an instant as her neighbors had done. When discussing one of her friends, Maribel noted, "Things slip out and it's not safe. [. . .] If he really wanted to even call [immigration officers] on my mom and he knows where she lives . . . where she works and lives so it's just. . . . I rather not." Sanctuary making for Maribel then necessarily entailed an element of concealment.

A few miles north of where Maribel lives, in San Marcos, Brenda Quesada, who is the oldest of three children, and her family have also seen immigration officers in their apartment complex. Sometimes officers waited outside the apartment complex's vehicle exit, which faced a public park. At other times they entered the apartment complex and waited in the parking lot. On occasion, officers blocked residents from backing out of their parking spots. Immigration officer sightings significantly increased following the 2016 U.S. presidential election. Brenda noticed, "There was like multiple people getting deported in these apartments at the same time, so that was kind of weird. Everyone was pretty scared of going to work early in the morning because [immigration officers] would be waiting for people here, outside in the parking lot." Her mother, Berenice, also noticed that immigration officers deported several of their neighbors, adding, "They may not be coming for them, but they find them, ask them [about their immigration status], and, well, they are undocumented, and they take them away." As the geographies of deportability deepen into apartment complexes, they serve as fertile ground for immigration officers conducting targeted *and* collateral arrests, of the kind Berenice noticed.

Frequent sightings of immigration officers, news of their neighbors' recent deportations, and their direct experience with a loved one's immigration arrest transformed the Quesada family's apartment complex, and the neighborhood more broadly, into hot spots. Consequently, the Quesada family and their neighbors found themselves looking over their shoulders, altering their schedules, and diligently checking in with loved ones whenever they left their homes. Their neighbors similarly changed their routines and living arrangements. Brenda noted, "Several people, they changed their schedules. They called their work and said, 'I have to go in later because I run too much risk.' A lot of people are moving, too, because of the risk." When immigration officers transform a home into a hot spot, families like Brenda's often consider relocating. However, for most families financial circumstances make relocating a challenge, as many simply do not have the means to cover the expenses associated with breaking a lease, securing a new place, and moving their possessions—especially on short notice. Even if a family could relocate, there is no guarantee that they would be safe at the new location.

In lieu of moving to a new place as a family, the individual member who is the most vulnerable to immigration enforcement may decide to temporarily relocate outside of the hot spot by themselves. They may be compelled to do this because of their undocumented status, because of their family's enforcement status, or because immigration officers are actively targeting them. When an individual member decides to relocate, the family often relies on their social networks to find a relatively affordable, short-term, and nearby room to live in—a type of liminal housing—while maintaining their previous residence. This type of relocation involves an intricate balance between creating enough physical distance from the immediate threat of immigration officers and staying close enough to their primary home so that they can continue managing their household responsibilities. Under these circumstances, they experience prolonged time away from loved ones and an added commute between two homes. Even though the family may be able to avoid an arrest, physical and social separations for an indeterminate period are suboptimal conditions for families.

The expanding geographies of deportability by which homes transform into hot spots effectively function as a mechanism for evicting immigrant families, if not through a formal process of eviction, then through an informal process of self-eviction fueled by fear. Recall the experience of Maribel's mother, who was terrorized in her own home to the point that her only option was to relocate to a separate, smaller, and distant location away from her family. At the time of my interview with Maribel, it was unclear if her mother would return home. Given the precarious nature of living in a hot spot, families consider moving altogether. This type of self-eviction often goes unaccounted for in both studies of enforcement and national statistics, but it nevertheless poses similar harms for young adults and their families. Much like formal evictions, self-evictions require entire families to contend with material hardships, instability, and negative effects on their mental health.[25] Many individuals experienced these effects repeatedly because undocumented and mixed-status families have already been uprooted at least once during their immigration journey.

The expansion and intensification of immigration enforcement constrain young adults' ability to find respite from the threat of deportation. While we typically associate time at home as an opportunity to rest and relieve stress, young adults and their families whose homes are transformed into hot spots are deprived of this essential opportunity. As Guillermo, a 24-year-old U.S.-born citizen whose father was arrested by immigration officers in their home, remarked, "Even though you have your own home, are you even safe in your own home?" He added, "People assume that you go to your house [and] nothing is going to happen to you, but I don't know why [immigration officers] came knocking to my dad's home. I don't know why they came knocking on our door." Guillermo's remarks bring to light the state's constant boundary making between two parallel worlds.

For most of the general population, which remains untouched by the tentacles of the enforcement apparatus, the walls of their homes continue to represent relative sanctity and privacy. For undocumented and mixed-status families, on the other hand, these rights and protections are being challenged. In the process, the expanding geographies of deportability terrorize immigrant families, and in the words of Guillermo, prevent individuals from having a "home to come to. A safe place." As a U.S. citizen, Guillermo's legal status should have protected him from invasions of privacy in his own home. However, both of his parents were undocumented and therefore highly vulnerable to enforcement actions. Moreover, his family's enforcement status—marked by expulsion following his father's deportation after being arrested at home—placed them in a particularly vulnerable reality. The geographies of deportability framework illustrates how immigration enforcement practices on the ground erode the rights of entire families, regardless of individual legal status.

As immigration officers permeate immigrant families' most private and intimate spaces, the lines between risk and safety are blurred, making it difficult for individuals to counteract the thoughts and emotions associated with hypersurveillance. For the Quesada family, something as simple as an unexpected knock on the door is now frightening. Brenda Quesada shared that whenever they hear a knock on the door, she and her siblings "get into this crazy panic." She also recalled a specific instance when one of their cousins unexpectedly visited them late in the evening and decided to playfully knock on the door very loudly. In that moment, Brenda's youngest sister, who was closest to the door, "started screaming like crazy." Brenda described how they all fell into a panic. The day immigration officers arrested Brenda's father, and specifically the place and way they did it, left a powerful imprint on the entire family. Brenda's observation that "every time someone knocks on the door, and it's late at night, it's the scariest thing," also suggests that even during the moments in-between enforcement activities—without active threats—individuals still experience a general feeling of uneasiness, vigilance, hyperawareness, and suspicion. These emotions could be triggered and heightened at any given moment.

ONCE A HOT SPOT, ALWAYS A HOT SPOT?

How the geographies of deportability are socially and physically mapped out is not fixed or neutral. The use of space is constantly being contested by multiple actors, including immigration agents, police officers, policymakers, young adults and their families, immigrant rights organizers, lawyers, and allies. In the process, the meaning that is associated with localized sites of enforcement is changing. As people come in and out of contact with these hot spots and change their routines (e.g., by avoiding a hot spot altogether), space is both transformed and transformative. It changes the ways people interact (or not) in such spaces and the memories associated with them.

Geographies of deportability are subject to change: they shift, expand, deepen, intensify, or weaken over time. In the state of California, a combination of policies has helped to weaken the geographies of deportability. For example, eligible undocumented young adults could obtain a driver's license in California through DACA. As of January 2, 2015, eligible undocumented immigrants could also obtain a driver's license in the state of California under Assembly Bill (AB) 60. Within three years, more than one million people received a driver's license under AB 60.[26] Now that police officers in Escondido could not cite undocumented immigrants with access to a driver's license under AB 60 or DACA, DUI checkpoints arguably became less profitable and were subsequently conducted less frequently.

Marcelino Molina attributed the recent shift in the frequency of DUI checkpoints in Escondido to these policies. He is a 55-year-old father of three who has lived and worked while undocumented in North County San Diego for over two decades. He mentioned, "[Police officers] don't set them as often. Ever since we could get driver's licenses in California, they don't bother as much with setting DUI checkpoints." Although the police department continues to conduct DUI checkpoints, it does so with less frequency, as Marcelino has observed. Immigration officers also do not solely rely on DUI checkpoints by law enforcement and instead maintain other forms of formal and informal collaboration, as well as a greater presence in other parts of the city through other forms of monitoring.

By focusing on immigrant families and immigrant rights organizers, we can better capture changes in the enforcement of immigration law on the ground. Members of undocumented and mixed-status families like Marcelino are keenly aware of enforcement activities. They pay attention to its nature, timing, location, and frequency. They need to be sensitive to these spatiotemporal dynamics as a matter of survival. As Carlos, who was born in Michoacán, México, and grew up in North County San Diego, expressed: "We're both [him and his brother] undocumented. We don't have a driver's license, so we're always hyper-aware when there's a cop around." The lived experiences of young adults and their families compel us to rethink our understanding of space—not as a static, external object, but as a dynamic, central force that shapes and is shaped by the features of the era of enforcement in the shadows. This includes the role of the law (such as the passage of immigration policies at the state level), and social actors (like police officers who dictate when and where to set up DUI checkpoints in the city) in (re)shaping the function and meaning that is associated with a particular setting.

As a method of inquiry, the concept of the geographies of deportability facilitates the ordering of seemingly isolated and ordinary facets of lived experience. It allows us to gain a rich portrait of the social world through the lens of undocumented and mixed-status families. By centering the role of space, this framework illustrates the set of social practices that transform a wide range of settings (public roads, stores, parks, worksites, homes), objects (orange cones, forms of identification), and social actors (landlords, employers, police officers, coworkers) into representations of immigration enforcement, thereby heightening the fear of deportation. Through the appropriation of space, the state produces, spreads, deepens, and exacerbates the threat of deportation.

Through the lens of young adults and their families, deportability is understood as a state of being that is shaped not only by legal structures but also by the everyday spaces and social interactions that define immigrant life. While changes in U.S. immigration policy play a significant role in determining who is at risk, enforcement extends beyond policy alone; it is embedded in the places where individuals live and work and in the relationships that they build with others in those spaces. From workplaces to schools to encounters with law enforcement and community networks, the threat of deportation is both spatially rooted and socially mediated. These insights help illuminate the profound spatial and relational vulnerability that permeates the lives of immigrant families, shaping their sense of security, mobility, and belonging.

The geographies of deportability represent the social, physical, and political terrain in which different meanings of space are made and remade. Take for example the presence of the federal immigration checkpoints, which are central hot spots. For immigration officers, the checkpoints represent fixed locations on main interstate freeways where they are tasked with enforcing immigration law. For commuters, the checkpoints symbolize the state's expanded power to "control" the border in the interior of the country. If the checkpoint is open, it represents an inconvenience. For young adults and their families, however, the checkpoints represent settings where immigration officers are concentrated. Whether open or not, the checkpoints are a troubling reminder of their vulnerability to deportation. For those who were arrested after driving through an open checkpoint—or whose loved ones were detained there—the checkpoints remain an open wound. In our analysis of the lives of young adults and their families, it is important to capture the dynamic features of space, including its changing and competing meanings over time.

The geographies of deportability are also remarkably expansive, especially for individuals who are entirely undocumented and as such do not have access to any form of legal protection. This is an issue of growing concern as undocumented children are coming of age at a time when they cannot benefit from DACA. The same is true for individuals who have returned to the U.S. after deportation without legal authorization. Ernesto León, a 60-year-old immigrant father who returned to the U.S. postdeportation on multiple occasions, knew he was especially vulnerable during any encounter with the police. On one occasion, a police officer told Ernesto explicitly that when they ran his name in their system, they noticed that he had an "ordén de que te entreguemos" (an order to be transferred to immigration authorities). Ernesto was ultimately safe during that encounter; the police officer used his discretion to let him go while encouraging him to speak to a lawyer. At other times, Ernesto did not have the same luck. For both segments of the immigrant population—those who are undocumented and those who have returned to the U.S. postdeportation without authorization—a wide range of settings function as hot spots. This includes hospitals, dental clinics, schools, banks, and public transportation. This makes it imperative to examine individuals' experiences in navigating the geographies of deportability based on their immigration status *and* their family's enforcement status.

When the state transforms a wide range of settings into landmarks of enforcement, young adults drastically reorient their understanding of the social world.[27] They navigate a topography of public and private coordinates with heightened vigilance, on guard against the possibility of being suspected, monitored, entrapped, and excluded from their homes and communities. In this environment, young adults are conditioned to feel as though the threat of deportation is omnipresent—embedded in the institutions they participate in, people they interact with, and spaces they occupy. They are primed to react to subtle changes or discrepancies at a moment's notice. As Claribel Gonzalez, a 29-year-old DACA beneficiary, expressed, "It's always a risk.... [J]ust walking out of the door felt like that sometimes." Other young adults used adjectives such as "extremely" or "hyper," or expressed the need to be "extra careful" to describe their state of mind when navigating the geographies of deportability.

My conversations with Claribel and others helped me to understand that their experiences with navigating the geographies of deportability are not just about an elevated concern: young adults and their family members have a set of preoccupations, sensations, emotions, and behavioral changes that are consistent and intense in ways that are indicative of deeper transformations. Young adults learn to quickly notice and process cues from their physical surroundings that signal imminent threat, such as the presence of ordinary objects like orange cones, stadium lights, and blocked roads, all of which could mark the start of a DUI checkpoint. They become wary of strangers and intrusive questions that revolve around their countries of birth or legal status. At a deeper level, young adults develop a high level of sensitivity to risk, which they continue to fine-tune over time with direct experience, observations, and insights from others.

These findings suggest a need to reconsider how we understand the development of children's legal consciousness, particularly in ways that capture the subtle and often profound transformations that occur. In this regard, the framework of geographies of deportability offers valuable insight, especially when paired with methodologies such as photo-elicitation or art workshops with young children. Sociologist Marisol Clark-Ibáñez and ethnic studies scholar Silvia Rodriguez Vega have used these methods to explore how children internalize the threat of deportation from an early age.[28] The geographies of deportability framework can assist with creating prompts that children are asked to engage with, offering a more nuanced approach. For instance, children might be invited to take photos or create drawings of settings that their families avoid. These portraits can make visible other objects or figures that have come to represent enforcement and in turn inflict symbolic violence on young children.

These findings are also in conversation with the work of Cecilia Menjívar and Sarah M. Lakhani on the "transformative effects of immigration law," which demonstrates how the legalization arm of the immigration system can alter immigrants' sense of self and mindsets.[29] I find that the restrictionist arm, with its focus on enforcement, has a similar effect. Specifically, the spatial distribution of enforcement alters the meaning attached to certain places, not only disrupting daily routines and travel routes, but also compelling young adults and their families to reconsider their understanding of the law as it is tied to place. It also reshapes their assessments of risk and safety over time and across space. These transformations begin early in life—and persist into young adulthood—for children in undocumented and mixed-status families. The memory of these hot spots lingers, allowing enforcement-related thoughts and emotions to resurface long afterward—sometimes months or years—even when far removed from the original sites. Both undocumented immigrants and U.S. citizens undergo these transformations.

Such findings also join efforts like those by sociologists and geographers that reveal the kinds of consciousness and emotions that emerge from distinct geographies.[30] By shining a bright light on the geographies of deportability, we recognize the state's ability to produce an uneven emotional landscape in which a segment of the population is taught to live in chronic fear, anxiety, stress, and pain, while grappling with a sense of being monitored, trapped, and persecuted. Such emotions and sensations can persist even among individuals who eventually gain access to some type of legal protection like DACA or a green card many years later. While segments of the public may experience feelings of control and legitimacy that enforcement brings, this is done at the expense of immigrant families, who must endure extreme suffering—a process that is inextricably linked with the racialization of legal status, the construction of illegality, and race-based enforcement.[31]

The geographies of deportability ultimately aid in the boundary-making work that is necessary to sustain sociolegal categories of exclusion and inclusion. It communicates to undocumented and mixed-status families that the threat of deportation is omnipresent and that one must carefully consider every move and interaction. Young adults and their families exist in a constant state of being watched. This dynamic—of seeing and being seen—is central to young adults' legal consciousness. The mere possibility that they might encounter immigration officers at an ethnic grocery store, a Wal-Mart, a swap meet, or just outside of their home increasingly means that there is at least one place where they are unsafe. Similarly, the ability of non-immigration actors like police officers, landlords, employers, and estranged partners to function as part of the pseudo-migra at a moment's notice illustrates the fragility embedded in ties and the vulnerability present in any given situation. Thus, whether consciously or unconsciously, young adults and their families find themselves on edge, primed to act, everywhere they go and with whomever they interact.

THREE

Sanctuary Making and Young Adults

ELENA AND MATEO RUIZ have lived in National City, California, with their three children for over a decade. This is where their children were born, where they completed their K–12 education, and where they formed meaningful relationships with teachers, friends, and neighbors. It is also where Mateo has worked in construction and landscaping—occupations that required him to drive to several locations daily. I first met with the Ruiz family during the winter of 2019. When I arrived at their home, Nidia, the eldest daughter, greeted me and introduced me to her parents, both of whom were undocumented. We gathered in the living room as the family recounted their immigration journeys and the children's upbringing in National City. They also spoke about recent sightings of immigration officers in their neighborhood.

The Ruiz family said that at the onset of Trump's first presidential administration, they saw immigration officers park in front of their apartment complex multiple times. On one occasion, officers entered the premises. According to their neighbor, the officers had an old photograph of Mateo from his deportation more than a decade earlier. The neighbor warned him: "You know what, Mateo? [Immigration officers] are looking for you, but they're not sure that you're here because it's been a while since they deported you." With the passage of time, Mateo's photograph on its own became obsolete. Because Mateo looked different now that he was much older, immigration officers could not solely rely on his old photograph to identify him. Instead, the officers hoped to pin down his whereabouts with the assistance of other residents. Unbeknownst to the officers, however, Mateo's neighbor refused to play the role of the pseudo-migra and instead used that information to warn him.

Mateo and Elena spent a sleepless night figuring out how to alter their routines and living arrangements to prevent immigration officers from finding them. Elena explained that they told their children "we had to leave. They would stay with the apartment, and we would move. We found a room for rent," and they set about fulfilling their parental duties from afar. Elena recalled, "Every evening after my husband returned from work, we would have to come back and make sure everything was okay with our children, make something to eat, grab it really quick for two to three days and leave once again." Mateo and Elena ensured their children had a place to live. They continued to work and cover household expenses. This was all while attempting to protect themselves.

As immigration officers transform homes into hot spots and envelop other social actors as part of the pseudo-migra, families like the Ruizes are forced to contend with a new ordering in how they navigate certain spaces over time. The home no longer represents a place of safety and is instead experienced in a heightened state of fear and anticipation as families dread the moment when immigration officers could return. Among some families, the home splits into two separate physical spaces, with a secondary location providing relative relief by being away from the immediate threat of immigration officers yet close enough to attend to their responsibilities at home, school, and work. These arrangements foster a sense of increased safety, but such efforts also come with significant material and emotional costs. For example, the Ruizes' living expenses doubled. Moreover, spatial and temporal disruptions significantly fracture family life, weakening bonds and dislocating shared memories.

These new arrangements also did not eliminate the Ruizes' mental anguish over the possibility of being found by immigration officers. The couple's brief moments of reconnecting with their children had to be carefully orchestrated around the times immigration officers might be the least active. But for them, survival was not just about addressing immediate threats and needs—it was about staking a claim to the life they had built. After a few months of these arrangements, there was a brief period of relief when immigration officers had not been spotted there for some weeks. Elena and Mateo felt it was safe to return to their home. Mateo also explained, "No vive uno agusto en otros lugares. No hay como su casa de uno [One does not live comfortably in other places. There's no home like your own]." Mateo's reflection is illustrative of the dynamic process through which space is actively contested. Despite immigration officers' attempts to transform their home into a hot spot, Mateo and his family were intent on reclaiming the space where they raised their children. While the Ruiz family could not completely reject immigration officers' use of the apartment complex as a hot spot, they could attempt to reclaim it with the passage of time and recalculations about their safety. In returning, they were not just resisting displacement—they were fighting for the right to remain in the place they had made their own. This was, after all, the Ruizes' home.

Upon their return home, it did not take long before undercover immigration officers showed up again. This time, a handful of plainclothes officers arrived in unmarked vehicles with tinted windows. The officers began to park right outside of the apartment complex. They would wait to approach and question Latino men who were leaving for work early in the morning. In some months officers were there as often as three times a week for an hour or more. This reality, Mateo said, prompted him to drastically alter his routine. He "grabbed an old mattress that someone was about to throw out. I put it in the back of my truck, and I took it. I also took a pillow, and I would leave at 3 a.m. I would get to work, and I would sleep in the back of my truck so I wouldn't be at risk." Work did not begin until six, but leaving three hours early seemed like the only way to avoid a potential encounter with the officers who parked outside of the complex later in the morning. This reality not only caused a tremendous amount of stress for Mateo and his family, who worried every night for his safety, but it also interfered with his ability to rest and emotionally connect with his spouse and children. While we often think of the hours outside of work as an important moment to rejuvenate and reenergize for the following day, undocumented immigrants and their loved ones are increasingly deprived of this basic need as they contend with the expanding geographies of deportability.

As a U.S. citizen, a college student, and the eldest of three children, Nidia played an important role in helping her parents navigate this period of acute fear. She was the first in the household to spot the undercover immigration officers. On a par with the era of enforcement in the shadows, the officers were dressed in plain clothing, driving three separate cars with tinted windows. Neither their clothing nor their vehicles displayed the emblems of ICE or CBP. In fact, one of the cars had regular license plates, while the other two did not have them at all. Nidia was able to identify the men in the cars as immigration officers after learning their telltale signs at a local immigrant rights session. One of the vehicles had antennas and sirens, accessories that are common to police or immigration enforcement vehicles. She also took notice of their behavior. The undercover agents exited their car only to approach Latino men who were leaving for work, including neighbors who stood by the entrance waiting for a ride. Once Nidia confirmed they were indeed immigration officers, she grabbed her phone and began recording them. This is a tactic that other young adults and immigrant rights organizers employ to document immigration officers' actions on the ground. These efforts can sometimes compel agents to leave the neighborhood or help garner support from others (if the video is shared via text message, news media outlets, or social media platforms).[1]

During this period, Nidia also provided emotional support to her mother and siblings as they grappled with the possibility of immigration officers detaining their father. This required substantial time and energy on Nidia's part. She traveled back home frequently from her college campus, which was more than 100 miles away. She checked in regularly to see how her relatives were feeling, spent additional time with them, offered emotional support, and comforted them.

As a college student who was also deeply embedded in parts of the immigrant rights organizing network in San Diego, Nidia's efforts also extended to the level of the community. During the days when Nidia was home from school, she stood near the entrance of the apartment complex at dawn to scope out the area and warn residents about immigration officers' presence. Since officers could not enter the gated apartment complex without a key or by having a resident prop the door open for them, Nidia warned her neighbors about officers' presence well before they needed to leave for work or to do errands. More generally, she stayed up to date with the work of organizations like Unión del Barrio (UdB; Union of the Neighborhood),[2] which alerted immigrant families about hot spots. Nidia helped spread the word about these efforts within her immediate network of friends and neighbors.

As families like the Ruizes navigate the expanding geographies of deportability, they are not without agency. In response to constant changes in immigration policy and practices that ultimately shape the environment they must contend with, families participate in what I refer to as "sanctuary making." To create sanctuary, families assert their presence in the spaces they inhabit by fostering a shared sense of safety, protection, and belonging. Sanctuary making is not merely about risk management or coping strategies; it is a collective, socioemotional process of reclaiming the right to live in the city, in the very spaces where immigrant families have built their homes, raised their children, and pursued their dreams.[3] Parents, like Elena and Mateo, seek out alternative living arrangements or change their travel routes to prevent encounters with immigration officers during their daily commutes to work. In the process, parents remain deeply committed to keeping their children in the place they know as home, prioritizing not only their essential needs—housing, food, and transportation—but also a sense of protection and normalcy. To make sanctuary, entire families constantly shift roles, responsibilities, and routines based on individual members' varied levels of vulnerability and privilege within the context of the expanding geographies of deportability.

At the core of families' sanctuary making efforts is the emotional and material labor of young adults like Nidia who are compelled to adopt a new set of roles. There are three main roles to which young adults dedicate a significant amount of time and energy: "backup parents" (or substitute parents in some cases), "emotional anchors," and "legal brokers." First, young adults become backup parents for their siblings by gradually assuming parental responsibilities to minimize their parents' risk of deportation, mitigate the effects of deportability, or prepare for the possibility of their parents' arrest or their potential deportation. As backup parents, young adults with access to a driver's license accompany their parents to hot spots or volunteer to drive them to work when there are rumors about raids. They also make significant financial contributions to the household and craft emergency plans. Then, in the event of an immigration arrest, young adults' contributions significantly increase and new responsibilities are introduced. They perform an increasing number of household tasks such as cooking and cleaning and make even greater financial contributions. For these reasons, young adults' roles come to resemble that of a "substitute parent," given the sheer number of parental responsibilities they assume following a loved one's arrest, detention, or deportation. Second, young adults become emotional anchors, which entails the process of being acutely aware of both their siblings' and parents' emotions and coping mechanisms and subsequently adopting strategies to help manage particularly negative emotions. This includes helping to lower stress levels within the family as needed. Third, young adults take part in legal brokering, whereby they help mediate information between the state and their family as it pertains to legal processes or matters of the law. This includes tasks such as identifying a trustworthy immigration lawyer, searching for immigration relief options available to their parents, and in the event of a detention, locating a loved one.

Young adults are typically balancing all three roles, and there are instances when one or two roles take precedence. When young adults are in the process of consulting immigration officers for potential options of relief for their parents, they are not only acting as legal brokers; often they are also performing emotional anchoring as they help manage the sense of frustration and hopelessness that can often arise from these conversations. In families with multiple children aged 18 or older (or close to it), siblings distribute responsibilities among themselves based on factors such as gender, birth order, age, and immigration status.

Children in undocumented and mixed-status families become aware of their parents' vulnerability in relation to the geographies of deportability at a young age. As they grow older, this awareness crystallizes and drives them to become backup (or substitute) parents, emotional anchors, and legal brokers. Through their sanctuary making efforts, young adults are determined to alleviate the burden their parents face—raising a family while undocumented in an environment increasingly defined by the threat of deportation and to keep their families intact in the spaces where they have built their lives—either by preventing their parents' arrest or working to reunite them after detention.

GROWING UP UNDER THREAT: CHILDREN'S EVOLVING AWARENESS OF PARENTAL VULNERABILITY

Children in undocumented and mixed-status households contend with the geographies of deportability at an early age, sometimes by virtue of their own undocumented status and other times because of familial ties with someone who is undocumented. Like all children, they both influence and are influenced by their surroundings, construct their identities, and negotiate relationships, all while attuned to the ways their caretakers do the same.[4] For children in undocumented and mixed-status families, this attunement also involves observing how their parents react to and discuss immigration-related news on the television, on the radio, or in conversations with others, and how they manage their own direct experiences.[5] They watch their parents' reactions to authority figures like the police and develop their own strategies for avoiding detection, such as wearing a seat belt, acting "normal," or being "quiet."[6] Maritza, a 23-year-old DACA beneficiary, remembered learning from an early age to stay seated and composed while in the car with her parents at the sight of a police officer or a checkpoint. Children also notice differences in treatment, access to resources, and living conditions, which they come to understand correlate with one's skin color, socioeconomic status, country of birth, or language.[7]

These observations unfold in space: in public roads, schools, doctors' offices, hospitals, local community clinics, parks, stores, and homes. In this environment, children begin to develop an understanding of which places and spaces across the geographies of deportability to avoid or navigate with extra caution. They also learn who to trust and what information to share during interactions with others. Along the way, they experience fear and uncertainty. Over time, this awareness solidifies, eventually driving young adults to take the lead in their family's sanctuary making efforts.

Karina, a 22-year-old U.S. citizen whose mother was undocumented for over two decades, recalled that when she was younger her family was "very vigilant about everything." She recounted that her grandfather "had this little white truck, and it only sat three people in the front so it would be my grandpa, my mom in the middle, and my grandma on the passenger seat and then my aunt and I would be in the back." When driving, Karina would sit in the back "just in case someone stops us, they can't see that you're like lying down behind." Karina was aware that while her grandfather was a green card holder, her mother and grandmother were not. She realized that if they got stopped by law enforcement her grandfather could get a ticket for not having his driver's license but "he won't get thrown out like my mom or my grandma would." Since an early age, children like Karina become acutely aware of differences in experience and risk based on immigration status.

Karina also recalled instances when her family heard about sightings of immigration officers in their neighborhood. "Since I was small," she explained, "I would like pick up on, *oh, we can't go to certain places because they don't have like a piece of paper.*" At the time, Karina lacked the language to describe different types of legal status or their implications in detail, but she had already developed an awareness of (il)legality and its connection to space, shaped by the understanding that activities like driving could lead to exposure to enforcement—an awareness similar to that of the adults around her. Such awareness was spatial and relational. Karina came to understand that different spaces carried varying levels of risk, and that there were different degrees of risk between her family members. Her attunement to her surroundings and the people around her and the actions (or inactions) they prompted—like wearing a seatbelt, crouching in the back of a car, or staying quiet in public places—reflects the unique legal consciousness that children develop at an early age.

As children and their families navigate the geographies of deportability, they learn about the underlying risks their parents contend with. By the time they reach young adulthood, many children of undocumented parents have witnessed police officers setting up DUI checkpoints. They are aware of certain hot spots and the prevalence of racial profiling. They know that immigration officers often make assumptions about the legal status of Latino men based on their skin color, the vehicles they drive, the language they speak in public, or their country of origin. In many cases, these young people have witnessed such enforcement practices and their effects firsthand.[8]

By young adulthood, children in undocumented and mixed-status families have a clear and nuanced understanding of deportation. Luna, a 25-year-old DACA beneficiary, told me about what happened after her father was arrested, when her younger sister asked, "What does a deportation mean?" Their family was mixed status, and Luna herself had DACA. Luna struggled to come up with an adequate answer: "I know what a deportation is. But I didn't know what to tell her, because for us a deportation means having your family split, going from being with all your family living together to having some member outside of the country. *Not knowing* where he is, *not knowing* how he is, or *not knowing* how you're going to reunite again, and the *implications* that it brings along [emphasis added]." In political and academic discourse, deportations represent the forceful physical removal of individuals from the nation-state, the ultimate form of exclusion. Deportability then entails the omnipresent threat of being removed.[9] Yet for young adults, the threat and reality of deportations signify much more. Luna's nuanced description encourages us to move beyond the conventional, denotative meaning of a deportation to highlight the type of social loss and profound uncertainty that a deportation creates. Tellingly, she used the words "not knowing" multiple times in the same breath. She also placed emphasis on the impact that this has on the entire family. Other young adults used similar language when describing the state's ability to tear their families apart, with words like "separation," "loss," "disappearance," or even "death."

For some families, deportations involved multiple and repeated separations, ranging anywhere from two to twelve times. Sara, a 26-year-old

DACA recipient, experienced multiple separations: her father was deported on two separate occasions, her mother was deported separately, and later, her siblings underwent de facto deportation to be with their father.[10] In other families, I heard of multiple members being deported, either simultaneously or at different times. Most often it was both parents who were deported, but there were also instances when a parent and an adult child were deported. When family members manage to return to the U.S. after deportation, the fear of a subsequent arrest often looms even larger than before.[11] This is in part because a history of deportation would prevent their loved ones from adjusting their immigration status under current U.S. immigration law.

Young adults are also keenly aware of instances when others grow impatient over their parents' requests, especially when these are made in Spanish or in "broken" English. Outright racism is common. These circumstances in turn mean that children are not only fearful of hot spots and the pseudo-migra, but they also dread instances when their parents must go to a store, restaurant, hospital, bank, or work for fear that their parents may be discriminated against or treated unfairly. Katrina Serrano, a 28-year-old DACA recipient whose mother was undocumented, recalled walking into stores only to be repeatedly ignored by employees who focused on greeting other customers. Katrina explained that this is "your daily interaction that you would think going shopping would be a stress-free activity but sometimes it's not." In the same way that she felt compelled to protect her mother from deportation, she wanted "to shield my mom from seeing or noticing that." Katrina tried her best to comfort her mother with reassuring messages like, "Oh, they just didn't see you," but she knew deep down her mother sensed the truth. At the end of a shopping trip, Katrina often felt anger and exhaustion. Over time, young adults like Katrina develop an awareness about the ways in which legal status *and* race operate together across settings to shape their parents' levels of risk of discrimination or deportation within the geographies of deportability. They strive to mentally prepare for such scenarios while also shielding their parents or reassuring them of their belonging.

Camila Iglesias, a 29-year-old DACA recipient whose parents were undocumented, was concerned about her father being deported or exploited. This was in part because he drove to multiple locations for work, which forced him to navigate the geographies of deportability for a living. He also frequently interacted with strangers and customers, some of whom knew about his immigration status. Camila was particularly worried that her father might be stopped by the police or immigration, or that he might be the victim of "racist comments" or exploitation. "Sometimes he has a hard time making a deal with a person or an employer just because they know about his status. So, they don't want to make the deal with him, and he starts to lower the price and lower the price and lower the price," she explained. He settled for these prices because he had scant options. If he pushed back, people may have threatened to report him to the authorities, and he feared the same thing Camila did: his deportation.

For these reasons, young adults often feel a sense of privilege and responsibility, which is in sharp contrast to their parents' vulnerability. Camila continued:

> I feel like if I have an encounter with the authorities, I will be okay. Not 100% okay. But I think I will be okay. But if I . . . just having that idea of my parents encountering . . . having to go through a checkpoint, it really scares me a lot. There are times where we all leave to work at the same time. And then we're on the same freeway and then all of the sudden my dad goes on the I-15 [. . .] and I just get that fear of him facing like racist comments.

Regardless of their individual immigration status, children in undocumented and mixed-status families experience the effects of illegality and racism in relational terms.[12] They worry about their parents' safety and well-being. They dread the moments when they know their parents will be by themselves, especially if there is a high likelihood of their encountering immigration officers, entering a hot spot, or interacting with the pseudo-migra.

When loved ones are unaccounted for outside of the expected time windows—perhaps they did not reach their intended destination, did not follow their typical routine or travel route, or did not answer their phone— time slows down. Minutes become hours. The mind begins to imagine possible explanations, ranging from benign to worst-case scenarios. Mariana, a 23-year-old DACA recipient, said, "It's stressful because if somebody doesn't come home at the time that they usually do, when you know they are off work. You start wondering, 'oh, he didn't go anywhere else.' So, it's stressful." Even upon confirming their loved ones are safe, the ongoing state of worry takes a toll on young adults' well-being and changes the way they relate to their family members. Emotional undercurrents of fear, anxiety, stress, dread, anger, and loss course through the lives of young adults, and in response, they take the lead in their families' efforts to make sanctuary.

Because enforcement in the shadows and its expanding geographies of deportability primarily target undocumented parents, a key facet of sanctuary making among young adults entails the gradual assumption of their parents' responsibilities. To this end, young adults often volunteer to provide rides, check on the status of a hot spot, accompany their parents to hot spots, or travel there alone. They also make financial contributions to the household. Young adults are also proactive about preparing for the worst-case scenario: a parent's deportation. This entails both grappling with the thoughts and emotions associated with being separated from a parent (mental preparation) and taking steps such as opening an emergency savings account or looking into the process of becoming a legal guardian for their younger siblings (material preparation). Backup parenting is done on a regular basis as the need arises.

There is also an important element of backup parenting that is prompted by physical distance. Unable to be with their parents during crucial times of the day, young adults keep track of their parents' departure and arrival times and the time it takes to drive between locations. This type of awareness of their parents' whereabouts helps to ensure that their parents are safe, and should they be at risk, it prompts young adults to act on a moment's notice. Guillermo, whose father was deported and mother was undocumented, told me that his concerns about his mother's whereabouts were, like Mariana's, "constantly there." He explained, "Every night I'd wait for her to come home, anxious because I didn't have a job and didn't have anything." Guillermo kept track of his mother's work schedule and knew that she would arrive home by six o'clock at the latest. If she was not there by then, he would "be really worried [and] give her a call, but of course she'd be driving so she wouldn't really answer my calls." He would go through the same worries when his mother started attending church meetings.

Having a meticulous memory of their parents' routines, whereabouts, and routes is not just a habit—it is a socioemotional adaptation and a form of sanctuary making that allows young adults to foster a sense of safety and protection. By keeping track of these details, young adults gain reassurance that their parents are where they are expected to be, reducing uncertainty and fear. If any deviations occur, they are prepared to act, whether by anticipating potential risks or by traveling to their location. While this form of backup parenting involves material adjustments, such as regularly texting or calling to confirm their parents' safety, its deeper significance lies in the emotional weight it carries. Awareness of their parents' whereabouts becomes synonymous with security, while any unexpected changes signal a need to intervene and protect. Through their sanctuary making efforts, young adults actively work to create a sense of protection within an otherwise precarious reality.

This form of sanctuary making requires near constant communication with their parents via frequent messages or calls. Natalia Cervantes, whose parents are undocumented, was particularly worried about her mother because she did not have a driver's license. Her father was able to get a license, so Natalia felt he was relatively safe at least when it came to a potential encounter with law enforcement. As part of her backup parenting efforts, Natalia would contact her mother whenever she was not home. She would check in with her to know where she was and to obtain confirmation that she was safe. She would promptly ask her mother: "Where are you? How long are you going to take? Call me if you need anything." Young adults like Natalia meticulously keep track of their parents' whereabouts on a regular basis, to the point that for many it seems like second nature. It is a behavior they have often deeply internalized and largely normalized. While recalling her daily routine, Gabriela Martínez aptly observed, "Now that I even say it, like I notice it, that we do call each other a lot, just to see where we're at." Any prolonged gaps in information—either because they cannot reach their parents or because their parents unexpectedly deviate from their routine—are cause for significant concern.

Young adults also remain on call for their parents, especially when they need to travel to a hot spot or when there is a possibility that they might interact with the pseudo-migra. For example, when a parent needs to go to the hospital for an emergency or the DMV for their vehicle registration, young adults are on standby to provide advice on how to answer probing questions from staff about their forms of identification, home address, social security number, or country of birth. Even when they are unable to be with their parents physically at certain times of the day, young adults foster a sense of safety and protection through their emotional accompaniment. In this case, their efforts to check in via text or call serve to reassure their parents that they are safe. Their children are just a phone call, text, or short drive away. This allows young adults to create a sense of closeness and proximity, and subsequently of protection, in relational space-time away from the immediate threat of deportation.

Young adults with DACA, permanent residency, or U.S. citizenship volunteer to drive their parents whenever possible. Natalia said she told her mother, "If she doesn't need to be behind the wheel to not drive if at least somebody is here that has their driver's license. And if I'm sleeping, you wake me up, and I'll go." Family members with legal status may travel to hot spots alone, allowing more vulnerable relatives, often parents, to avoid these locations, though not always permanently.

Sometimes, young adults volunteer to travel to the hot spot first to check whether it is safe for their parents to go there, too. For example, when driving through the federal immigration checkpoint for a family trip, young adults may go on separate cars even if they are heading to the same destination as their parents, so that they can first verify whether the checkpoint is open or closed. This requires significant effort on the part of young adults, who first mentally prepare for the possibility that the checkpoint may be open, a burden that often begins during the days leading up to the family's planned trip.

These concerns and adaptations are also prevalent between spouses. Vanessa, a 31-year-old U.S. citizen, texted her husband, who is undocumented, every morning as he drove to work: "And we literally live like a mile away from his job, but I was like, 'Are you at work? Did you make it safe? Are you ok?'" By contrast, being at home together brings families a level of comfort. This is less about how being at home acts as a physical shield against outside forces and more about the relational aspect of being together. If not completely safe from the threat of deportation, family members can nevertheless count on each other's support if immigration officers show up. Many young adults told me that they longed for this type of closeness as much as possible, particularly during periods when there were rumors about raids, frequent sightings of immigration officers, or news about major changes in immigration policy.

Backup parenting sometimes involves multiple households. During periods when the checkpoint is regularly active, some young adults ask friends for help verifying if it is open or closed on the day their parents are scheduled to drive through it, if they themselves cannot do it because of work, school, or other commitments. On social media, private groups allow young adults to ask for advice on whether it is safe to travel to a particular area. They can also browse through similar threads started by others to assess the likelihood of a checkpoint being active. The purpose of these private groups is for members who are driving through a checkpoint to provide real-time updates. Many young adults belong to a broader network in which information sharing about hot spots through text or social media is a common practice.

Many young adults check notifications from grassroots organizations like Alianza Comunitaria or UdB about any sightings of immigration officers or DUI checkpoints to gauge if it is safe for their parents to leave their home or travel to a particular place.[13] This type of information sharing not only helps families safely navigate the geographies of deportability, but also lessens some of the burden that young adults shoulder in their roles as backup parents. Rather than having to travel somewhere to check for themselves whether immigration officers are there or not—an activity that requires significant time and traveling distance—young adults could rely on the work of immigrant rights organizations for some aspects of backup parenting. These efforts bind families and organizations together in a network of trust and solidarity in ways that chart new terrains away from hot spots, crucial for both survival and reimagining the use of public space.

Aware of their parents' vulnerability and limited opportunities in the context of the geographies of deportability, many young adults feel compelled to financially contribute to household expenses. Among young adults whom I interviewed, their contributions typically made up anywhere from 30 to 50 percent of the family's income and as such went to covering the costs of rent, groceries, cable, internet, or utilities, among other expenses. This was all while taking care of their own personal expenses like clothing, gas, cell phone data plans, tuition and books (if enrolled in college), and costs incurred during outings with their friends. Cassandra, a 23-year-old DACA recipient who was raised by a single mother, shared that she helps "with the bills, paying taxes. I have to work part time when I'm still in school to be able to help out with the bills. So, I work, I go to school and do my internships and all the money that I get just goes to bills to help her out." Young adults' contributions are notably highest among single-parent households.

In addition to helping financially, young adults sometimes accompany their parents to work, especially if their occupations are in landscaping or cleaning. From a young age, some of them also go to work. While they do not necessarily earn an income at their parents' worksites, children are nevertheless working. They help translate for their parents, secure clients, and fulfill work orders.[14] Gabriela Martínez explained, "Since I started working with my mom, [my younger brother] started working with my dad. He would be translating. He wouldn't be like necessarily doing the physical work but translating for my dad." Gabriela's younger sister, too, occasionally went to work with her mother. Other young adults complete individual work orders for their parents, particularly when the task requires traveling to a hot spot. This can include delivering party rentals on their behalf. Through their labor, young adults ease some of the stressors and concerns associated with working and commuting in the geographies of deportability while undocumented.

FROM BACKUP TO SUBSTITUTE PARENTING: TAKING ON PARENTAL RESPONSIBILITIES DURING TIMES OF CRISIS

If, despite a family's best efforts to circumvent risk, a parent is arrested by immigration officers, young adults' efforts take on a different form better described as "substitute parenting," given the sheer number of parental responsibilities they must adopt. The transition from backup to substitute parenting is often abrupt and intense. The experience of Sara, who was a community college student at the time her father was deported, illustrates the process through which a young adult may transition from backup to substitute parenting. Her father's deportation both forcefully separated him from his family and prevented him from financially providing for the household. Her mother was deeply affected, as Sara recalled: "That's when it was really downhill because she used to always take care of the kids and everything.... But when my father was deported, she couldn't support them.... He was the breadwinner, so she gave in to alcoholism." Given that immigration enforcement practices largely target Latino men, mothers like Sara's suffer tremendously, both financially and emotionally.[15] Sara sought out mental health and rehabilitation services for her mother, as well as financial support, but many of these resources had restrictions based on immigration status, gender, income, and insurance coverage. Sara's frustration was clear as she recalled encountering multiple closed doors: "I took her to the hospital a lot of times, and every time they'd be like, 'We don't have services for her. We don't have anything.'" Sara also called various rehabilitation facilities, "but one told me they couldn't because of her immigration status. The other one told me they couldn't because they didn't accept women. Apparently, they only took men. And then another place that I called ... didn't accept anybody, period, that had—I forgot what it was—unless they had a lot of money or insurance." This was during a time when Sara's mother needed extensive support to cope with the aftermath of her husband's deportation and the sudden loss of a significant portion of their household income.

Without the institutional support she needed, Sara's mother's situation worsened. Her alcoholism soon began to interfere with her ability to care for her children, all of whom were living at home with her, except for Sara. Then one day, when Sara went to visit her mother and siblings, she was shocked to find out that her siblings had been left by themselves, without adult supervision. She asked them, "How long have you all been here?" Her siblings replied, "Mom hasn't been back in a couple days." At this point, Sara said, "I grabbed them, I showered them, I took them to eat, and then I took them to their school, and that's when the school started questioning me about my mom." The school wondered why her siblings had not come to school and where their mother was. It was then that Sara "broke down and told them about the alcoholism." Sara very much needed and thought she had found a sympathetic ear in the school personnel.

However, she had not anticipated that the school staff would end up calling Child Protective Services (CPS). Upon CPS becoming involved, circumstances worsened for the entire family. Sara's mother lost custody of her children. As the oldest sibling, Sara tirelessly fought for custody, but CPS eventually ordered her siblings, all U.S.-born citizens, to live with their father in Mexico, where he had been deported. In this instance, the school staff effectively functioned as part of the pseudo-migra by calling CPS on the family; this was an action that eventually resulted in Sara's younger siblings undergoing de facto deportation.

Consequently, Sara went from backup to substitute parenting. "I was hurdled into all these responsibilities and all these really hard decisions that people shouldn't make so young," Sara said about the effect her parents' deportation had on her life. "So, it went from that to like, *where am I going to stay while I send money to the kids? Or when they got sick.* Every day it was a stress about whether they are eating." She elaborated: "I didn't realize how much work my mom put into raising all these kids. It was kind of like I became a mom overnight." Although Sara tried to regain custody of her siblings—a task that entailed securing a larger apartment and new job—her request was ultimately denied. When we spoke four years later, only one of Sara's three siblings had returned to the U.S., to live with their aunt. Sara remained hopeful that she would be able to bring her other two siblings back home in the future.

Following a parent's arrest, young adults like Sara are compelled to abruptly assume the role of a substitute parent. This is a process whereby young adults adopt an even larger share of their parent's responsibilities such as driving, cooking, cleaning, and disciplining younger siblings. At a deeper level, substitute parenting is about more than just taking on responsibilities; it is a way for young adults to reclaim a sense of belonging in the spaces where they and their parents have lived. This involves maintaining hope and normalcy while fostering a sense of unity, working to keep the family together both physically (in the U.S.) and socially (across borders).

Adrián Guerrero recalled drastically shifting his routine and responsibilities after his mother's arrest: "For me, it was a lot of responsibilities because I would drive. I would keep the house clean. I would keep up with the clients. The big thing is, I would wake up early. I never wake up early, so I would wake up early and every day I would have to call someone just to get a job, every day." Adrián added, "That was my mom's job to do. I would just go to school, help her out sometimes with the job. But since she was gone, I did all this alone." Adrián stepped in to fulfill his mother's previous role as the primary caretaker and financial provider. In a separate interview, I spoke with Adrián's sisters: Susana (an 18-year-old U.S. citizen) and Daniela (a 20-year-old U.S. citizen). Both sisters agreed that their mother's arrest "was the toughest for him to be honest," in part because he lived at home with her and had gotten close to her, whereas both sisters lived with their father. (Their parents had divorced when all three children were young, so they lived separately.) As substitute parents, young adults often see a significant increase in their financial responsibilities, sometimes assuming both parents' previous roles as primary providers. The transition from backup to substitute parenting often occurs immediately after a parent's immigration arrest with greater repercussions as time passes.[16] It requires spending even more time and energy on their previous responsibilities and contributions. It also entails new and related responsibilities, such as that of emotional anchoring.

EMOTIONAL ANCHORS: MANAGING EMOTIONS AND COPING STRATEGIES FOR SIBLINGS AND PARENTS

Parents and young adults alike often do their best to emotionally support one another. Mothers generally reassure their spouses and children, talk with them, and listen to them. Fathers express their care and support for their children through gestures like reserving them a parking spot in busy apartment complexes or side streets near their homes, preparing them lunch or snacks for work and school, filling up their gas tanks, or washing their cars. These nontraditional types of emotional support are meaningful to young adults. While these acts are relatively small, they are nevertheless frequent and thoughtful. Young adults recognize these gestures as different than their mothers' and interpret them as their fathers' attempts to show that they are thinking of them and supporting them. Maricela noticed this difference between her own parents: "I don't talk to [my dad], but he's there for me. For example, the other day, he went to Walmart, and he bought bottles of water for me to take to work." While her father did not necessarily ask about her day or her feelings, his small gestures communicated to Maricela that he cared and was thinking about her.

Without much dialogue, young adults like Maricela sense their fathers' care through these gestures and occasional conversations about their days. On the other hand, mothers generally make themselves available to discuss their children's emotions. They often ask their children about their days, including how they are feeling. Young adults for their part engage in backup parenting and consequently concentrate much of their efforts on their younger siblings. They tend to their needs and emotions as needed and mentally prepare for a future when they might become sole caretakers following a parent's deportation.

Yet as young adults transition from backup to substitute parenting, the nature and direction of the emotional support they provide to their loved ones also drastically changes. This is in large part because of the profound effects that a parent's arrest has on the entire family. Young adults whose parents are arrested notice abrupt and drastic changes to their loved ones' health and general well-being. Mothers in particular, who were once the primary sources of emotional support, often become distraught following their husband's deportation, to the point that it severely interferes with their ability to fulfill their previous roles. More specifically, mothers may experience frequent emotional breakdowns; trouble sleeping; a lack of appetite; and difficulty completing their daily routines and responsibilities, including caretaking, cooking, and cleaning.

Under these circumstances, there is often a role reversal between young adults and their mothers whereby young adults become the primary sources of emotional support—the anchors—for the entire family. These roles are qualitatively different from the typical emotional support young adults might offer as backup parents, due to both the depth and direction of care involved. It is one thing for young adults to provide emotional support to their younger siblings; it is quite another to extend that support to their parents as well. Supporting both generations not only broadens the scope of responsibility but also deepens the emotional demands placed on the young adult within the family. Substitute parenting then is a dynamic role that not only encompasses a larger share of financial contributions and other kinds of material responsibilities, but also entails emotional anchoring, which I define as the process of learning how each family member is feeling and coping and subsequently adopting responsibilities to support them.[17]

Maribel, whose father was detained after their neighbors turned their home into a hot spot (see chapter 2), explained that her mother was "really trying to be strong but [broke] down" after her father's arrest. Consequently, there was a role reversal between Maribel and her mother; it was "hard to see her like that because it's usually . . . [h]er giving me strength, and I had to give her [strength] for a change." This is a type of role reversal that is well-documented in the context of divorce or a severe disability within the family and is often referred to as a form of "parentification."[18] Parentified children often take on caretaking responsibilities for or toward their parents, including cooking and caring for younger siblings. I find that parentification can also result from a parent's immigration arrest. Moreover, it is possible for young adults to willingly adopt these behaviors as a strategy to foster a sense of stability and normalcy during periods of upheaval. In this context, parentification leads to significant shifts in both the direction and distribution of emotional support among young adults. The experiences of young adults like Maribel highlight that a key aspect of substitute parenting involves offering emotional support not only to siblings but also to parents. This dynamic can persist even when a deported parent returns to the U.S., as the roles and responsibilities established during their absence often remain entrenched.

As emotional anchors, young adults prioritize their family's well-being and needs. They devote more time to attending community events or social gatherings with their family and consistently check in to understand how their loved ones are feeling, seeking ways to ease stress within the household. Others mimic aspects of their parent's behavior or personality, such as their strong work ethic. They also strive to keep their parents' "spirit" alive by playing their favorite songs around the house. Following his father's deportation, Guillermo, the eldest of three children, tried his best to figure out how his mother and sisters were feeling at any given moment. He also supported them emotionally by helping them stay distracted. He felt particularly responsible for being the emotional anchor in the household. While some "people think it's kind of cliché to live with your mom," Guillermo shared, he was not bothered because he prioritized his family and their ability to be together. He noticed that sometimes his younger sisters were sad "because they don't get to see my dad as often, and so I'm usually there just to try and make them happy. I'll tell them, 'Let's go and do something fun' or try to keep their mind off things so they don't have to worry about it." After their father's deportation, Guillermo took a proactive role in supporting his family—tuning into their emotions and organizing activities to help them cope.

During the process of emotional anchoring, young adults like Guillermo often turn to outside activities to cope with the challenges of life at home in a parent's absence. These are efforts that first and foremost require young adults to be emotionally aware and to assess how their family members are feeling and coping. They gather this information from conversations, observations, or personal reflections about changes in their loved one's demeanor.

Viviana Valencia, who was 26 at the time of her father's deportation, noted that during the first week after he was separated from the family, "it was so hard for [my mom] to function. She was just crying and crying. She didn't want to talk." Reflecting on the lingering effect of the deportation, Viviana shared that "even to this day, my mom still lives in that house.... She smiles, but it's not the same way.... I feel like she's suffering from anxiety and depression." In her role as the emotional anchor for her family, Viviana acquired an intimate and nuanced understanding of her mother's well-being. She made an important distinction between her mother's outward expressions and the subtle changes in her smile, which were more revealing of her emotional state. As emotional anchors, young adults like Viviana are keenly attuned to their loved ones' behavior, appearance, emotional expressions, routines, and interactions with others. This attunement necessitates both a sustained level of care and close observation of their loved ones, especially to account for subtle changes over time.

LEGAL BROKERING: MEDIATING LEGAL INFORMATION AND NAVIGATING IMMIGRATION PROCESSES

In addition to their roles as backup (or substitute) parents and emotional anchors, young adults also help broker legal information between their families, legal actors, and the state. Young adults often help their parents navigate legal processes, understand their legal rights, secure legal services and resources, or obtain information about their legal options. The set of responsibilities young adults adopt in the legal realm varies in large part by the family's enforcement status.

For families in which a loved one has never been arrested but nevertheless lives with the fear that one day it could happen, young adults primarily take the lead in developing their family's emergency plans. This entails searching for resources online, such as emergency preparedness templates they can use in the context of immigration enforcement, identifying emergency contacts, and facilitating difficult conversations about the possibility of a loved one's deportation. To prevent an arrest, young adults share resources like Know Your Rights cards.[19] They either hand them directly to their parents or strategically place them in key spaces where their parents spend much of their time—at home (near the front door, on top of a table or dresser) or inside the car. Keeping these cards visible and easily accessible prepares their parents for a possible encounter with an immigration officer. Beyond their practical use, these visual tools help foster a sense of security in everyday spaces. For young adults, knowing that their parents have the means to assert their rights offers a small measure of solace, reinforcing their efforts to create protection and stability within liminal landscapes.

Following a family member's arrest, access to legal information, support, and resources are most needed. Without prior knowledge about the inner workings of the immigration system or deportation proceedings, families often struggle to secure adequate and trustworthy legal representation for their loved one. They also need to search for a loved one across the various detention centers (and in-between transfers); secure funds to pay for legal services and a potential bond; and compile evidence that may help to prevent their deportation, such as letters of support from relatives, friends, or coworkers. There is also the issue of time as families race against the clock to secure enough legal support before their loved one is deported without due process. Under these circumstances, young adults take the lead and prioritize their legal brokering responsibilities. This includes locating their loved one who is detained and translating legal documents.

Ana, who was a college student when her brother was first apprehended, recalled that at the time she was the only one in the family who spoke English, and "when it came time to call the officers, calling the detention center, and stuff like that, I had to do all of that." Ana explained that this required a substantial amount of effort, as it "took a lot of my time, a lot of my energy, a lot of stress." This was especially the case because immigration officers and lawyers were asking technical and legal questions, some of which Ana did not fully understand.

Such circumstances can be particularly stressful for young adults, as they are not just tasked with effectively communicating information between multiple figures of authority, but they also need to make careful decisions about the type of information they can safely exchange with others, which often carries significant implications for their family. They need to consider the potential repercussions information sharing may have on their loved ones who are undocumented, including those who have already been detained and those who have not been detained but nevertheless live in heightened fear. For example, when employers probe young adults about a parent's indefinite absence from work, young adults need to promptly and carefully frame their responses so as not to reveal their parent's detention and subsequently their immigration status.

Across the spectrum of enforcement, young adults also search for trustworthy immigration lawyers who can explain their parents' options for relief. This often requires young adults to ask their mentors or friends for recommendations; search online for the lawyer's areas of practice and fees; and even conduct preliminary discussions with immigration lawyers to determine their trustworthiness and affordability before formally requesting their legal services. Taken together, these efforts are exemplary of young adults' legal brokering, which require them to stay informed about immigration news, events, resources, and immigrants' legal rights during encounters with law or immigration enforcement.

Clara, a 21-year-old U.S.-born citizen, was proactive about searching for options for relief for her parents, who were both undocumented. More than a decade earlier, Clara's parents were apprehended at a clothing store in San Diego. One of the store employees wrongfully accused her parents of stealing and called the police. At the time, Clara was separated from her parents for weeks. Both were eventually released from the detention facility, and their cases were temporarily closed. Aware that their cases could be reopened at a moment's notice depending in part on the political climate, Clara stayed up to date with immigration-related news and events and shared this information with her mother, who would tell her not to worry about it. Clara, however, could not help but do so: "How can I not worry about it if they're my parents?" She frequently searched for resources, but when she would tell her mother about them, she "wouldn't reach out to them anymore. It was just like I connect her, but she doesn't really try, because she's just tired of everything." In the process of legal brokering, young adults inevitably participate in emotional anchoring, too, working to keep their parents' hopes up.

In the case of Clara, legal brokering entailed encouraging her mother to seek resources and helping her sustain a sense of hope. Her mother's hope, however, diminished over time as it became clearer that short of significant changes in U.S. immigration law, it would be near impossible for her to adjust her status given her existing immigration and criminal records. Emotional anchoring during the process of legal brokering can be particularly difficult to sustain because of the pain and sense of hopelessness that families often contend with upon realizing that there are limited avenues for relief, if at all.

Young adults whose parents are hopeful that they could adjust their immigration status through U.S. citizen children once they turn 21 may experience such emotions quite intensely when they learn that despite their ties, they may not be able to proceed with the case because of a previous deportation, criminal record, or unauthorized entry. Under these circumstances, young adults consult with multiple immigration lawyers, often exhausting their resources to no avail. They try to encourage their parents to remain hopeful that one day policies might change in their favor. They also hold onto the hope that there could be some kind of exception that would apply to their parents' case. As the rates of criminalization and deportation of immigrants continue to increase, alongside blocked legal pathways and diminishing protections, it is likely that more immigrant families must contend with this reality in ways that compel young adults to adopt a greater number of responsibilities within the realms of legal brokering and emotional anchoring.

Young adults' legal brokering can also extend to other aspects of daily life, such as securing housing and employment. In these instances, young adults help their parents navigate concerns that deal with their tenants' or workers' rights. Carmen explained how her parents relied on her help to navigate the process of securing employment and a new home to live in. She attributed this in part to her age and level of education: "Now that I'm older and that [my parents] know that I'm obtaining more education and stuff they definitely always expect me to know the answer to everything." However, like other types of legal brokering, this was "a huge pressure to have because sometimes I don't know or sometimes it's just hard to explain things to them." Carmen's legal brokering (to help her parents find a new home and job) was prompted by immigration officers' presence at their workplace.

Such roles intensify as the expanding geographies of deportability penetrate deeper into the realm of social reproduction for families. Carmen described a level of codependence between her parents and her. By virtue of living at home, and therefore being around them more often, Carmen felt that her parents expected her help more than her brother's.

Other young adults are uniquely positioned to engage in legal brokering because of their political and civic engagement. As immigrant rights organizers or activists, some young adults have access to a large network that can assist them in keeping up with immigration-related news or addressing pertinent questions and concerns. Camila Iglesias mentioned that since she received a college education and was an activist, her parents expected her to know more about immigration policies. However, this was a difficult task because "everything is changing daily, so you don't know everything, so you have to check in with other people, like I have to check in with you, or Naomi, Guadalupe, or anyone. So, we're not fully informed but since I'm the one that went to college, I'm supposed to know more, so I'm supposed to have the answers to everything they ask me. And then I do get emotional." Staying up to date with changes in immigration policy and enforcement is an essential responsibility for young adults like Camila, as it assists with their backup parenting, emotional anchoring, and legal brokering efforts.

Nevertheless, legal brokering is a complicated and difficult task that requires young adults to constantly discern between rumors or facts, follow the latest news on immigration, and spend additional time researching and brainstorming the implications of such news. Keeping up to date with immigration news also brings emotional challenges, as the constant influx of information can be overwhelming for young adults. It forces them to confront their parents' vulnerability, making them acutely aware of the risks they face. This ongoing awareness can evoke feelings of loss, sadness, and anxiety, adding an emotional burden to their role in protecting their families. To assist them with these tasks, some young adults may lean on fellow activists and peers.

RESPONSIBILITY DISTRIBUTION BY AGE, STATUS, GENDER, AND THE FAMILY'S ENFORCEMENT STATUS

Young adults' ability to assume the role of backup or substitute parenting changes over time and is shaped by their own age and immigration status.

As minors, children are limited in the responsibilities they assume because they are unable to legally work or drive. If they are undocumented, children continue to face these limitations even into young adulthood. For those who have access to DACA, the ability to legally work and drive significantly shapes their backup or substitute parenting.

Brenda Quesada, who grew up undocumented and whose father was apprehended by immigration officers on two separate occasions within a span of 10 years, shared that she was 15 years old at the time of the first arrest. Given her young age, Brenda was limited in how much she could contribute to her family's sanctuary making efforts, especially materially. She explained that her mother was not working, so they relied heavily on savings. At the time, Brenda was unable to find a job to support her family due to her age and immigration status. When her father was apprehended a second time, Brenda was older (23) and was able to legally work under DACA. She explained that her mother was still not working because of an injury and illness, but Brenda was "not as worried about it, because I am able to work, and my sister just turned 18, so she can work as well. It's not the financial as much anymore as much as the emotional burden that it brings." Still, as Brenda shared, the family was contending with the emotional toll of their father's arrest and detention and the real possibility of being deported.

The eldest children or those with access to some types of legal protection (such as DACA or legal permanent residency) are most often in charge of making greater financial contributions following a parent's immigration arrest. Damián Aguilar explained how he had to find a new job with higher pay to financially support his family following his father's arrest and subsequent deportation. When I asked Damián if he could share how his role and responsibilities within the family changed since his father was apprehended, he explained that this happened "dramatically." At the time, Damián was about to move out of his parents' home and so he "was already in the mindset of just fending for myself." He remarked that his family came first, and so rather than continuing to prepare for his move, he made mental and material preparations for how his family would cover their household expenses now that their income was abruptly cut. In addition to eliminating expenses like cable TV and sticking to the "bare minimum of things," Damián explained that he also "immediately started looking for a new job because I was working at a store, and it was part time. I knew that wasn't going to be enough." With DACA, many young adults gained access to a driver's license and better employment opportunities.[20] The experiences of young adults like Damián and Brenda demonstrate that DACA is crucial for young adults' backup and substitute parenting efforts.

For Katrina Serrano, DACA not only "opened a lot of doors and made me realize that I could get better jobs" but also gave her "a chance to contribute to my household income" more substantially. Prior to DACA, young adults contributed financially to the extent that they could while often relying on their parents' help to cover their personal expenses. With DACA, many young adults gained relative financial independence from their parents and were positioned to make greater contributions to the household income.[21]

Some siblings share responsibilities. This is more likely to be the case if there are multiple siblings older than (or nearly) 18 years old. Recall the experience of Gabriela, who helped her mother keep up with rumors about raids while her younger sister accompanied their mother to work. Brenda and her sister also split their financial responsibilities.

The distribution of responsibilities in the aftermath of a parent's detention is also shaped by gender. The eldest daughters often become responsible for taking care of younger siblings, cooking, and cleaning, while the eldest sons contribute financially to the household and discipline siblings.[22] Valentina Jiménez, a 29-year-old legal permanent resident whose mother was previously detained, shared how she and her older brother, Alejandro, split their mother's responsibilities between them following her arrest. At the age of 15, when she was undocumented herself, Valentina took care of her younger siblings. This entailed "cooking for them and cleaning after them. Making sure they bathe, shower, and have clean clothes. Make sure they get to school on time. Make sure they come home and do their homework . . . just tasks that a mother would do to make sure that her kids are okay." Alejandro, on the other hand, became the primary financial provider and disciplinarian of the house. Valentina shared, "My older brother, he really did step up a lot where he started working and helping out [. . .] and being there in the financial sense of it. And many times, when I had a hard time disciplining my siblings where they wouldn't listen, I would just tell them that I was going to tell my older brother and they kind of feared him. He had this authority over them, over all of us really." By splitting responsibilities between siblings, sanctuary making at the family level becomes more manageable.

As is the case with backup and substitute parenting, age informs the extent to which children partake in emotional anchoring. Beatriz, a 20-year-old

U.S.-born citizen, for example, was too young when her father was first arrested. This is a day that was seared in her memory, as she recalled her mother crying while "trying to explain to me, and I could barely understand her." At a loss for words and unsure of how to help, Beatriz hugged her mother upon seeing her. She explained that it "was so scary at such a young age to see her breaking down like that." As a seven-year-old, Beatriz was limited in the type of emotional support she could provide her mother. She noticed that her mother got very lonely without her husband or emotional support. Because of Beatriz's young age when her father was arrested, the best she could do at the time was to keep her mother company and hug her. As Beatriz grew older, she began regularly asking her mother how she was feeling. In some ways, Beatriz explained, she was filling in the gaps of the type of support her father could not provide in part due to his own personality and his previous arrest. Beatriz became aware of her circumstances at a young age, and as she grew older, this awareness developed into a conscious ability to engage in emotional anchoring.

How legal brokering responsibilities are distributed within the family is influenced by several factors, including, as in Ana's case, knowledge of the English language. Legal brokering also often falls on the shoulders of the oldest children in the family. Nataly, a 26-year-old U.S.-born citizen, for example, explained how her older sister (Priscilla) played a critical role in helping their family navigate conversations with the lawyer and her father, who was detained: "My sister, yeah, I felt like she was feeling overwhelmed. She was also very helpful because with the move and she's the one who communicated with the lawyer and everything. She was saying that at the time she was 17 or 18, so she was dealing with the lawyer." Adding to Priscilla's sense of being overwhelmed was the fact that it is "a complex system and to be able to communicate with him, you have to fill out a form, you have to send in letters, and she's the one that deals with that. She's the one that deals with sending him money. You have to call a certain number. You have to put in some information on my dad's identification number and all this other crazy stuff." As the legal broker of the family, Priscilla became familiar with the visitation forms and process and with the steps involved to send him money. In this instance, legal brokering responsibilities were primarily dictated by age and birth order rather than gender or legal status. Notably, Nataly's older sister was undocumented, but her status did not deter her from engaging in legal brokering. Instead, her older age at the time of their father's arrest propelled her into that role.

When a family member is deported, sanctuary making revolves around efforts to keep the family emotionally and socially connected and to seek forms of reunification in either the U.S. or their loved one's country of birth. If all children in the family are minors, sanctuary making efforts often fall on both the parent who has remained in the U.S. and the parent who is in their country of birth postdeportation. Angelica Nuñez and her husband (Giovanni), for example, struggled for years to keep their family together despite multiple deportations and reunifications. At the time of my interview with Angelica, she was living in San Diego with their seven-year-old daughter. They were both U.S.-born citizens. Following one of his deportations, Giovanni lived in Tijuana, Baja California, Mexico, a city that is located approximately 25 miles south of San Diego. Although he had extended family members who lived farther south in Mexico, Giovanni was determined to live as close to San Diego as possible so that his wife and daughter would have a shorter distance to travel when visiting him.

To remain connected despite living across borders, Angelica and their daughter would drive to Tijuana every Friday evening. This allowed them the opportunity to spend time with Giovanni during the weekends while living in San Diego for the rest of the week, where Angelica worked and their daughter went to school. These living arrangements, however, were less than ideal. By the second year postdeportation, it became taxing on all accounts—emotionally, physically, and socially—for the Nuñez family to sustain these arrangements. Angelica and Giovanni brainstormed how they might live together again.

Because Giovanni was banned from reentering the U.S. after one of his latest deportations, the most feasible option was for all three of them to relocate to Tecate, Baja California, Mexico, a city located approximately 40 miles southeast of San Diego. Angelica and Giovanni concluded that housing was more affordable in Tecate compared to the other neighboring cities. Living in Tecate, they felt, would also allow Angelica and their daughter to commute to San Diego on weekdays for work and school. (The wait time to enter the U.S. in the mornings was shorter at the Tecate port of entry than at Tijuana's.)

An extensive body of literature examines the experiences of transnational immigrant families.[23] Scholars point to the hardships and violence that families endure across generations as a direct consequence of changes in immigration law and neoliberal policies in both the receiving country and their place of birth. Parents, children, and extended family members alike often grapple with significant periods of prolonged separation, feelings of abandonment and isolation, alongside guilt and regret.[24] What is unique in the context of the era of enforcement in the shadows is that a growing number of transnational families like Angelica's are being forced into these arrangements by deportation. Moreover, they are contending with a set of bars that legally prevent them from reuniting in the U.S., even if the member who has been deported has intimate ties to a U.S. citizen who could otherwise petition for them.

Under these circumstances, individual members long for the ability to be together as a family unit. Indeed, families sometimes decide that they will all relocate to Mexico.[25] What is unique about the San Diego context, and other cities similarly located near the U.S.-Mexico physical border, is that arrangements can sometimes be made so that some members continue to live in the U.S. while their loved one who has been deported lives a couple hours away. This setup allows those who are U.S. citizens to visit with some regularity. Such a decision is made immediately after a loved one's deportation or with the passage of time as it proves increasingly difficult to sustain other alternative arrangements.

Relocating to Mexico as a family unit, while maintaining connections in the U.S. vis-à-vis family ties, work, or school, can be challenging. When they moved to Tecate, Angelica was relived to be physically reunited with her husband again, though she lamented that she never felt quite at home in Mexico. She tried her best to take it day by day, not letting the prospect that these arrangements would last months, if not years, become overwhelming. However, when they neared their fourth year postdeportation, Angelica was struggling with depression. Living in Tecate meant that she lacked the time, resources, and support necessary to take care of her mental health; most of the time she was driving, working, or trying to rest. During the interview, Angelica broke down in tears as she recalled recently telling her husband, "I can't do this anymore because I've lost myself in the process." Confronted by the need to choose between her own mental health or her marriage, Angelica was driven to give Giovanni an ultimatum: either he would return to the U.S. despite the risks so that they could live together as a family in San Diego, or they would have to separate. The conditions that stop families from legally reuniting in the U.S. postdeportation also prevent them from fully healing. Under these circumstances, spouses face diminishing hopes, difficult decisions, and turbulent moments across borders.

Families' efforts to remain connected—whether physically or emotionally—following a deportation are varied and dynamic. In some families, there is only one member who can legally travel across borders and is thus tasked with visiting their loved one. Each visit represents an important moment to reconnect and exchange items. Sometimes these items help address essential needs (like money, food, or clothing). At other times the items are more sentimental in nature and include family photographs, favorite belongings left behind, and gifts. When more than one member can travel, young adults may accompany their younger siblings to visit their parent. Those who are undocumented in the U.S. and cannot legally travel try other measures to remain connected and be helpful, such as making frequent calls, sending money, or helping identify resources from afar. They also hold onto the hope that one day they will be able to see their loved one again. Or they mentally prepare for scenarios in which their other parent or younger siblings may have to relocate to Mexico to be with their parent who has been deported.

Deciding whether to stay in the U.S. or accompany their loved one to Mexico is a difficult choice with far-reaching consequences. When she was 12 years old, Ana moved to Mexico with her mother and younger brother to follow her stepfather, who had been deported. The family lived there for a couple of years but eventually decided to return to the U.S. because Ana and her younger brother were struggling to adapt to the new culture. Although Ana was born in Mexico, she had lived in the U.S. since she was four years old. She knew how to speak Spanish but "struggled with writing it, reading it, and just understanding and pronunciation." Her brother, a U.S.-born citizen, similarly struggled to adjust to life in Mexico and would often arrive home from school crying. After two years of living in Mexico as a family, her parents decided they would attempt to return to the U.S. The journey was the easiest for Ana's younger brother, who was a U.S. citizen. Ana and her father, too, had relatively easy journeys despite their undocumented status. Ana's mother, however, had a much more difficult time reentering without authorization. It took her three months and multiple attempts to cross the border, one of which involved a kidnapping by the very individuals who were ostensibly helping her migrate. This episode was not only deeply traumatic for her but also inflicted profound emotional and financial harm on the entire family. During this period, Ana's family was filled with uncertainty and fear for her mother's safety. The emotional toll was compounded by the material burden: in total, the family spent $23,000 to facilitate their separate reentry attempts and ultimately reunite in the U.S. The condition of "hyper-illegality", which subjects families like Ana's to repeated deportations and separations, also imposes greater vulnerability and financial costs on the entire household.[26]

Depending on young adults' age at the time of their parents' deportation, and whether it is a two- or one-parent household prior to the deportation, children sometimes require substantial help from other households to remain in the U.S. Daria, for example, is a 26-year-old U.S.-born citizen who was raised by a single mother. The family's living arrangements drastically changed when Daria's mother was deported. Daria remembered coming home from school one day and being confused about why her mother was not there. Suddenly, Daria "got this gut feeling that something went wrong. I didn't know what and then my aunts came in maybe an hour after and told me all that." It was then that Daria learned her mother was questioned about her immigration status while trying to enter a navy base where she was scheduled to work cleaning one of the housing units. Her mother was detained and was deported within a few days.

At the time, Daria was only in middle school. She wondered whether she would be able to continue her education in the U.S. While she had previously traveled to Tijuana to visit her grandmother, Daria never went to school there. After her mother's deportation, Daria's aunts offered to move in and help care for her so that she could continue her education in San Diego. This support allowed Daria the opportunity to finish the rest of middle school with the same teachers and friends. However, it became financially unsustainable for Daria's aunts, who eventually "decided that rent was too expensive, and they would go back to Mexico." At that point, Daria was older in age and determined to continue her education in San Diego, so she took the initiative: "I shared my story with some girls from my school, where my bus stopped, and they talked to their parents and one of them said that I could stay with them." That support from a peer's family allowed Daria to continue her education in a relatively stable living arrangement, albeit temporarily. Within two years, when tensions in her peer's household arose, Daria had to once again look for a new home. She went through two more separate households after that to make it through high school and college.

> DARIA: I think I started opening up to friends and then after that, I realized that I felt liberated that I wasn't hiding. Then I started sharing it with some of the teachers that felt like I could trust them. I did. Luckily, it didn't backfire on me, but as I reflect on it, I realized that I could have been taken to ... What's it called? I'm not sure what it's called, child custody?

CAROLINA: Foster care?

DARIA: Foster care, yeah. Because that's really where I should have been had I not been with family, but I didn't. I wonder if that helped or hurt me because I know that when I was in college, there are certain programs in place to help college students who have been in foster care. Because I hadn't been [in foster care], technically I wasn't able to access that help.

CAROLINA: In some ways, you felt like you faced similar challenges as kids who went to foster care?

DARIA: Yeah, because I was living with families that I didn't fully know, but I just wasn't placed in the system because it wasn't all official then that's why I didn't get to benefit from what they had to offer.

Having secured alternative living arrangements outside of formal systems, Daria was able to complete her high school degree. However, she still grapples with the question of whether it would have been better for her to have been placed in the formal foster care system. Initially, she felt grateful that her teachers had not reported her, sparing her from official intervention. But in hindsight, she wonders if that decision ultimately hurt her—she felt as though she had lived much like a foster child, moving between multiple households to finish middle and high school without her mother's presence, yet without the formal designation. This lack of official foster care status later prevented her from accessing certain support systems in college that were designed to help foster youth. At the time of our interview, Daria was in graduate school. To sustain their mother and daughter connection, Daria traveled every weekend to Tijuana, where her mother was now living. Nevertheless, with the passage of time and growing responsibilities, it became more difficult for Daria to keep making regular trips across the border.

DISCUSSION

As the geographies of deportability expand under the era of enforcement in the shadows, young adults are compelled to undertake roles as backup (or substitute) parents, emotional anchors, and legal brokers at an early age, roles that are often interlocking. Take for example instances when young adults investigate the process of becoming legal guardians for their siblings. At first glance, this task fits squarely with the notion of legal brokering, as it entails navigating a legal process, legal guardianship. Yet young adults primarily do this in preparation for the worst-case scenario as part of their backup parenting efforts. Young adults are apt to determine what type of efforts are needed and when. They often engage in backup (or substitute) parenting, emotional anchoring, and legal brokering simultaneously and for prolonged periods. Considerations of young adults' experiences must account for all three of these roles while acknowledging how one or more may take precedence in their lives at any given moment. We must also work to disentangle the various forms of sanctuary making that young adults are leading to gain a deeper understanding of how these intersect, the time and energy spent on each, and ways to alleviate the burden of each of these roles.

The distribution of responsibilities varies by age, status, gender, and the family's enforcement status. The oldest children typically assume greater responsibility and care for younger siblings. Young adults' immigration status also influences their ability to undertake such responsibilities. With DACA, young adults are often uniquely positioned to help their families with tasks that require legal protection, such as working and driving. Gender, too, shapes the distribution of responsibilities between siblings. Daughters may adopt greater responsibilities like caretaking, cooking, and cleaning, while sons assume increased financial responsibility. Movement along the spectrum of enforcement can also shift young adults' roles from backup to substitute parenting after a parent's arrest and introduce new roles such as emotional anchoring. The distribution of responsibilities matters for how we understand young adults' shifting roles within their families in the context of enforcement, including the toll that these circumstances may have on their personal lives.

Each of these roles comes with clear responsibilities, such as providing financial support and assisting with legal processes. However, beyond these practical duties, young adults also drive socioemotional changes, fostering a sense of safety and protection. Together, these material and socioemotional efforts help families navigate, mitigate, or cope with the constraints imposed by the geographies of deportability.

To understand young adults' varied perspectives and adaptations from childhood, it is important to track their experiences through retrospective interviews or interviewing them during childhood. From an early age, children become aware of their parents' sacrifices. As they grow, they not only hear these stories but also witness and experience tangible effects of immigration policies and enforcement in their daily lives. They become keenly attuned to the risks associated with navigating the geographies of deportability and gradually lead the charge in their family's sanctuary making efforts. In the process, young adults develop a consciousness that is attuned to both the vulnerabilities embedded within the geographies of deportability and the need to protect their families through sanctuary making efforts. Sociologist Leisy Abrego highlights how young adults' consciousness is shaped by early experiences of exclusion. From a young age, they come to understand their differences from peers—realizing they cannot legally drive, work, or apply for financial aid.[27] At the same time, they also recognize their responsibility to protect their families.[28] Building on this work, I find that young adults' consciousness extends beyond stigma and responsibility; it is also deeply shaped by fear, their family's enforcement status, and the spatial distribution of immigration enforcement.

Young adults develop a deep, personal understanding of deportation through their surroundings and family experiences. Whether as an imminent threat or a lived reality, deportation brings intense fear of separation and profound loss: emotional, social, legal, and financial. Beyond physical separation, they worry about younger siblings entering foster care and the burden of becoming primary caregivers. The term "deportation" is not an abstract concept but one tied to specific places, people, and routines, shaping their daily lives with persistent dread. This awareness heightens their vigilance—they track their parents' movements, assess risks, and guide their families in precautionary measures. In their communities, they foster safety and unity, displaying Know Your Rights cards and honoring deported loved ones through music and memory. Constantly adapting to shifting threats, they recalibrate their understanding of vulnerability, navigating an ever-changing landscape of deportability.

Through the framework of the geographies of deportability and sanctuary making, we can also recognize the wide range of spatial contexts that arise in absolute, relative, and relational space. We can also appreciate the daily rituals of sanctuary making that unfold in such contexts, including that of emotional accompaniment, which exists in relational space. Indeed, the kind of contexts that arise in relational space are equally consequential as those we can readily observe, as both prompt young adults to act. In this instance, young adults are compelled to keep track of their parents' whereabouts and schedules. It is imperative to fully account for young adults' perspectives and adaptations as they navigate the geographies of deportability and sanctuary making. This approach allows for a deeper understanding of how families define their relationship to the places they inhabit and the roles young adults adopt in the process—including those that may be detrimental to their well-being.

FOUR

The Emotional and Material Tolls of Enforcement

IN THE FACE OF heightened enforcement, Camila Iglesias, a 29-year-old DACA recipient, became a secondary mother to her siblings. The family immigrated to the U.S. some two decades ago, and Juana, her older sister by two years, used to fill a similar role. Juana explained that she would "stay home all the time," looking out for Camila and their siblings. That changed when she had children of her own, and Camila slid into the same role. Now their younger siblings "go to Camila. She takes care of them right now." Ever since Camila and Juana were young, their mother spent most of the day working to make sure they had a safe place to live in, food, and other essentials.

Camila spoke proudly of her caretaking responsibilities. She drove her younger siblings to school, helped them with their homework, and encouraged them to get good grades. Having graduated from college as an undocumented and first-generation student, Camila saw herself as a role model for her siblings, all of whom are U.S.-born citizens. Her next youngest sister, Lily, she said, more or less "had to go" to college. For her younger brother, still in high school when we spoke, college also seemed a given. If you asked him, "What are you doing after high school?," Camila said, he would reply: "I'm going to college, duh." Camila worked hard to go to college as an undocumented student, she told her siblings, but college should be a given for them as U.S. citizens.

For the most part, Camila's undocumented status did not interfere with her ability to care for her siblings. Once the DACA program was implemented in 2012, she became more secure in her role as the "second mom." She obtained her driver's license, which protected her while driving with her siblings. She also secured a higher paying job, which allowed her to purchase a new car and make greater financial contributions to the household. However, the 2016 U.S. presidential election results abruptly called into question her ability to be a caretaker for her younger siblings. With significant coverage of deportation on the news, she recalled, "Our communities got scared and my parents got scared." The temporary and limited nature of DACA seemed riskier than it had before.

As a mixed-status household, Camila and her family have contended with the possibility of being separated for as long as they have been in the U.S. Of primary concern was the future of Camila's youngest siblings: What would happen to them if their parents were deported? Following a parent's deportation, children might relocate outside of the U.S. to live with their parent who has been deported,[1] or they might remain in the care of an older sibling or extended family such as aunts or grandparents. In other instances, children under the age of 18 might be placed in the foster care system, where they would be legally separated from their parents.[2] To prevent such scenarios, some undocumented parents transfer the legal guardianship of their youngest children to their eldest child.[3] This is an important form of sanctuary making in which intimate ties help foster a sense of security and stability in the face of an uncertain future. Nevertheless, when Camila's mother revealed her plan to transfer legal guardianship of the youngest siblings to Lily, Camila's sense of herself was shattered.

Camila asked her mother, "Why Lily? I'm the oldest. I'm the one responsible for my brothers . . . of my siblings. Why are you having her be the responsible one?" Her mother responded, "Because you don't have a secure status either." From her mother's perspective, Lily was over 18 years old and had a stable future in the country by virtue of her U.S. citizenship. For Camila, however, it introduced a fear that Lily "was taking my position of me being the oldest and me being the second mom of my siblings." Camila's identity was deeply rooted in her caretaking responsibilities. She had poured a lot of her time and energy into that role over the years.

While the threat of deportation is a shared condition among undocumented and mixed-status families, there are important differences within the household regarding perceptions of who is most at risk and who is uniquely positioned to enact a form of protection and stability. From Camila's perspective, factors such as her parents' undocumented status and age, along with her father's darker skin complexion and occupation—which required him to drive to different locations—made them particularly vulnerable to being deported. At some level, Camila's mother also agreed with this assessment of risk. Where the two differed, however, was with respect to whether Camila or Lily was better positioned to fulfill the role of care-taking in the future if both parents were arrested. Camila's mother was fearful of the possible revocation of DACA and wanted to secure the most stable future for her younger children. Even just considering and discussing her mother's plan took a toll on Camila, who painfully shared: "That was the first time I would say, *Mom, you're taking that away from me.*" Camila, whose sense of identity largely stemmed from her role and responsibilities within the family as a backup parent, believed she was best suited to steer the family through any crisis that might come.

The restructuring of family life, as the Iglesias family experienced first-hand, is central to sanctuary making. In this context, young adults often assume roles as backup or substitute parents, emotional anchors, and legal brokers. Although these efforts are pragmatic and aimed at safeguarding the family, they carry significant psychosocial costs. These include grief, stress, a loss of identity, substantial personal sacrifices, and an intensified sense of responsibility. Indeed, while sanctuary making allows families to confront and better cope with the geographies of deportability, it also has its limits and can carry its own set of costs. This chapter examines the emotional and material tolls of immigration enforcement as they manifest through the burdens that sanctuary making imposes on young adults. Many of them are shouldering these burdens while simultaneously managing their own precarious status by virtue of being undocumented or DACAmented themselves and negotiating life in liminal landscapes. They are balancing the weight of their family's protection with the challenges posed by their own uncertain futures.

PROTECTIVE ROLES AND THE STRAIN OF RESPONSIBILITY: PERSONAL SACRIFICES, FINANCIAL STRUGGLES, AND DERAILED TRAJECTORIES

In North County San Diego, the Fernandez family has also contended with the possibility of being separated for over a decade, and they, too, have re-shuffled family roles accordingly. Renata Fernandez (a 28-year-old DACA recipient) and her siblings grew up with a single mother who worked tire-lessly for decades in both the service and manufacturing industries. However, about a year before our interview, their mother was laid off. When she began applying for new jobs during the summer of 2016, her children were concerned that her immigration status would be revealed. Many of the places that were hiring had implemented E-Verify, a system that enables employers to confirm applicants' eligibility to work in the U.S. Renata explained that with "people being detained, immigration coming to the work environment and taking people," she and her siblings were "just afraid that something [was] going to happen, that she [was] going to be stopped." All three children—who, as DACA beneficiaries, had work permits that enabled them to secure relatively well-paying and stable jobs—decided to distribute the task of providing for the family's finances among themselves. This strategy, they thought, would allow their mother to stay home and avoid the risk of being detected. As the youngest and only sibling living at home, Renata's brother became responsible for paying the rent for him and his mother. Renata and her two siblings split all other expenses, including groceries, health costs, and phone charges. Months into this arrangement, however, Renata and her siblings were struggling to afford their own household, medical, and personal expenses. Renata explained that she was continuing to give her mother "$500 every month," but that she could not "give more because of my rent, my food, my gas, my everything." With limited resources and a growing sense of responsibility, Renata and her siblings did their best to shield their mother from the risk of being detected. In turn, however, they had to make significant personal sacrifices and endure financial struggles. Renata's brother eventually made the difficult decision to drop out of school during his second year of college so that he could work more hours to pay for the increasing cost of rent. The added financial stress also affected his physical health. He was struggling to eat, sleep, and get out of bed on most days.

The Fernandezes' story is by no means unique. Following the enactment of DACA, young adults' newfound legal protection, albeit limited and temporary, instilled in many of them the need to make greater contributions to the household.[4] Many understood it as an issue of survival and commitment to remain together as a family. Renata explained that immediately after benefiting from DACA, her brother searched for jobs: "He told my mom, 'I'm tired of us struggling for food, struggling to pay rent, struggling for everything.' Ever since he got DACA, he's been working." With DACA, young adults have secured better paying jobs or work multiple jobs to make greater financial contributions to the household so that their parents do not have to experience continued financial stress or work. In the words of another young adult, Matías Herrera, parents of immigrant children "already have enough to worry about. They don't need more stacked-on top." Young adults often frame their financial contributions in the context of lessening the burden that their parents endure daily.

While not all undocumented or mixed-status families rely on young adults' financial contributions, most families I interviewed had at least three working members, including both parents and adult children. Among these households, where at least one member was undocumented but never apprehended, the self-reported average income was $45,706.[5] Notably, the average household income was lower among families in which a member was arrested ($37,142) or deported ($26,080). These numbers suggest that it is difficult for undocumented and mixed-status families to rely on any single individual for financial help.

Adding to the overburdened roles young adults take on, there are issues of under- or uncompensated time at work undermining families' sanctuary making efforts. Recall the experience of Mateo Ruiz, who was compelled to leave for work three hours before his scheduled shift to avoid running into immigration officers outside his home, at dawn. To ensure that he would be able to continue providing for his family, he spent extra uncompensated time at work, away from his family. The father (Emiliano) of another young adult I interviewed went off employment records following the advice of his boss. This was a strategy that protected him from immigration agencies in case of an audit of the company's employment records, but it also made him vulnerable to exploitation. Now that Emiliano was off payroll, he did not have a set schedule. His boss often asked him to come at unexpected hours and to work overtime without adequate compensation. This also meant that on some days, his boss asked him to arrive at work between 4:00 a.m. and 5:00 a.m.—a precarious timeframe when immigration officers typically roam the streets—to help set up before the restaurant's opening hours.

Issues of being underpaid also came up even among people with shared immigration statuses and from similar racial and ethnic backgrounds. Nayeli, a 51-year-old mother who was undocumented, recalled that she spent years working for someone who was also undocumented. Nayeli cleaned approximately four houses a day and received $50 in compensation for the day. Nayeli explained, "Abusan de uno por que uno está illegal. Pero ella está igual, pero como ella tiene más años aquí [. . .] se aprovechaba! [They take advantage of us because we're illegal [*sic*] even though she's also in the same situation, but she takes advantage because she has been here longer.]" Even though they were both undocumented, Nayeli was at a disadvantage because she desperately needed a source of income. Her boss also perceived that she could take advantage of Nayeli because she had lived in the U.S. longer. Other respondents shared similar stories about otherwise friendly and understanding employers taking advantage of undocumented workers, or in some cases, behaving with outright hostility—refusing to pay earned wages or subjecting employees to verbal abuse. In this context, young adults' financial contributions are crucial because they serve as a counterbalance to the structural forces that leave their parents under- or uncompensated.

Under the pressure that comes with sanctuary making, young adults may feel guilty for dedicating any time to themselves or their friends. They may also feel a strong need to always be with their families. Rubén Durante, an 18-year-old DACA recipient, felt this sense of guilt and urgency. Following the 2016 U.S. presidential election, Rubén stopped hanging out with his close friends "because I was scared that my dad would have to drop me off at their house and he would come back alone and maybe one of those times that he came back alone he was going to get detained or deported." He felt similarly frightened for his mother and sister. Rubén also felt an urgency to be close to them: "I didn't want to leave their side. I didn't want to hang out with anybody. If we were going to go somewhere we're all going to go." Young adults are keenly attuned to changes in the geographies of deportability based on the political climate, including the risk that is embedded in public roads where law enforcement may function as the pseudo-migra. As part of their sanctuary making efforts, young adults frequently think about the worst-case scenario so that they can take precautionary measures. This helps explain not only Rubén's fear that his father might encounter law or immigration enforcement while driving home alone, but also his decision to avoid spending time away from home with friends. In some instances, such risks can compel young adults to work alongside their fathers—in landscaping, cleaning, or construction—to accompany them as they navigate the geographies of deportability. This is the case even if it means foregoing relatively stable and better paying jobs.

Sanctuary making across borders also places significant strain on young adults, who must balance their daily responsibilities at home while being there for their loved ones from afar. For example, young adults determined to visit a parent or sibling in Mexico after deportation struggled to get enough time off work or school to travel. Additionally, transportation was a barrier for minors or those without cars, requiring them to coordinate with others for rides. Marcela, a 20-year-old U.S.-born citizen whose brothers were deported, explained that it was difficult to see them often because her employer "hardly give[s] me days off to go there. I don't have a car, or else I'd go. I'd have to go by bus with my mom or plan it out with my parents and say, 'Okay, let's go together for two days, and come back.'" Although Marcela was determined to visit her brothers regularly, particularly so her son could build a close relationship with them, she was limited by her work schedule and lack of personal transportation.

In some cases, young adults face the difficult decision to step out or drop out of school to focus on supporting their families. This is especially the case in the aftermath of a parent's immigration arrest or deportation and if such events occur when young adults are near their high school graduation or in college. Marcos Valencia, a 27-year-old DACA recipient, started working with his father at a young age. For years, Marcos kept up with both his work and school responsibilities. He graduated from high school and enrolled in a local community college, where he was pursuing a degree in mathematics. In 2014 he was just one semester away from obtaining his associate's degree when his father was deported. It was then that Marcos had to drop out of college and run his father's business so that he could help his mother cover their household expenses. He also had to care for his daughters and emotionally support his siblings after the loss of their father. This was when, Marcos noted, "Everything just fell apart." He added, "My marriage, my ex-wife, you could say she got bothered that I was tending my mom too much and [she] would say, 'What about us? You forgot your own family.' We just had personal problems, so we ended up divorced." Marcos, like other young adults who faced similar challenges following a parent's deportation, concluded that everything "piled up. It was a domino effect." Under the pressures of losing a parent to a deportation, young adults like Marcos dedicated substantial time and energy to their substitute parenting efforts in ways that severely impacted their own trajectories and relationships.

THE EMOTIONAL WEIGHT OF EVERYDAY WORRIES: OVERWHELMING STRESS, SUDDEN EMOTIONAL BREAKDOWNS, AND DECLINING HEALTH

Young adults contend with multiple daily stressors while navigating the geographies of deportability and participating in sanctuary making. The incessant worry of being separated from their families. The need to constantly look over their shoulder when driving and keep up with immigration-related news. The gut-wrenching worry over a loved one's departure or late arrival, especially when there are rumors about raids. The constant need to circumvent hot spots or avoid the pseudo-migra. The endless set of "what ifs" and "plans a, b, and c" over the worst-case scenario. The trauma of witnessing or directly experiencing the effects of a deportation. The need to hang on to hope even when it is diminished.

There is also an overwhelming pressure to repay their parents' sacrifices. Young adults are keenly aware of the sacrifices their parents endured during the immigration journey. This awareness further shapes how children understand what a deportation means and their sense of responsibility. Children in undocumented and mixed-status families realize that a parent's deportation would prevent the entire family from reaping the benefits of their collective sacrifices. This lesson represents two sides of the same coin: children often think about their parents' vulnerability when recalling their sacrifices and vice versa. This is an important issue to account for as it helps us gain a deeper understanding of young adults' internal pressures to protect their parents and subsequently the reasons many go to great lengths to prioritize their family's safety and well-being over their own.

Matías Herrera witnessed his parents' sacrifices at a young age. His father migrated first and would send money home to Mexico. To reunite with him, Matías immigrated alongside his mother and sister to the U.S. in 1999. Matías remembered his mother's fear of arrest and death during their journey, the trailer park followed by the garage that the family first settled in, and the inescapable fear that prevented his parents from living freely with peace of mind. When I asked Matías how often he thought about his parents' sacrifices, he responded: "All the time. Some people, I don't know if it just doesn't cross their mind, but for me it's all the time. I know that my parents are here for us." He looked into the distance and explained that his parents "can't be out too late; they can't do certain things." He referenced a popular regional band in Mexico, Los Tigres del Norte, and their song "La jaula de oro" (the cage of gold) to describe the sharp contrast between being in "paradise" yet "trapped." This entrapment comes from the way immigration law is implemented through the geographies of deportability, such that "you can't really do anything or go anywhere if you want to. I know that's what they want. They haven't had a break or vacation in a long time, and we can't just be like, 'Well, let's go fly out here, or go there,' because we have to watch out. We have to see if there's a checkpoint." In the end, Matías reflected, his parents endured these fears and anxieties for him and his siblings: "They don't do it for them; they do it for us." Young adults like Matías possessed a deep understanding, admiration, respect, and gratitude for their parents' sacrifices. In detail, they recalled the various reasons that motivated their parents to make the difficult decision to immigrate. For some, the decision to immigrate was fueled by growing insecurity and violence in Mexico. Others described a hopeful search for better economic, health, and educational opportunities for their children. Whatever the motivation to migrate, children witnessed their parents making real sacrifices to pursue it—leaving behind previous homes, jobs, and familial ties in their countries of birth.

As children navigate the geographies of deportability and sanctuary, they not only carry with them the determination and inspiration that derive from their parents' sacrifices, but they also bear the weight of the stress and guilt that come with what Carmen described as "the pressure to have to succeed in an extreme way." This is a heavy weight to carry for young adults, who often feel compelled to shoulder many of the responsibilities for their family's safety and well-being even at the expense of their own mental health.

Children born in the U.S. also face an unspoken pressure to petition for their parents' adjustment of status. Sandra Villa, an 18-year-old, felt this pressure at a young age "because I was told that once I turn 21, I can get my parents papers and stuff, and so I think, even in the back of my mind I'd always think, *okay, I have to grow up, I have to be older.* And I think that's one of the reasons why I said, *I will graduate early from high school. I'm going to try to do things faster* [emphasis added]." Sandra found solace in reaching milestones such as graduating from high school and enrolling in college earlier than many of her peers. It was her attempt to become older even though she knew her biological age would not change: "I'm still going to be 21 when I'm 21, you know?" At the time of our interview, Sandra was only three years away from turning 21. However, after speaking with an immigration lawyer, Sandra realized that it would be complicated for her parents to adjust their undocumented status. Sandra said, "Now I hear that it still doesn't make a big difference when I'm 21," to which her sister (Emilia) added, "We spoke to a lawyer, and it just seems like for my parents' situation it's definitely a longer process than just having their child ask for them." As U.S. citizen children consider the possibility of helping their parents adjust their undocumented status, time may seem to speed up or slow down. Families may encounter challenges such as financial difficulties that make it hard to cover legal or administrative fees, delaying their ability to apply as soon as they become eligible. In more complex cases—such as those involving a prior deportation, multiple unauthorized entries, or a criminal history—families often discover they must wait longer before applying to ensure they meet the eligibility requirements. This can be a frustrating moment for children, especially when they have grown up believing that they can help their parents adjust their status as soon as they turn 21.

A young adult whose parent has been deported also experiences guilt, frustration, stress, and a sense of powerlessness when contemplating how to reunite with their loved ones. Sara had not seen or spoken to her mother since she was deported in 2014. Since then, Sara had struggled to take care of her younger siblings (first in the U.S. and later from afar) and to locate her mother and find a way for her to be able to safely return to the U.S. This was particularly challenging and distressing for Sara because as a DACA recipient, her own immigration status prevented her from freely traveling to Tijuana, where her mother was last seen. During our conversation, Sara mentioned that she finds it difficult to be at home and have idle time, as that is when she is more likely to think about her mother's whereabouts. She added: "So, that's why every single day I got home I didn't want to be home. Because every single time I got home, I have all this stress and stuff I'm thinking about, and you sit down and it's like *there's the kids and my mom, where's my mom? I should be looking for her.*" In the process, Sara felt a tremendous amount of guilt, along with a sense of pressure and responsibility to find her mother and reunite with her siblings.

These pressures, fears, and worries have a lasting impact on young adults' mental health. Carmen was born in Ensenada and immigrated with her family to the U.S. at the age of seven. She lived undocumented in San Diego for over a decade. It was the place where she attended school, developed friendships, and created family memories, and where her parents secured employment opportunities. The fact that the neighborhood (and surrounding cities) where Carmen lived was imbued with a growing number of hot spots interfered with these experiences. This limited where her family could safely shop, travel, socialize, attend school, work, and rest. It also functioned as a source of chronic and sustained suffering. At one point Carmen shared that she "was so young when I was brought here, and everything just affected me, and I've carried that with me as I've been growing up." This weight, she suspected, "has been the reason for a lot of things I struggle with mentally and everything. The fact that I'm undocumented and how we've had to navigate our life that way." Young adults like Carmen commonly used words such as "weight," "load," "bricks," or "buildup" when describing the set of fears, pressures, traumas, pains, and preoccupations they carried with them as they navigated everyday life while undocumented (or as U.S. citizens with undocumented parents). This weight was a defining feature of their experiences circumventing and coping with the geographies of deportability. It regularly influenced young adults' emotions and energy levels, to the point where it often interfered with their ability to sleep, concentrate, rest, or enjoy outings with their family and friends.

For young adults in undocumented and mixed-status families, both the weight of navigating the geographies of deportability (on their own and with their families) *and* participating in sanctuary making give rise to their legal consciousness, which often becomes too heavy to bear. Inevitably, this weight can be debilitating and difficult to overcome. Katrina, who grew up undocumented for more than a decade, identified the weight of it all as the cause for her depression. Although Katrina was the youngest of three and her oldest brother was a U.S.-born citizen, she felt compelled to lead their family's sanctuary making efforts. By the time she reached young adulthood, Katrina had assumed all three roles—of backup parent, emotional anchor, and legal broker—in her family. Even after her mother became a legal permanent resident and eventually a naturalized U.S. citizen, Katrina kept fulfilling many of the same responsibilities and knew that she would be "the one to take care of her when she gets older." The burdens associated with sanctuary making can at times extend far into the future even when the family's enforcement status becomes less vulnerable. As a young adult with DACA, her income now covered at least 50 percent of their shared expenses, and sometimes much more. Meanwhile, Katrina's personal ambitions had fallen by the wayside. By the time she was granted DACA, Katrina felt she was already "stuck" in her role at home. Although in theory she could have searched for a job that better aligned with her passions and interests; realistically, Katrina felt she could not just "abandon" her mother. In Katrina's eyes, pursuing her true career aspirations would jeopardize the stability and pay that her current job offered her and subsequently prevent her from financially contributing to the household. These circumstances took their toll on Katrina over the years: "The mental aspect is just feeling drained after going out, which is supposed to be like a fun day, a free day. Feeling really tired after work and then if I start thinking too deeply about my situation, about my future." These thoughts bring up acute anxiety, "to the point where I just get so afraid that I don't want to do anything anymore . . . that I don't want to continue with anything." Looking back, Katrina sensed that such circumstances led to her depression, which went undiagnosed for several years.

Maricela is a 33-year-old college graduate who has similarly lived undocumented in the U.S. for over a decade. Despite achieving her dreams of obtaining a bachelor's degree in nursing, it was difficult for Maricela to find meaning in her work, relationships, and plans. Contributing to the distress that she was experiencing was the fact that she did not qualify for DACA because of its exclusionary age requirements, and as such she was unable to legally work in the country.[6] Moreover, the prospect of any form of relief was out of reach. With a college degree and passion to work in the medical field on the one hand, and the inability to secure employment without a social security number on the other, Maricela had instead been relegated to working in the service sector. She was working from 8:00 a.m. to 9:00 p.m., going from one part-time job to the next, on most days of the week.

Under these pressures, Maricela was not eating well. She had recently been diagnosed with anemia because her iron levels had reached an all-time low. She was also unable to get enough rest. During the interview, I could tell this had all taken a toll on her emotional well-being. She broke down on multiple occasions, especially when we spoke about the political climate under the first Trump administration, her jobs, or her plans. In her own words, Maricela painfully told me, "I am not living a normal life. It is affecting my stress. My emotional, physical, everything. . . . There are days that I am very energetic and very positive, but there are days that I feel very down." For some time, Maricela had been experiencing sudden emotional breakdowns. "There have been times where I am at work, and I can't control my emotions, and I start crying at work," Maricela started to cry as she continued, "and then I have to hide because I don't want anyone to see me. It's hard. [. . .] There are times when I don't want to, but all of [a] sudden I just cry. When I get home after a long day, I feel super tired. I have my to-do list, but for the most part I never follow my to-do list because I am so tired." Throughout the interview, Maricela reflected on the weight of having to lead two separate lives. At work, she learned to hide her emotions and the fact that she had a college degree to avoid probing questions from others about why she was not pursuing her career aspirations. In her dating life, she did not tell others about her immigration status, work, or college degree.

She feared coworkers and prospective partners could report her to immigration authorities with relative ease. Young adults like Maricela used phrases such as "not living a normal life," "living a double life," or "living in a third dimension" to denote the sheer instability and fragility of navigating everyday life while undocumented. This is one of the many tolls of enforcement on young adults that can often go unnoticed and therefore unaddressed, since it is often experienced as an internal battle.

There are times when the tolls of enforcement become visible. Accounts of difficulty eating are consistent with rapid weight loss. Signs of difficulty sleeping are evident in undereye bags or fatigued bodies, trouble concentrating, or irritability. For some, feelings of hopelessness and depression are visible through self-inflicted wounds. Most of the time, however, the effects of enforcement are hidden from the outside world. Young adults experience chronic headaches or migraines, stomach or abdominal pain, suicidal contemplation, shortness of breath, and chest pain. They also endure sudden emotional breakdowns, depression, debilitating anxiety, growing distrust of others, recurrent immigration-related nightmares, and at times a sense of hopelessness. Young adults often keep these internal battles private. Such battles only occasionally prompt them to schedule doctor appointments to find out possible causes. On some days the weight of it all results in sudden mood changes and makes it difficult for young adults to get out of bed.

The weight of navigating parallel, or double, lives is particularly distressing when legal protections are threatened. This has been the case for many undocumented young adults since 2016, when the then presidential candidate Donald J. Trump first threatened to terminate DACA. Right before Trump was inaugurated for his first presidential term, several news reports surfaced about the precarious state of DACA and its beneficiaries. On September 5, 2017, the Trump administration officially terminated the program. This placed thousands of young adults in limbo once again. For undocumented youth who turn 18 years old and meet all other eligibility requirements, USCIS has stopped granting approvals on initial requests for DACA for more than seven years. This means in part that undocumented high school graduates have been contending with particularly acute uncertainty and vulnerability over their futures for the last few years. For those with DACA who remain eligible for renewal, fear lingers that their protections could be abruptly revoked. This anxiety is compounded by the threat of losing their jobs, income, and ability to drive safely—all essential opportunities for navigating the realities of deportability and engaging in sanctuary making.

In separate interviews, young adults described the emotional turmoil they faced during the 2016 U.S. presidential cycle, Trump's 2017 inauguration, and the prolonged uncertainty surrounding DACA. Perla Torres, a 28-year-old DACA recipient, explained that following the 2016 U.S. presidential election, it was "a roller coaster of emotions," adding that "the first few days I was just very sad. I was crying half the time just for no reason." Perla was particularly concerned about her ability to continue working should Trump fulfill his threat of terminating DACA. Gabriela Martínez was similarly distressed about the uncertainty surrounding DACA under Trump's first presidential term. Days before Trump's official announcement on September 5, 2017, Gabriela had trouble sleeping and eating and experienced frequent headaches. She recalled, "This week I had a lot of headaches just thinking about everything. And eating, sometimes I'm like, *okay, I'm just not going to eat anything.* Or I try to focus on work and it's just I forget to eat. Sleeping too, I mean, I just want to sleep all day." Young adults like Gabriela often did their best to stay distracted, with either work or school, as a coping mechanism. While temporarily helpful, it is difficult to sustain such efforts for a prolonged period.

Over a year after Trump was inaugurated in 2017, young adults continued to grapple with this emotional turmoil in ways that significantly impacted their mental health. Paulina, a 21-year-old DACA recipient, reflected on the point that although she was aware of her situation, she preferred not to think about it. However, she could not continue to ignore it once Trump was elected, at which point "that scaredness [*sic*] that I felt when I was little came back [she cries]." Despite Paulina's best attempts to cope with the sheer uncertainty and acute levels of fear she felt at the time, "it's still there, it won't go away." In tears, she shared, "That's why with the whole political talk that I hear every day with DACA going on, it just got to the point where I'm just like, 'I'm done, I'm over it' [she cries]. And it sucks because I want to have that mentality where I'm just like, 'I'm done. I want everything to be done. If they're going to send me back, send me back,' but I just can't be living like this." Ever since the 2016 U.S. presidential election, Paulina had experienced an acute sense of vulnerability and fear in waves. Each time, it was becoming more difficult to overcome these emotions.

Throughout the years getting to know young adults like Perla, Gabriela, and Paulina both in and outside of the research setting, I have observed the tendency to repress the thoughts and emotions associated with the threat of deportation. It is emotionally difficult to consciously confront one's (or a family member's) deportability. Yet daily reminders of deportability course through the lives of young adults and their families in the era of enforcement in the shadows, both those that are obvious (sightings of immigration officers) and those that are more subtle (orange cones, stadium lights, helicopters). For many young adults, the interview setting represented one of the first sites in which they paused to reflect on the weight of the mounting fears, worries, and pressures they had endured for years.

ADDITIONAL HIDDEN TOLLS OF ENFORCEMENT: MISSED OPPORTUNITIES, LEGAL LAGS, AND COMMUNAL ERASURES

In the context of the geographies of deportability and sanctuary making, young adults also contended with missed opportunities. Many of the young adults I interviewed opted to attend colleges that were near their homes. While the high cost of attendance and lack of federal financial aid inevitably influence these decisions,[7] another often-overlooked factor also plays a role: young adults may choose to stay physically close to their families to avoid driving through immigration checkpoints and to be nearby in case a family member is arrested. Carmen explained that while "she did kind of hope" to attend school out of state, she ultimately only applied to schools in Southern California and decided to attend school in San Diego, where her family lived. "My family is my number one priority," she said. "I always kind of made-up my mind to stay here simply because of the fact I was not comfortable with leaving my family in case anything happened." Crystal, who was in her second year of college when we spoke, also decided to stay close to home. She explained, "I got into all the schools that I applied to, and I got into my dream school which was Los Angeles University, and I was like, 'Oh my God. I can't believe it!'" Crystal's family encouraged her to enroll there, but she ultimately felt that she could not just "get up and leave" her family, especially given her parents' undocumented status, so she decided to attend a university in San Diego. A few weeks before we talked, Crystal's father was apprehended, and she was trying her best to support her family during this difficult time. "I mean I thank myself right now that I trusted my gut feeling," she continued. "I know realistically everything would crumble if something were to happen and if I wouldn't be here." For young adults, choosing to stay close to San Diego for college is not just about academics or the lack of financial aid—it is a deliberate decision shaped by their family's vulnerability. Aware that an immigration arrest could separate their family at any moment, young adults feel responsible to remain nearby. This awareness, coupled with the foresight that they might need to take on a greater role in supporting their parents if such an event occurred, leads many young adults to imagine the worst-case scenario and plan accordingly. Their decisions reflect a relational understanding of familial vulnerability in which young adults weigh their educational aspirations against the ever-present possibility of family separation in the expanding geographies of deportability.

This relational understanding of familial vulnerability continues to shape young adults' aspirations beyond college, influencing their career choices and decisions about graduate school. As the only U.S. citizen in his family, Nicolas, a 22-year-old college student, felt an immense responsibility to protect his parents—especially his father, who, with a prior deportation record, faced heightened risks within the expanding geographies of deportability. This is why he ultimately chose to attend a four-year university close to his parents' home in San Diego. Five years later, these same circumstances continued to influence his decision about where to attend graduate school. While he was eager to attend graduate school out of state and submitted some applications, he wondered, "How am I going to be there, miles away, hours away . . . comfortable?" When we met, he was in the process of finishing the rest of his applications and experiencing these conflicting emotions. "I'm submitting them because I want to have options available but at the same time, I'm scared. . . . [H]ow am I going to just leave my parents? Anything can happen at any moment." Notably, young adults like Nicolas are foregoing significant opportunities due to the threat of deportation. This decision-making process is often shaped by a profound sense of responsibility, guilt, and vulnerability that weighs heavily on them as they navigate critical life choices. For many, the fear of family separation compels them to prioritize staying close to home to provide emotional and logistical support, even when it means sacrificing educational or professional opportunities elsewhere. These internal conflicts not only shape their immediate educational trajectories but can also have long-term implications for their personal and professional growth, as their aspirations are constrained by the ever-present specter of deportability.

Attending a school that is even a short distance away can still pose great challenges. Naomi Gutierrez, whose family resides just a few exits past the checkpoint in Temecula, worried that her parents would not attend her college graduation in North County San Diego. She was the first in her family to graduate from college, so this was an important milestone and moment of celebration. Yet Naomi explained, "My parents are actually scared to come down here. My sister was like, *I don't know if they're going to come.*" Armando, another college student, similarly explained that as much as he wanted his mother to attend his upcoming graduation, it was simply too risky to ask her to travel, because she is undocumented. She had only once before made the trip to San Diego from Orange County to visit her son, and on the drive home, the possibility that the checkpoint could be open had shaken the entire family. Armando described the drive there as follows: "On our way there, we took the wrong turn and then we got into major traffic. She has an app called Waze [. . .] where people communicate about traffic. And so, we asked what was going on." At that point, Armando and his mother learned that the checkpoint was open. Armando recalled, "We were screaming at each other. I had my license, so I told her, '[L]et me drive. Pull over. Let me drive. I'll drive from here.' She insisted, '[N]o, because regardless of the fact if I drive or not, they are still going to check for everyone's papers.' It was just really bad." Once Armando and his family got closer, they realized that immigration officers had just closed the checkpoint. Despite a sudden sense of relief, there was tension. He added that on the rest of their drive back home, "it was just dead silent." On that day, they were safe, but the reminder that the checkpoint could be open at any time was enough for Armando to decide that he would not let his mother take the risk again—not even for his college graduation: "Now she's prohibited from coming to San Diego and it's one of the reasons why I hate going to school here because I know I really want my mom to see me, but she can't come." Parents and children alike make deliberate choices to limit movement and exposure, prioritizing safety over emotional or celebratory connections.

These findings underscore how the geographies of deportability not only constrain physical mobility but also fracture familial bonds and the ability to share pivotal moments. Parents' absence from their children's milestones, while often invisible to outsiders, represents a tangible loss that reinforces the isolating effects of enforcement policies. The spatial and emotional constraints imposed by the geographies of deportability thus ripple across generations, reshaping how families experience success, joy, and connection.

There are high school students in undocumented and mixed-status families who pursue a higher education outside of San Diego County. Some feel compelled to move far from home to escape the sense of confinement they experienced growing up. Having access to a large support network plays a critical role in their decisions. There are high school educators and counselors who help undocumented students connect with recent graduates who are attending (or have attended) a college outside of San Diego. These connections are crucial to attending college beyond San Diego and navigating the challenges of travel and long-distance travel support. However, students who attend college away from their families often experience feelings of vulnerability and guilt, an urge to graduate early, and a sense of disconnection from their hometowns.

In the context of the geographies of deportability, young adults also grapple with "legal lags," a term I use to describe their tendency to delay applying for various benefits they are eligible for and their inability to immediately take advantage of legal protections. This includes applying for DACA, financial aid, or an adjustment of status. Some young adults hesitated to apply for DACA when it was first announced even though they were immediately eligible.[8] Ximena, for example, was "incredibly nervous because I was giving up everything. I was giving up my family because by me telling [USCIS] where I live, I was giving up my parents." Her fear was particularly acute because the U.S. presidential election was near. Ximena added, "I was scared. Do I apply? Do I not apply? This president could come in and who knows what the heck is going to happen and so I waited." While DACA became available during the summer of 2012, Ximena did not submit her application until the following year.

Tellingly, Ximena described the DACA application process as one that required her to "give up everything," because of the type of sensitive information that USCIS collects when processing DACA applications. Ximena was particularly concerned that USCIS could function as a hot spot. While the agency is responsible for reviewing a host of immigration relief applications separately from the work of U.S. ICE officers, growing distrust about USCIS circulates in the immigrant community. This is in part because since its enactment, DACA has been at the mercy of any given presidential administration and as such could be terminated. It is also because there have been reports of ICE officers conducting arrests at USCIS field offices when immigrants whose applications are under review show up for their scheduled appointments or interviews.[9] Ximena was also worried about exposing her parents' immigration and enforcement status (they were both undocumented with an existing deportation record). Notions of being excluded, surveilled, and vulnerable were especially prominent in Ximena's decision-making process, to the point that she delayed submitting her DACA application for close to a year. Even when a hot spot is not actively present, individuals feel compelled to delay legal opportunities due to their understanding of the dynamics of the geographies of deportability. They recognize how easily a location can become a hot spot and remain aware of the increasing data sharing among agencies, reinforcing their caution in navigating legal processes.

Even after benefiting from DACA, young adults contend with another type of legal lag. Namely, they are unable to fully reap the benefits of their newfound legal protection. DACA beneficiaries may not immediately feel safe driving despite their legal protection from deportation. The possibility of encountering DUI checkpoints or driving through the fixed federal immigration checkpoints can remain stressful. Veronica explained, "Even after I had DACA and I was able to cross the checkpoints, I would still feel fear. I think it probably took a few months or up to a year for me to be like, *Okay, nothing is going to happen to me.*" Forms of temporary legal protection such as DACA have undoubtedly expanded recipients' access to a wide range of educational and economic opportunities.[10] However, given the all-encompassing nature of the geographies of deportability, DACA is unable to fully address the long-lasting psychological effects of growing up undocumented. Indeed, it can take years to undo that damage. A similar pattern emerges when considering the enactment of Assembly Bill 60, which provides eligible undocumented immigrants with a driver's license in the state of California. Recipients may remain fearful of their encounters with the police despite having access to a driver's license.

The type of legal lags that I document here are different from delays caused by the state. We know that the state frequently makes people wait for months, if not years, as it processes their applications, whether it is in the context of an adjustment of status application or asylum.[11] This type of waiting is harmful and could be significantly addressed by allocating more resources and expanding the availability of visas to reduce wait times. A geographies of deportability framework makes visible another type of legal lag. Namely, it is possible for a person to learn to fear the unimaginable—that which is most dreaded and exists in the realm of possibilities and imaginations—to the point that it prevents them from applying for certain legal protections or fully reaping its benefits. This type of legal lag is often rendered invisible, as it operates at a psychosocial level and undermines the benefits of obtaining legal protection by preventing individuals from feeling safe.

Service providers, immigration lawyers, organizers, and workers in community health clinics may also enact and prolong legal lags. Brenda Quesada explained that when DACA was first announced, she did not know others who were in a similar situation or organizations that provided pro bono or low-cost legal assistance. Consequently, she consulted an immigration lawyer who intensified her fear of the unknown by telling her, "It's only one try and if you mess that up, you ruin all of your chances." The lawyer then charged her $1,700 in legal service fees to prepare her application.[12] After the lawyer spent six months working on her application and did not submit it, Brenda decided to submit it on her own. She was approved for DACA some months after, but in the process, she had had a bad experience with an immigration lawyer who cost her a lot of money and amplified her fears. When legal lags are enacted by service providers, immigration lawyers, organizers, and workers in community health clinics—the very same institutions and social actors meant to serve immigrant families—it can be especially distressing, frustrating, and dehumanizing. When young adults are going through these periods of time that have been extended, they may experience acute feelings of anxiety, frustration, fatigue, and a return of immigration-related nightmares and unexplained physical ailments.

During the process of sanctuary making, young adults may also engage in a form of "communal erasure"—intentionally omitting personal information about their family members from institutional records, such as those maintained by schools, medical clinics, and nonimmigration courts. Nataly experienced this firsthand, navigating both the routine interactions within her educational setting, such as completing school forms, and the deeper fears her family faced with the broader geographies of deportability. She is a young adult whose family was worried about Hector, the head of the household, after his immigration arrest. To protect him, the family refrained from including any of his personal information on forms, including those necessary for Nataly's school. Nataly explained that she "would help my mom with school sign-up and registration," adding that, "I would fill out the paperwork and when it would come to the guardian, I wouldn't put my dad." Her primary concern was "what if they find out and chase us down?" In addition to removing her father from school records, Nataly also "wouldn't talk about it or him in school. He was invisible, like he wasn't part of our family." Aware of the possibility that information shared with schools could reach immigration agencies, she took deliberate steps to protect her family. As a backup parent, she not only left her father's name off school records but also avoided mentioning him in school altogether. Her need to shield him was particularly urgent, as he had previously been arrested by immigration officers. Indeed, young adults whose parents were arrested, detained, or deported were the most likely to engage in communal erasure as part of their backup parenting efforts.[13]

Young adults whose parents had never been arrested still engaged in such erasures as a preemptive measure, but with far less frequency or urgency, while prioritizing other aspects of their backup parenting efforts. This did not make such efforts less harmful or painful. Young adults still grappled with a sense of fear and shame in the process of erasing. *Am I doing the right thing? How will this make my parent feel?* Spouses whose husbands have been deported also engage in communal erasures, either to avoid having to answer probing questions about their partner's whereabouts or to prevent others knowing about their deportation history, which could raise questions about their own immigration status or plans for reunification. These strategic erasures are communal in that they effectively remove individuals from networks and social institutions like schools, workplaces, and health clinics.

The hidden costs of communal erasures and their implications in the short and long terms warrant further exploration. When Beatriz's father was able to return to the U.S. undetected postdeportation, he was rehired by his previous employer. He was "working there for a long time" and "was really close" to them, Beatriz shared. Aware of his immigration status and deportation record, his boss suggested that they remove him from employment records and instead use his wife's information to "make it look like they're paying my mom." For Beatriz and her mother, this meant "getting financial support" from her father while minimizing his risk of being apprehended once again. These arrangements brought great relief to the family, but when Beatriz was applying to college years later, she learned that it came with an unanticipated financial cost. On financial aid applications, she explained, it looked "like my mom is making all this money and it's just me and my sister and her [in the household]. So then when it came to applying to colleges and stuff, my financial aid packages were pretty shitty." Beatriz did not express any form of regret or anger toward her father for this outcome, and she understood the precarious situation both he and the rest of the family were in. Nevertheless, she did have to contend with the reality that despite financial need, she did not qualify for federal financial assistance and thus had to work extra hours and jobs to be able to afford the rising cost of tuition. The effects of her parents' financial decisions, she said, "sneaked in" on her own time in college. The unequal distribution of legal status and rights within families, coupled with the power differential present in decisions about who in the family unit needs protection and how responsibilities should be redistributed, can become a potential source of tension for families.

COPING IN ISOLATION

How do young adults cope with the realities of navigating undocumented life for their families and themselves? Who do they lean on for support? Although young adults' strategies may vary, one pattern remains consistent: they are often by and large coping in isolation. Young adults provide substantial financial and emotional support to their parents but largely hesitate to ask for help. Often, young adults do not want to place additional burdens on their parents. Moreover, children gradually become accustomed to their own overburdened roles. Beatriz "didn't always feel comfortable putting that weight on them and talking to them about it." Instead, she felt compelled to repress her emotions and keep them to herself. She added, "Even when I was self-harming or smoking or drinking and stuff, I would still [hide it], I didn't want it to affect my mom or my family in any way. I didn't want to come home all drunk and stuff and see her reaction. So, I really kept it under wraps." Beatriz explained that even while engaging in behaviors that were self-harming, she "would still do good in school" to hide the depths of her suffering from her parents.

Guillermo explained that ever since he was young, he would often stay up at night contemplating what the future might bring. After his father's deportation, those worries became much more pressing. Although his mother was still in the U.S., her immigration status rendered her vulnerable to deportation and low-paying jobs. Guillermo adopted the role of head of household and cared for his two younger sisters. He became responsible for contributing financially to the household, helping his sisters with their homework, making sure that they were coping with their father's sudden deportation, and arranging trips to Mexico to spend time with their father. This was in addition to helping care for his own child and covering his girlfriend's expenses. He explained, "This is kind of what I've been conditioned to ever since my dad got deported, just try to help other people. I just kind of lost track of working on myself. Helping myself out doing something to better myself, my future as opposed to other people's future." Ever since his father was deported, Guillermo had prioritized his family and their needs, including "making sure my sisters have everything they need for school, making sure that their future is fine, making sure my baby's future is fine, making sure my girlfriend's future, college, just making sure she stays on track." At some point, Guillermo stepped out of college to work more hours. When I asked him if he had reached out to anyone for support, he explained, "Throughout this time, I haven't really talked to anyone about it. I haven't really sat down with anyone and told them [that] this happened to me, and this is how I feel, this is what I've been going through. No one really." With his girlfriend, Guillermo only shared the news in a very broad sense: "I gave her a general overview [and said], 'my dad was deported, and I didn't know how to feel about it at first, that's why I'm so close with my family.'" Despite the emotional and financial impact of his father's deportation, Guillermo learned that "a lot of people depend on me, but I don't really have anyone to depend on but myself." Many of the young adults I interviewed similarly played critical roles within their family units. As young adult children adopt additional roles and responsibilities to support their parents and siblings, they often hesitate to seek support, either because they do not want to cause additional stress on their parents or because they have been conditioned to cope in isolation.

Young adults also hesitate to disclose their undocumented status or family's enforcement status, fearing they may be reported, discriminated against, or treated differently. Paola, a 22-year-old DACA beneficiary, explained that despite struggling during her first year in college after her father was arrested, she refrained from telling others about their situation. At school, she only told one professor, whom she trusted. In general, Paola explained, "It's something that I didn't want to share because there are so many people out there that have strong opinions about people going through those situations, and I felt like if they knew they would see me differently because of what my dad was going through. I didn't want them to think of me as a different person." Paola was also guarded with some of her friends and acquaintances. While she told them that she was going through a difficult situation, she did not disclose any details.

The Nuñez family largely concealed Giovanni's deportation history from those outside of the family unit. In San Diego, Angelica worried that if her daughter's school found out they were living in Mexico with Giovanni, they would expel her since she was outside of the school district boundaries.

While she told a trusted support group she met with frequently about Giovanni's deportation, she refrained from disclosing information about his subsequent attempts to return. She was hopeful about the prospect of reuniting in the U.S. but did not want to share that with others, to protect her family's privacy and safety. Should Giovanni manage to return clandestinely, he would be even more vulnerable to undergoing a subsequent deportation. In Mexico, Giovanni was careful not to disclose his circumstances to many others either, because of the stigma associated with having been deported. The handful of people he told included a psychologist he was seeing and several other men who had also been previously deported. Even then, he told me, discussing his experience was hard: "Es difícil hablar del tema. Si, es un poco personal. [It's difficult to talk about it. Yes, it's personal.]" He also added, "El momento que yo me abro a compartir es volver a revivir esos momentos, esas experiencias. [The minute that I open to talk about it, I relive those moments, those experiences.]" The pain and trauma that individuals like Giovanni must endure even years after a deportation can often be paralyzing and prevent family members from accessing support. The process of disclosure can also be retraumatizing—requiring individuals to recall painful moments.[14]

Children, too, hesitate to disclose their parents' deportation history. Some are afraid of putting their other parent or themselves at risk should others begin to question their own immigration status. Others are concerned that they will be judged or treated differently. Cecilia, a 31-year-old U.S.-born citizen whose husband had been deported close to two years earlier, shared that her children refrained from telling their friends about their father's deportation. Instead, her children "make it seem to their friends that their dad is here." Cecilia suspected they did this because they were not quite ready to emotionally confront the reality of their father's absence.

The decision about whether to disclose or conceal a loved one's deportation history is complex. Often, families are already careful to conceal information related to their immigration status. In the event of a deportation, they now have another secret to keep. Fabiola, a 21-year-old who grew up undocumented in San Ysidro (a city in San Diego located right next to the U.S.-Mexico border), explained that she never disclosed her immigration status or her brother's deportation. She mentioned, "I don't think I ever told anyone at school, but I guess I just feel like you're scared of something happening, or like you're even scared of the cops. If you ever see a cop, you're just scared of that. To see if they're going to ask you for your papers or if you're going to school." While studies on illegality have increasingly examined undocumented young adults' decisions to disclose or conceal their immigration status,[15] we know much less about how entire families approach the process of disclosure about a member's deportation history. The decision to disclose or conceal a member's deportation history is complicated because although families often need significant support at this stage of the spectrum of enforcement, the risk of undergoing another separation in the future is high and palpably felt. Families are concerned about undergoing extended periods of separation if a loved one were to be apprehended upon reentry and subsequently incarcerated, detained, and deported. Each period of incarceration, detention, and deportation can translate to significant time spent apart.

The inability to lean on others can take its toll. Fatima explained how having to show strength to both her siblings and parents deeply affected her: "I realized that was emotionally draining, not having to show emotions, not being able to cry." This is not to suggest that parents or younger siblings are always on the receiving end of support and that such support is never reciprocated. Family members overwhelmingly try their best to support one another, in ways that are both small and large. Indeed, the family unit is often the only source of support for individuals. What the experiences of young adults like Guillermo and Fatima instead point to is the sheer legal-spatial violence that is marshaled against entire families in ways that are particularly burdensome on young adults, which we have yet to recognize.

Even if some people opt to disclose their immigration status to trusted friends, they conceal information about a family member's deportation. Paula, for example, disclosed her immigration status to teachers and counselors during her college application process, but she never approached anyone for support on the two separate occasions when her father was deported. Even years later, Paula had not shared this information with anyone outside of her family. She noted, "What happened with my dad is something that my parents told me, *no, you can't tell anybody.*" The decision to conceal is relational in nature, prompted by concerns from multiple members.

Young adults who disclose their loved one's deportation often do so to a limited number of people and for specific reasons. For example, they might confide in friends who are undocumented or have similarly experienced the deportation of a loved one. María, a 21-year-old whose brother was previously deported, only told one of her friends. She felt she could trust her because both of her parents were undocumented, and her father had once been deported. Except for her friend, María kept this information to herself because she would regularly "hear a lot of those stories, living in the community, of people being deported." The constant news of others being deported instilled fear in María.

Other young adults told me they reached out to extended relatives or friends for support when family members were deported but were met with an unwillingness to help. After Jaime was deported, his friendships quickly dissolved because of their lack of reciprocity. His wife, Leila, explained, "When he got out and was in Tijuana, he decided to call his friends [. . .] Well, he thought they were his friends, but they weren't really his friends because they helped him once only. They went to TJ and gave him money but after that they haven't called him or visited him or nothing. So, now he knows they were not his true friends." Leila also recalled instances when their friends would instead spread gossip or judgment about their family upon learning about Jaime's deportation. Since then, Leila and Jaime had relied solely on each other for emotional support. Leila's parents also occasionally helped them with rent or food.

Another young adult, Hugo, who had been deported more than two decades earlier, echoed that feeling of isolation. His friends were initially willing to help. When they had asked him for help in the past, he said, "I would help them because I wanted to." They promised to do the same for him, saying, "Whenever you need anything, let me know. I'll help you out." But when he called them, "They [hung] up on me, they sa[id], 'Let me call you back in a few,'" and they never did. In fact, he said, they "disconnected their phones." He felt "drop[ped] under the bus," and "abandoned," and he declared those friendships "dead." It was, he said, "one of the reasons I fell into a depression because people that I thought were my friends, they just stabbed me in the back so many times. All those friends I had, they stabbed, they stabbed me in the back. For me, I have no confidence. I have no trust, no confidence for nobody. For nobody." Despite young adults' efforts to identify resources and support, they were often left on their own.

A handful of the people with whom I spoke accessed support from a therapist or psychiatrist, though this came with its own set of challenges. Ximena went through multiple therapists in search of someone who would understand that her fear of deportation was not irrational and that it was grounded in the conditions she had to confront every day. On various occasions, therapists recommended that she try techniques that she found wholly unsuited to the reality of her life. For example, one therapist suggested to "do a color wash, where you're imagining yourself being washed over in a very calming color." Ximena immediately thought, "When I'm sitting there in front of border patrol, I don't think a freaking coloring wash is going to help me." Ximena felt that "standard ways of dealing with anxiety just don't work with undocumented people. They just don't. I want to meet the undocumented person that says, 'I have meditated, and my fear has left me.' I haven't met one yet, and I don't think I will because you can't." Ximena was skeptical that techniques like color washing or meditation would do much to undo the harm that U.S. immigration policies and enforcement practices have inflicted on her. The only way "this is all going to change," Ximena felt, is once the "laws begin to change." She clarified that "it's not just about getting residency." At its core, Ximena thought, "It's about knowing that the people in Congress, that the people that are elected, believe that we belong here. That we're people, that we're human beings, because I think that is lost on them that they are dealing with people's lives." Ximena's reflections reveal the limitations of current approaches to treating stress, trauma, and anxiety. They also underscore the need for meaningful change—both at the policy and societal levels—to recognize undocumented immigrants and their families as human beings and treat them with the dignity they deserve.[16]

One challenge with addressing the trauma that accompanies the geographies of deportability by using established treatments is that clinical practice is largely predicated on the assumption that the trauma is from the past. Attention is centered around helping the person move away from their trauma, to realize that they are no longer threatened in the present, that the moment has passed. Yet as Ximena observes, for undocumented immigrants and their loved ones, the source of trauma remains ever present. It is deeply embedded in the geographies of deportability and the tribulations associated with sanctuary making—manifested through the people, places, and moments that shape where and how they are permitted to live. This reality presents significant challenges to addressing individuals' mental health needs and exposes critical limitations in conventional mental health treatment that continue to go unaddressed.

Over time, young adults develop various coping mechanisms to deal with the fears, uncertainties, and stressors of navigating the geographies of deportability. This includes confiding in trusted friends or partners about their situation, exercising, or keeping busy. At times, young adults turn to coping methods they recognize as unhealthy or destructive, such as drinking excessively or self-harming.

Beatriz, who at one point became overwhelmed by constant news about sightings of immigration officers in her neighborhood, described this reality as one in which the fear of deportation comes in waves and requires constant repression. She added, "I think a lot of me tries to push away things like that. I don't like keeping that. I guess I like to disassociate from things that make me anxious and stuff. Because if not, then I feel like I really obsess over it and get super paranoid and stuff. So yeah, I try and put-up walls." Referencing the dominant political discourse at the time when then president Trump repeatedly led chants to "build the wall" during rallies, Beatriz qualified her reflection by adding, "That's a bad metaphor, but yeah." Like a relentless wave, young adults like Beatriz and their loved ones are forced to grapple with a sudden rush of endless possibilities and imaginations on a frequent basis when navigating the geographies of deportability and needing to carve out their own strategies of sanctuary making. If given the attention that these waves demand at a moment's notice, it can be quite debilitating—even paralyzing. Young adults do what they can to block these thoughts and emotions and subsequently carry out their lives.

Some do this by being fixated on staying busy. Between school, work, household responsibilities, friendships and other distractions, they fill almost every minute of the day with tasks. This leaves very little time, if any, to consciously reflect on their worst fears. As Matías Herrera described, "When you work that much, you don't have time to think about anything. You go home, the only thing you're thinking about is finding food, eating it, and going back to sleep and then doing it all over again. I found that's a way to hide away from all that. You're not dealing with it; you're running away from it." This does not mean young adults are unable to experience carefree moments. Rather, the daily anxieties and stresses that stem from the geographies of deportability are often buried deep in the subconscious.[17] It is there that many of their worst fears reside and continue to subtly influence all aspects of everyday life, even the literal content of their dreams.

DISCUSSION

Deportations, both threatened and realized, compel young adults to prioritize their family's safety over their own goals and aspirations, imposing material and emotional costs that often go unnoticed. Through the framework of the geographies of deportability and sanctuary making, we see how these costs manifest in subtle yet profound ways. Their understanding of deportability, particularly in an era of enforcement operating in the shadows with continuous data sharing between agencies, compels them to assess potential dangers. The mere threat of deportation can pressure young adults to remain close to home for college, foregoing opportunities available out of state to stay near their parents. Similarly, young adults may delay critical applications, such as those for financial aid or DACA, postponing legal benefits they are otherwise immediately eligible for. In some cases, young adults remove their parents from official school or employment records out of fear of detection, effectively erasing their familial relationships. In doing so, they deprive themselves of fully recognizing and affirming their own families, illustrating how enforcement shapes not only material realities but also profoundly personal and emotional experiences. Ultimately, the need to safeguard their families often takes precedence, forcing them to choose safety over their own preferences and aspirations.

In the era of enforcement in the shadows, the risk of deportation looms everywhere for young adults and their families. As a result, young adults must constantly assess and distinguish between tangible or hypothetical, imminent or distant risks. Consider a common scenario: when a young adult applies to college, they are required to complete the Free Application for Federal Student Aid (FAFSA). For U.S. citizens with undocumented parents, this routine process involves a unique and unsettling concern. Despite their own legal protection as citizens, they worry that sensitive information—such as their parents' names, physical addresses, and forms of identification—could be recorded, shared, and potentially accessed by federal immigration agencies. Completing a FAFSA form, in their eyes, might inadvertently expose their parents to immigration authorities.

Although it is generally believed to be safe for students to submit FAFSA applications, uncertainty remains about the extent to which immigration agencies currently have—or could obtain—access to student records under different circumstances. None of the participants in this study knew anyone who had been deported due to information submitted through FAFSA or school records. Yet an underlying fear persists: policies could change, and what seems safe today may become a risk in the future. Under these conditions, some young adults choose to omit their parents' information from FAFSA, delay submission, or proceed only with the guidance of a trusted staff member who can ease their concerns.

What initially feels like a hypothetical risk can suddenly become imminent or tangible, shaping the decisions young adults make as they navigate their education in the shadow of uncertainty. This reality became especially evident during the 2023–2024 and 2024–2025 academic years, when U.S. citizens with undocumented parents faced significant delays and anxieties following the rollout of a new FAFSA system and the inauguration of the second Trump administration.[18] Across the country, these disruptions led to basic needs crises for students who relied on financial aid for essentials such as food, housing, and transportation.[19] Meanwhile, staff working in undocumented student services faced overwhelming workloads. Many struggled to stay up to date with the latest FAFSA guidance, assess students' risks and safety, and reassure them that it was safe to apply—all while hosting FAFSA workshops, troubleshooting application glitches on a one-on-one basis, and searching for ways to help students meet their basic needs.

Numerous factors can expand or restrict the geographies of deportability, and consequently the scope of hypothetical risks. These include changes in policy and practices, the political climate, and electoral results. For these reasons, young adults are constantly grappling with shifting liminal landscapes in which at any moment a setting may become a hot spot or an actor may function as part of the pseudo-migra. This is in addition to contending with ongoing changes in policy and practice that seek to further undermine legal protections otherwise associated with DACA and U.S. citizenship. This includes Trump's attempts to end DACA during his first presidential term and his efforts in his second term to redefine birthright citizenship so that it excludes U.S.-born children of undocumented parents. As a result, young adults often live in cycles of two to four years, constantly anticipating potential threats and uncertain policy changes.

As the geographies of deportability expand and intensify, families face increasing pressure to engage in sanctuary making. The stakes are high, as encounters with hot spots create lasting ripple effects. Even when such encounters do not lead to an arrest, family members remain vulnerable to lingering trauma, in which everyday symbols and objects (such as orange cones, helicopters, and stadium lights) become enduring signifiers of enforcement, even in the absence of an immediate deportation threat. Under these conditions, the pressure on young adults intensifies. They frequently take on increasing responsibilities, often at a personal cost. Consequently, young adults grapple with depression and anxiety, often in isolation, while others experience physical health effects linked to chronic disruptions in sleep and eating patterns.

Young adults often articulated their emotions through spatial metaphors, revealing how deeply intertwined their emotional worlds were with their physical and social environments. The phrase "put in a black box" suggests an attempt to compartmentalize or contain difficult emotions. Similarly, expressions like "running away" reflect a desire to escape not just physically but emotionally from distressing realities. The notion of "putting up walls" further underscores the protective mechanisms young adults employ, both in terms of guarding their emotions and in maintaining distance from situations or conversations that may expose them (or their loved ones) to risk. These spatialized expressions illustrate how young adults navigate both the emotional and physical geographies of deportability.

To more fully account for the emotional and physical terrain that young adults navigate with their families, it is essential to attend to the dynamics that sustain the geographies of deportability. These include the capacity of immigration officers and the pseudo-migra to transform everyday settings into hot spots; the ease with which various social actors can assume the role of the pseudo-migra; and the pervasive nature of data collection, surveillance, and institutional information sharing. Such features are inherently fluid, challenging static or binary conceptualizations of space as either "welcoming" or "restrictive." These realities are especially critical to consider amid ongoing and intensifying tensions across institutional, local, state, and federal levels regarding the enforcement of immigration law. By attending to the mechanisms that expand and deepen the geographies of deportability, we open possibilities for reimagining the meanings and uses of space—grounded in trust, care, and solidary with immigrant families.

FIVE

Reclaiming the City

ON AUGUST 26, 2020, UdB organizers were alerted about a sighting of immigration officers near a public park in Sherman Heights, a community located approximately 15 miles from the U.S.-Mexico border. On that Wednesday, more than a dozen immigration officers were attempting to conduct an arrest inside a multifamily residence. When UdB organizers arrived there, they began to live stream the attempted arrest via the organization's main Facebook account.[1] In the stream, immigration officers were seen surrounding the house. Most of them were wearing bulletproof vests, some were displaying guns, and one was wearing plain clothing without a vest. On a par with the era of enforcement in the shadows, the officers at the scene were mostly driving unmarked vehicles with regular license plates. A few minutes into the live stream, two police vehicles arrived.

As the attempted arrest unfolded, concerned organizers, passersby, and neighbors gathered on the sidewalk. There was at least one UdB organizer near the residence who shouted legal rights information so that those inside the house could hear. At one point, at least 50 people can be seen on the stream bearing witness to the attempted arrest. Several of them were recording what was happening on their personal phones. On Facebook, the video received close to 50,000 views.

At about the 26-minute mark of the stream, more than a dozen immigration agents were seen leaving the house without making an arrest. The police followed suit shortly after. People could be heard in the background shouting, "el pueblo unido, jamas sera vencido," which roughly translates to "the people united will never be defeated." It is not entirely clear what led officers to this specific location or what prompted them to eventually leave without making an arrest. It is clear, however, that UdB organizers drew attention to the arrest both offline and online and rallied others around the individual(s) being directly targeted. Through their participation, UdB organizers and community members alike fostered a sense of community and solidarity that was felt among those who witnessed the attempted arrest as it unfolded and those who watched the live stream afterward.

Their efforts prompt us to consider the following questions: If every immigration arrest unfolded in plain view with the public bearing witness, how many more families would be able to remain together? How much longer would we, as a society, tolerate the existence of agencies that terrorize immigrant families every single day with the threat and reality of deportation? In the era of enforcement in the shadows, immigration officers rely on tactics that allow them to remain camouflaged and avoid scrutiny. This is how officers can conduct arrests in a manner that is relatively swift and uncontested. The efforts of organizations like UdB play a critical role in disrupting immigration officers' tactics by exposing the dynamics that sustain the geographies of deportability, while simultaneously participating in sanctuary making efforts at the community level to support immigrant families directly impacted by enforcement.

UdB is part of a growing network of immigrant rights organizations in San Diego County that provide information, support, and resources to undocumented and mixed-status families. Some of these organizations, like UdB, alert the immigrant community about sightings of immigration officers or the use of DUI checkpoints through their social media networks and text message notifications. Others host workshops to help people learn about various legal benefits and opportunities. This includes assisting individuals in applying for different types of relief from deportation and work permits through programs such as DACA or Temporary Protected Status (TPS), or U.S. citizenship through naturalization. There are also organizations that aid families with identifying and assessing their current needs regarding housing, finances, food security, and health so that they can connect with social service providers who may help meet their needs. Many organizers and volunteers also frequently attend rallies and marches and host Know Your Rights informational sessions at which they explain to people what they should do if they encounter a police or immigration officer.

This chapter features the work of immigrant rights organizers in San Diego County to support immigrant families, often on a volunteer basis and with limited resources. I first provide a brief discussion of immigrant rights organizing in the U.S., and among young adults more specifically, to set the context for the type of work that is unfolding in San Diego. I then look at the various factors that compel San Diego residents—both those who are undocumented and those who are U.S. citizens—to become active in immigrant rights organizing. These insights reveal that while a legal consciousness that is primarily characterized by fear, stigma, distrust, and vigilance is detrimental to the well-being of children in undocumented and mixed-status families, it is possible for young adults to leverage their consciousness to obtain a deeper and shared understanding of the condition of illegality and its effects in order to counteract it as best as possible. When this happens, their consciousness motivates political action. It functions as a source of empowerment and collective resistance to the very social and physical violence that the state inflicts.

I also discuss the work of immigrant rights organizations in greater depth, including alert-based systems, Know Your Rights workshops, and emergency preparedness plans. In doing so, I argue that these are key examples of the ways in which other social actors can bolster families' sanctuary making. In the process, organizers equip immigrant families with helpful information and tools to navigate the geographies of deportability. Through their efforts, organizers chart terrains based on solidarity, trust, and a sense of agency alongside immigrant families. In this chapter we see how sanctuary making can grow from the family level to the community level, creating a cycle that ultimately strengthens support for families.

A BRIEF NOTE ON IMMIGRANT RIGHTS
ORGANIZING IN THE UNITED STATES

The efforts that I document in this chapter are part of a long history of immigrant rights organizing in the U.S.[2] This includes mobilization efforts witnessed during nationwide protests in 2006 following the passage of H.R. 4437, a bill that if enacted would have further criminalized the state of being undocumented by making it a federal felony.[3] It also includes efforts by immigrant workers advocating for their labor rights,[4] religious leaders providing sanctuary,[5] and young adults pushing for the enactment of the DREAM Act.[6] Leading these efforts are organizers across all levels—national, state, and local—working to shape the stated goals of the immigrant rights movement and influence policy and practices. Such goals have shifted over time as priorities and narratives across all three levels change and tensions arise.[7]

During parts of the Obama administration, for example, sociologists Walter J. Nicholls, Justus Uitermark, and Sander van Haperen found that there were notable differences in priorities that emerged between large national organizations and local grassroots organizations. Despite their limited resources and capacity, grassroots organizations were able to take a leading role in shaping the immigrant rights movement by establishing networks across the country.[8] In California, in particular, there has long been a robust network of immigrant rights organizations, both those that are grassroots and nonprofits.[9] This includes organizations like the Coalition for Humane Immigrant Rights (CHIRLA) in Los Angeles and the California Immigrant Youth Justice League.[10] These networks continue to play a critical role. They provide immigrants with direct services alongside opportunities to become civically engaged and politically active.[11]

Among undocumented youth and young adult organizers specifically, one of their primary goals at the onset of the 21st century was to pressure legislators to pass the Development, Relief, and Education for Alien Minors (DREAM) Act.[12] If signed into law, the DREAM Act would have provided eligible undocumented young adults with a pathway to U.S. citizenship based in part on their educational achievements, contributions to the U.S., or military service.[13] To garner enough support for the DREAM Act, young adults mobilized and participated in rallies, marches, film screenings, fundraisers, and phone banking events over the years.[14] Organizers also staged "Coming Out of the Shadows" rallies, sit-ins at various congressional offices, and hunger strikes in ways that challenged the invisibility and stigma that are often associated with being undocumented.[15] These efforts have not been in vain and in part led to the announcement and implementation of the DACA program under the Obama administration.[16]

Despite being ineligible to vote, undocumented young adults participate in a wide range of civic engagement and political organizing efforts.[17] They do so for various reasons, including the need to raise awareness about their experiences, protect their families, and advocate for pro-immigrant policies (or against anti-immigrant legislation). Through their efforts, in both formal organizations and informal groups, young adults foster a sense of belonging and collective identity and challenge the notion of physical borders.[18] They also build important networks across movements to bring light to other issues, including police violence and LGBTQ+ rights.[19] Here, too, local contexts matter for the type of sites and ties that can be created (or challenged) in the process and the range of strategies and tactics that organizers adopt.[20]

In recent years the narrative that undergirds immigrant youth-led campaigns has also evolved. At the onset of advocacy for the DREAM Act, such efforts largely relied on a narrative that portrayed undocumented children as individuals who arrived in the U.S. through no fault of their own and were particularly high achieving.[21] Youth and their allies often highlighted notable aspects of their educational journeys such as their grades, diplomas, certificates of achievement, and a strong work ethic to position undocumented children as members who belong in U.S. society and deserve legal recognition. This unified DREAMer narrative, however vital it proved to be during the early stages of the undocumented youth-led movement, nevertheless left out the experiences of undocumented parents, deportees, and those who have been pushed out of the educational system.[22] After the DREAM Act failed to pass in Congress by five votes in 2010, undocumented youth and young adults began to increasingly challenge this narrative through organizing, art, and academic literature.[23]

During this time, grassroots efforts were underway to broaden the scope of demands beyond the DREAMer narrative. Namely, undocumented young adults from various parts of the country began to exert pressure on legislators to stop deportations as part of two growing campaigns on social media: #Not1More and #AbolishICE.[24] What began as local campaigns soon gained traction and challenged the previous reformist approaches to immigration policy led by national organizations.[25] These efforts also marked an important shift in the immigrant rights movement. That is, while much of the immigrant rights movement historically centered around legislation such as Comprehensive Immigration Reform (CIR) or the DREAM Act in hopes of creating pathways to U.S. citizenship for segments of the undocumented population, growing parts of the movement began to call into question the role of immigration policy and the enforcement apparatus in criminalizing, dehumanizing, and legally excluding noncitizens. These efforts have continued during Trump's presidential terms.[26]

It is in this context that immigrant rights organizers and volunteers in San Diego have mobilized to shed light on the collaboration that exists between police and immigration officers, the devastating consequences of deportations for entire families, and the tactics that immigration officers employ to surveil families and conduct arrests. While this chapter is by no means a comprehensive representation of immigrant rights organizing in the county, I hope that it provides a window into the wide range of efforts presently underway to provide direct support and services to immigrant families and to expose some of the dynamics of immigration policing from the ground up. Some of these efforts parallel those seen on the national stage (such as anti-deportation campaigns), yet others stem from local specificities that are unique to the U.S.-Mexico borderlands region (like information sharing across households about the federal immigration checkpoints). As such, this chapter is in direct conversation with the growing literature on immigrant-led organizing efforts across the country.[27]

WHY YOUNG ADULTS BECOME INVOLVED

Immigrant rights organizers often intimately understand the lived experience of undocumented immigrants and their families. They have either grown up undocumented or have parents who are undocumented. They may know relatives or friends who have been deported. They have also heard numerous stories from the broader community of individuals being arrested. Some have personally witnessed immigration officers conducting arrests. This shared understanding about U.S. immigration policy and enforcement and its effects forms the basis of young adults' legal consciousness and can subsequently foster a sense of agency among members of undocumented and mixed-status families or those closest to them (such as a best friend, spouse, partner, or extended relative).

Erika is an immigrant mother who recently became involved in immigrant rights organizing in San Diego County. She has multiple relatives who have been deported. Erika also vividly remembered the day she witnessed an immigration arrest. She recalled driving her children to school one morning when her son noticed one of his friends in the car next to theirs. When they both came to a stop, she noticed several undercover immigration officers "approached the car to detain the father of my son's friend." She continued, "I felt the light took forever to turn green, and while we were stopped, we witnessed a family being separated, in front of our eyes." Erika felt hopeless and at a loss for words, unable to explain what was happening to her children.

In this instance, time effectively slowed down for Erika and her family as they saw the immigration arrest unfold. This was an unsettling occurrence that left a powerful imprint on her, and potentially on her children as well. Sometime after this incident, Erika learned about the work of immigrant rights organizations in San Diego through social media and one of her friends. This was an opportunity for Erika to join efforts to prevent immigration arrests and document sightings of immigration officers. Since then she has been volunteering her time to shed light on the type of enforcement practices that are happening on the ground and helping to recruit others.

Jesús is an undocumented young adult who was similarly motivated to join an immigrant rights organization because of his lived experiences. Growing up in San Diego, he frequently heard about families being separated by a loved one's deportation. Jesús referenced the fear that he and others like him had endured for years. It can be a type of all-consuming and paralyzing fear that is difficult to overcome. At the onset of the first Trump administration, his levels of stress, fear, and depression were at an all-time high. He noted that at that point he "became paranoid" and "was under a lot of stress and was suffering from depression." The expanding geographies of deportability were encroaching into his community: "I constantly heard about ICE activity in my neighborhood, and whenever I saw a large gathering of police around my neighborhood, I feared they were looking for me." It was at this moment that Jesús decided to become politically active and attended events that "rescued" his mental health, including a human rights observer training and a Know Your Rights workshop.

Emily, who is a U.S.-born citizen and has multiple relatives who have been deported, was similarly motivated to join immigrant rights organizing efforts following the results of the 2016 U.S. presidential election. She felt that she "just couldn't sit and do nothing about" the anti-immigrant rhetoric that president elect Trump was fueling. Both of Trump's presidential administrations have undoubtedly created climates of fear among undocumented immigrants and their families.[28] It is a reality that has discouraged some from becoming (or continuing to remain) politically active because of fear for their personal safety and future.[29] For others like Jesús and Emily, however, there often came a point when the level of fear and anti-immigrant sentiment became unbearable and compelled them to join larger efforts to enact change.

Given the acute levels of fear and uncertainty that Trump's presidential administrations have created, much of the landscape of immigrant rights organizing has centered on pressuring localities and states to adopt sanctuary policies, informing immigrants about their rights, and working to meet families' most immediate needs when faced with the threat or reality of deportation.[30] It is in this context that young adults like Jesús and Emily became involved.

Others joined immigrant rights organizing efforts years ago but became even more vocal and active when faced with a direct threat of family separation. Luna, for example, is a DACA beneficiary whose father was detained while on his way to work with his brother. During our interview, Luna explained that she was immediately motivated to seek support from the broader community because she had previously seen other individuals being open about their immigration status and family's enforcement status. Even though her father's arrest signified a time of great uncertainty and hardship, she found courage in others' stories. She thought, "If I don't speak up, my dad's probably going to be deported. I'm not going to see him. I don't know what's going to happen to my family." Luna elaborated on the emotions she experienced when making the decision to speak out about her father's case: "Part of me speaking up and being open about my status and my situation was courage, but it was also fear of not seeing my dad again, of not knowing what was going to happen with my family. Like I said, it was the courage. I guess fear turned into courage." It was a very "uncertain" and "scary" moment for Luna and her family after her father was detained. Luna remembered that there were nights when she and her mother would "sit and cry because there were so many things that we didn't know what was going to happen." In some ways, Luna felt that her only option was to become politically active to garner support for her father's case. That decision gave her the support and the strength "to be really, really strong in my family" and to tell her mother in confidence that "things are going to be okay. My dad's going to come home. I don't know how. I don't know when. I don't know how long this is going to take, but he's going to come home. We're going to do whatever it takes." During that time, Luna not only dedicated substantial time and energy to supporting her family as a substitute parent, emotional anchor, and legal broker, but she also worked closely with fellow immigrant rights organizers to create an online petition, "calls to action," and candlelight vigils, and spoke with news media reporters to spread the word about her father's case.

Young adults' decisions to publicly disclose their immigration status or family's enforcement status is not necessarily about repressing or ignoring the very real emotions of fear, distrust, uncertainty, suspicion, and isolation that entire families experience in the era of enforcement in the shadows. Young adults recognize the risks that are involved in such public disclosures. During their search for support, resources, and other forms of community building, youth are simultaneously contending with fear, uncertainty, courage, innovativeness, and hope. In this context, young adults' legal consciousness can become a source of strength.

From this type of critical consciousness, individuals are compelled to participate in a wide range of immigrant rights organizing efforts. These include, among other activities, attending workshops, volunteering at events, signing petitions, raising awareness about local or national organizations, and encouraging others to act. In the era of enforcement in the shadows, concerted efforts to shine a bright light on police and immigration officers' tactics are underway in San Diego County. Many young adults were involved in these efforts at various levels.

MAINTAINING ALERT-BASED SYSTEMS

In San Diego County, two immigrant rights organizations alert immigrant families about sightings of police and immigration officers in the city: Alianza Comunitaria and UdB. There are also informal sharing networks via text and social media that similarly alert undocumented residents about sightings of immigration officers near or at the federal immigration checkpoints. There is one coalition, the San Diego Rapid Response Network (SDRRN), that occasionally alerts people about immigration raids in the county. From different vantage points, these organizations and networks play a crucial role in exposing and contesting the geographies of deportability through their organizing.

The first of these, Alianza Comunitaria, is an immigrant rights organization in North County San Diego whose primary mission is to inform undocumented residents about DUI checkpoints. For more than a decade, organizers with Alianza have maintained a text-based notification system that has reached over 30,000 people.[31] On its Facebook page, Alianza has more than 32,000 followers.[32] The organization also maintains an Instagram account with more than 5,000 followers.[33]

Its notifications typically alert people about DUI checkpoints either when these are underway or about to commence. On occasion, organizers can notify people about planned checkpoints a few days in advance.[34] They issue their notifications in both English and Spanish. On their social media platform, organizers will sometimes include photographs of the confirmed checkpoint or a map showing the exact location. In the comments on their Facebook and Instagram pages, community members typically thank the organizers for their notifications, ask clarifying questions, or share related information. For example, someone might confirm that they just drove through the checkpoint, or they might share information about other places they have recently seen DUI checkpoints. Considering that the Escondido Police Department (EPD) frequently conducts DUI checkpoints, most of the alerts that Alianza issues are for Escondido, although organizers occasionally share similar reports of checkpoints in the nearby cities of San Marcos, Vista, and Oceanside.

This type of information sharing intervenes in the police-to-deportation pipeline and renders hot spots visible. By documenting the precise timing, location, objects, and dynamics that police officers use when conducting a checkpoint, organizers expose some of the mechanisms that transform otherwise mundane settings into hot spots. Families can use this information to be especially wary about signs that may signal the start of a checkpoint. Information sharing among organizations and immigrant households can reveal patterns about the state's strategic use of space and render the geographies of deportability more maneuverable. For example, because police officers generally set up DUI checkpoints on the weekends, immigrant families have come to expect them during those times. As the end of the week approaches, some young adults will periodically check Alianza's social media feed before they (or their parents) leave the house. Others will time their errands so that they are home by 6:00 in the evening, when DUI checkpoints are more likely to be active. Ultimately, information sharing across households can help families pick up on distinguishable patterns and use this knowledge as they carefully navigate the geographies of deportability.

Additional efforts are underway to gradually reduce the effectiveness of DUI checkpoints that are used for immigration enforcement under false pretenses. For example, there are instances when Escondido residents have protested the checkpoints on-site by displaying warning signs a few hundred feet before their location to alert drivers about their presence.[35] These efforts in part help render police officers' strategic use of space through the DUI checkpoint visible and subsequently subject to questioning and contestation.

UdB similarly contests the state's use of space, in part by focusing on the work of ICE and CBP officers on the ground. UdB is a national organization that was initially founded in 1981 with a mission "of building a peoples organization capable of defending the democratic rights and class interests of la raza."[36] There are chapters of UdB in the cities of San Diego, Los Angeles, Sacramento, and New York City.

In San Diego, one of the main tasks of the organization has been to identify, document, and expose immigration officers' whereabouts and activities when these are underway. More specifically, the organization deploys what they refer to as "patrullajes comunitarios" (community patrols) or "comites de resistencia" (self-defense patrols). These units are tasked with documenting immigration officers' whereabouts and subsequently alerting immigrant families about them. UdB encourages community members to share information with them about any suspected immigration enforcement activity via the organization's Facebook page or phone number. Oscar, an organizer with UdB, shared that under the Biden administration they were typically receiving anywhere from five to ten reports each week.

When the organization becomes aware of a suspected immigration enforcement activity, it will distribute this information to organizers so that someone can go to the reported location and confirm the information. The locations of suspected enforcement activities can vary significantly. Organizers will sometimes need to drive to a specific shopping center or apartment complex. At other times organizers might have to drive several blocks in a neighborhood to find the officers' precise location. Those who live closest to the area and are available at the time of the suspected activity will be the first to arrive. UdB organizers are also mindful of their personal safety and decide who will go to confirm suspected enforcement activities based on legal status. For this reason, the responsibility to go and check often lies on organizers who are U.S. citizens.

Once on the scene, UdB organizers monitor the situation. They often video record immigration officers on their phones and upload these to the organization's Facebook and YouTube accounts. UdB organizers are sometimes able to support those being directly affected, albeit from a distance and without physically interfering with the officers' actions. If organizers have megaphones with them, they use them to instruct undocumented residents not to leave their homes or vehicles because of the presence of immigration officers.

UdB also proactively and regularly schedules patrols. For instance, a group of organizers may drive around neighborhoods that are commonly targeted by immigration officers. They will usually do this in the early morning, when officers are known to target immigrant families. Through scheduled patrols, the organization can assure the community that immigration officers are not present in the neighborhoods that are most frequently targeted and if they are, they alert undocumented residents.

UdB organizers are aware that immigration officers often drive un-marked SUVs with regular license plates and tinted windows. They are also mindful that undocumented residents have learned to fear any vehicle that fits this general description. For these reasons, UdB organizers clearly mark their own cars with a UdB banner. This can be particularly helpful for residents so that they do not confuse unfamiliar UdB vehicles for those of immigration officers and so that they can find some comfort knowing that there is a community organization working to support them.

The organization's community patrols play a central role in contesting the geographies of deportability. Namely, their efforts reverse central dynamics of "predator-prey" and "watchful-watched" and in the process push immigration officers out of the neighborhoods being targeted. When UdB organizers arrive at a particular location to identify and record immigration officers, their cover is effectively removed. In those moments, it is the community that is doing the watching. Once this happens, immigration officers typically leave the scene.[37] Here we see a clear example of sanctuary making at the community level directly reshaping the geographies of deportability by effectively extinguishing the hot spot. Organizers also use the information that they collect during their community patrols to inform undocumented residents about the tactics that immigration officers typically employ so that they can more easily spot them during their daily commutes. This includes information about the telltale signs of undercover immigration officers (such as the antennas and tinted windows and the models of the vehicles that officers typically drive). Organizers encourage undocumented residents, equipped with this information, to be watchful and alert the organization when they suspect that there are undercover officers in the neighborhood.

Many immigrant families depend on the existence of formal and informal systems that can alert them about hot spots to navigate them with caution or avoid them altogether. Individuals learn about which places to avoid from several sources, including news media coverage on immigration, word-of-mouth stories about immigration arrests, reports about immigration or police activities on social media networks, and both firsthand and secondary exposure to enforcement and policing practices on the ground.

Young adults are familiar with both formal and informal types of information sharing and stay up to date with notifications issued through these networks. They help spread the word about these notifications and share information about checkpoints with others, both inside and outside of their households. They might take a screenshot about an alert from Alianza issued on social media from their personal phones and text it to their parents. They may reshare any alerts on their social media profiles so that their friends who are not subscribed to UdB's Facebook account can still see them. Although there are no established guidelines or expectations for this type of information sharing, the intent is to distribute information about enforcement activities in a manner that is timely, helpful, and accurate.

Notably, the use of communication tools plays a critical role in maintaining and expanding sanctuary making across households, including this type of alert-based system. With social media, information about hot spots can instantly reach many people. Social media users can also cultivate a safety network by only befriending individuals they personally know and trust or by subscribing to notifications from organizations they are familiar with. This can help filter out information that may be false or unreliable. Through live streams, social media users can also instantly document an immigration arrest and broadcast it to others.

These notifications are crucial for members of undocumented and mixed-status families. Daniela Guerrero is an undocumented young adult who is not formally affiliated with an immigrant rights organization but often volunteers at events. She became aware of immigrant rights organizing at a very young age. During our interview, Daniela recalled meeting some of the organizers with Alianza Comunitaria years ago when there were frequent reports of immigration officers boarding public buses and trolleys in Escondido. As a young adult, Daniela relied on information that she received from Alianza Comunitaria and her friends to help spread the word about DUI checkpoints or sightings of immigration officers. She explained the importance of this type of information-sharing network and the ways in which people in the same community might not understand the experiences of undocumented and mixed-status families. Indeed, she has gotten comments from peers asking, "Why do you post where the checkpoints are at? People that don't have a license and are drunk driving should be able to get caught." Daniela, however, knew that the issue is far more complicated, and she would respond: "I'm not doing it for the drunk drivers. I was doing it for the parents who work late at night, and don't have papers, and they go through a checkpoint, obviously they're going to get in trouble and stuff like that. Immigration will come in and things like that." She knew about such effects at a personal level as she recalled her parents' fears of driving through a checkpoint.

Police officers commonly portray DUI checkpoints as efforts to apprehend individuals who are driving under the influence of drugs or alcohol. It is not surprising then that the public either does not question or defends the use of DUI checkpoints. However, through the legal consciousness of young adults and their families, DUI checkpoints function as hot spots. Daniela's efforts to help spread the word about DUI checkpoints therefore represented an attempt to protect others from immigration enforcement. In the process, she also made sure that others in her network were aware of the unique set of challenges that undocumented parents and their children confront.

The SDRRN is a relatively more recent effort aimed at providing information and resources to immigrant families directly impacted by immigration policies and enforcement practices. It is a coalition of more than 40 organizers, attorneys, and faith leaders in San Diego.[38] The SDRRN was founded during Trump's first presidential administration in December 2017. Its work includes operating migrant shelters in the county and maintaining an emergency immigration enforcement hotline. Undocumented residents in San Diego are encouraged to call the SDRRN emergency hotline to report any type of immigration enforcement activity, including checkpoints, raids, arrests, or harassment. Upon calling the hotline, they are asked to leave a detailed message with information about the enforcement activity. The SDRRN operates on weekdays between 8:30 a.m. and 5:00 p.m. Organizers are tasked with reviewing each voicemail and returning calls on a case-by-case basis.

These organizations, informal networks, and coalitions are part of a robust network of immigrant rights organizations in San Diego County, which also includes Border Angels, the Unitarian Universalist Refugee and Immigrant Services and Education (UURISE), the San Diego Immigrant Rights Consortium (SDIRC), Universidad Popular, the North County Immigration Task Force, the San Diego Dream Team, Alliance San Diego, Jewish Family Services of San Diego, the ACLU of San Diego, the American Friends Service Committee, Catholic Charities of San Diego, and the San Diego Border Dreamers. This is not a complete list, and there are many other organizations and informal networks throughout San Diego similarly advocating for the rights of undocumented immigrants, asylum seekers, and refugees.

There are also organizations and centers throughout San Diego that are affiliated with institutions of higher education. Examples are the COMPASS program (formerly known as the Dreamer Resource Office) at CSU San Marcos, Dreamer Center at Southwestern College, and Undocumented People Rise in Solidarity and Empowerment (UPRISE) at Mira Costa College.[39] Campus-based efforts typically center around helping currently enrolled undocumented students and those in mixed-status families. This includes providing students with academic counseling, financial assistance, emergency housing, legal services, mentorship, and networking opportunities. There are also other centers across university campuses whose primary mission is not centered on the topic of immigration, but whose resources are nevertheless open and helpful to students in undocumented or mixed-status families. These include, for example, the National Latino Research Center and the Cougar Care Network at CSU San Marcos. Some of these efforts have been underway since the 1980s, while others were created more recently.

Many of these organizations also host Know Your Rights workshops, meant to inform immigrant families about their legal rights and protections. Catalina, an immigration lawyer and community organizer, facilitates this type of workshop, in which she encourages families to document immigration officers' tactics so that they can be held accountable. Ismael, a recent college graduate and organizer, similarly believes in the power of recording immigration enforcement activities. During a follow-up conversation we had after his interview, he stressed the importance of garnering community support through live streaming or video recording. He recalled a recent experience of an undocumented mother who was released shortly after being detained. It appears her daughter, a U.S.-born citizen, had rallied other San Diego residents to support her case after she live streamed her mother's arrest. The recording was later shared by local news media outlets.

These types of support are an important example of how organizers can bolster families' sanctuary making efforts. By providing information, resources, and support to immigrant families, organizers help cultivate trust and solidarity amid growing state surveillance. Moreover, by documenting and disrupting immigration officers' attempts to conduct an arrest or raid, even if from a distance, organizers are actively contesting the use of that space. Their efforts bring forth an alternative meaning of space that is based on solidarity, agency, and protection. Organizers' efforts also help counteract the thoughts and emotions that arise out of the geographies of deportability by fostering a sense of inclusion among immigrant families.

THE LIMITATIONS AND RISKS OF SUSTAINING A COMMUNITY ON HIGH ALERT

Immigrant rights organizers confront numerous challenges while carrying out and sustaining their efforts. One of the biggest limitations for organizers is that the demand for their services and support often far exceeds their capacity. Indeed, the era of enforcement in the shadows demands a tremendous amount of energy and resources from immigrant families and organizations alike. These needs are vast and increasingly difficult to meet. Consequently, some of these organizations must occasionally pause or significantly scale back their efforts.

UdB is a grassroots organization that operates with limited funding. Because they do not receive federal or grant money, organizers mostly rely on membership dues, donations, and fundraisers. Although the organization has sought to establish partnerships with other local nonprofits to expand community patrols, one organizer commented that many of the other organizations they have had conversations with "are not ready nor want to recognize that we must 'abolish ICE' to avoid the attacks of our communities." Immigrant rights organizing efforts are not uniform, static, or free from tension. There may be competing political aims and missions, shaped in part by funding allocations and restrictions that can ultimately hinder collective efforts.

With limited funding available, organizers largely volunteer their time for a shared cause. This means in part that many individuals who, like them, believe in the cause and want to join their efforts, simply cannot afford to do so because they need to work. It also means that those presently volunteering may struggle when trying to balance the demands of work, home, school, and organizing. These conditions can prevent individuals from staying involved. One of the most often cited challenges that organizers mentioned was the lack of funding, and relatedly, the need for more volunteers.

In the era of enforcement in the shadows, predicting the movements of immigration officers has become increasingly difficult. Unlike the relatively predictable patterns of DUI checkpoints, their operations are marked by continual change. Organizers do their best to train people to identify and locate immigration officers. During their Noches de Defensa y Resistencia (Nights of Defense and Resistance), UdB organizers highlight the make and model of the type of vehicles that immigration officers typically drive, including any noticeable changes over time.

Nevertheless, there is an unequal balance of power and an uneven proportion of knowledge between immigration agencies and grassroots organizations. The former has a massive infrastructure—tools, budget, and personnel—to constantly surveil millions of people (often in collaboration with other agencies) and to make this information readily accessible to immigration officers on the ground. Grassroots organizations, on the other hand, are limited in their capacity. Thus, what immigration agencies know about families is disproportionately greater than what organizations know about officers' tactics. Although organizers' efforts are an important part of the solution, significant changes at the policy and institutional levels are also necessary to overcome this knowledge gap.

Moreover, organizations like Alianza largely depend on reports from undocumented residents or allies regarding suspected enforcement activities. While some notifications are timely and accurate, others arrive too late or contain unreliable information. In the absence of clear evidence, organizers often travel to the reported location to verify the presence of immigration enforcement. If confirmed, they act swiftly to alert the community. If the initial reports prove to be false, organizers reassure the community that they are safe. Either scenario requires significant effort from organizers, who often volunteer their time to stay aware of these notifications, verify their validity, and disseminate accurate information.

In the days following Trump's inauguration for a second presidential term, numerous rumors circulated about immigration officers conducting raids and questioning people at various locations. This created panic among immigrant families, who became particularly fearful of traveling to school and work or utilizing public transportation. These circumstances also compelled organizers to quickly create and disseminate helpful information on what to do during an encounter with an immigration officer, how to spot an immigration vehicle, and what to do if someone is detained. As the geographies of deportability intensify and expand, organizers and families must act quickly to identify potential hot spots to ensure their safety. This urgency partly explains why rumors circulate quickly within immigrant communities, often before they have been verified. Relatedly, because the timing of enforcement activities is unpredictable, it can be difficult for organizers to stay alert around the clock. Volunteers often work full time to make ends meet while also trying to be part of these efforts.

Transportation is also an issue for volunteers. Tomás, an organizer familiar with many of the networks in San Diego County, noted that many volunteers often live in the central or southern parts of San Diego. This means that when someone reports a suspected enforcement activity from North County San Diego, it can take a volunteer 30 minutes or longer to get to the location, at which point immigration officers may already be gone. Ultimately, organizers' reach is limited by the distance between their homes and where enforcement activities take place, the travel that is inherent to this type of work, and the lack of resources.

There are also important issues regarding personal safety for organizers involved in community patrols. Vilma, an organizer with UdB, shared that there have been occasions when organizers are targeted and arrested. Because there is a significant amount of risk involved for organizers, Vilma explained that organizers typically stay at a distance. They cannot physically intervene lest they risk arrest, but they remind people of their rights, including the right to remain silent or not open their doors without a warrant. Those involved with community patrols must walk a fine line between providing support while at the same time doing so from a distance for their own personal safety. Similarly, other organizers with UdB were mindful about personal safety and the limitations that come with the nature of community patrols. For these reasons, UdB organizers may limit active participation in community patrols to members who have some type of legal protection, like legal permanent residency or U.S. citizenship.

There are also pressing challenges that emerged from the COVID-19 pandemic. Among these, organizers referenced the shutdown of in-person services at the start of the pandemic; issues with accessibility to online services for those without a reliable internet connection or a computer; and a growing demand for basic needs support regarding food security, housing, and employment. Pilar, who helps provide popular education courses to the immigrant community in North County San Diego, mentioned that attendance significantly decreased at the onset of the pandemic. Whereas they used to have 150 to 200 participants on a weekly basis, in more recent years they had about 50 people, sometimes far fewer.

On the one hand, organizations can expand their reach by using platforms like Facebook, Instagram, or YouTube to inform community members about their legal rights and immigration enforcement activities on the ground. On the other hand, it may be more difficult to sustain interest and participation in events that require greater engagement from people. When the COVID-19 pandemic began and many organizations shifted their services online, the nature and reach of their work inevitably changed as well.

Like families' sanctuary making efforts, which take a toll on young adults over time, organizers similarly endure emotional difficulties when participating in this work. Erika explained that one of the main challenges is "having to witness parents [and] families dropping off their children at school and being arrested." She added, "having to witness and not being able to help." The act of witnessing an arrest, without being able to ultimately prevent it through physical intervention, can engender feelings of guilt and powerlessness. Ultimately, the extent to which organizers can contest the use of space is curtailed and fraught with an emotional toll.

There can also be tension within family units when one family member feels empowered and relatively safe to join immigrant rights organizing efforts, but their relatives do not agree. Relatives may fear for their loved one's safety or their own. They may be concerned that others might begin inquiring about the immigration status of family members through association. Penelope is a 29-year-old DACA beneficiary whose mother was concerned about her involvement in immigrant rights organizing. Her mother was upset that Penelope occasionally attended protests and spoke at some events. Penelope attributed this to her mother's fear that immigration officers might go after the family. Penelope, however, felt relatively safe with DACA and was eager to use that protection, she told her mother, "to be your voice." Ultimately, Penelope could not convince her mother that it was safe for her to be involved, so she later opted not to share much information with her mother about her political involvement. DACA beneficiaries like Penelope may be compelled to act, especially for others who do not have the same opportunities.[40] It can nevertheless be a point of added fear and a source of tension within the household.

Julio, a 22-year-old undocumented college graduate, similarly contended with these concerns and pressures at home. At one point his parents told him to discontinue his organizing efforts out of concern for his personal safety. This was "a whole other level of stress" as Julio argued with his parents over his decision to be politically active. This situation reminded Julio that "it was just not myself that was putting myself at risk, but my parents as well, and just our overall well-being as a family." It is important to recognize that young adults like Julio and Penelope are grappling with a form of "disclosure by proxy" that can occur through public political participation. The concern is that others may make assumptions about family members' immigration status based on their political participation. This was the case for Vilma's brother, who was questioned by his friends after they saw Vilma on TV during a protest she participated in. Vilma remembered getting a call from her brother, who was upset about her decision to protest: "He was like, 'why don't you think about us, or our mom?' Because my mom has a fake social security number. 'They're going to know.' After that, I called my mom and I was like, 'I'm so sorry, I'm so sorry.' She was like, 'I'm proud of you.' And I was like, 'really?' And then my brother now after that, he was like, 'I'm sorry. You made me come out of the shadows. I didn't know how to feel about that.'" Disclosures by proxy bring up complicated emotions for all family members involved. It is a tense situation to be in because young adults are aware that political organizing can expose the entire family to the vulnerability of being detected. As Julio added, "I was like punishing myself, like, *You can't be as selfish*, right? *You are putting your parents at risk to a certain degree*, so yeah." Other young adults like Julio may feel conflicted and guilty about their decisions to participate in immigrant rights organizing efforts, despite having good intentions.

For these reasons, the extent to which individuals draw on their legal consciousness to become politically active varies within the family unit; changes over time; and is shaped by factors such as age, educational level, legal status, and varying levels of risk tolerance. Ismael has been active in immigrant rights organizing efforts for years. However, in contrast to Luna's experience, wherein she felt compelled to become more active following her father's arrest, Ismael at one point distanced himself from community organizing. This was at a time when immigration officers apprehended and detained his mother. Ismael very acutely felt that he was next, adding, "It got scary because this is a very real thing that can happen where we can get detained and placed in jail, literally just for fighting for our rights." Ismael also valued the importance of an education because of her mother's sacrifices and ultimately felt that school was a haven for him during this challenging time.

DISCUSSION

The dynamic of seeing and being seen is central to the era of enforcement in the shadows as immigration officers prey on immigrant families. In this context, the work of immigrant rights organizations plays a crucial role in temporarily and partially reversing this dynamic. Immigration officers operate with a vast arsenal of digital technologies, actors, and tools to surveil and monitor families. However, by tracking and confirming officers' whereabouts in real time, organizers shine a bright light on officers' presence and tactics while issuing timely alerts to the community. Through social media and text messages, they document sightings and strategies, creating an archive that captures enforcement operations from the perspective of those directly impacted.

This archive makes visible the terrain of enforcement, pinpointing apartment complexes, parking lots, worksites, and parks where immigration officers have been observed. In doing so, it exposes the areas most affected by their presence. This practice aligns with what ethnic studies and undocu-scholar Rafael A. Martínez describes as "undocumenting"—a process in which undocumented youth organizers document their own activism.[41] Beyond the political realm, I find that undocumenting also encompasses efforts by immigrant family members and their allies to record their everyday practices and surroundings, illustrating how these are deeply shaped by U.S. immigration policies and enforcement practices. This form of undocumenting is essential for revealing the inner workings of the era of enforcement in the shadows.

Sanctuary making is about staking a claim to space, carving out protection in an environment of constant risk, and claiming one's right to remain in the city. While this often takes place at the family level, where individuals take steps to shield themselves and their loved ones from immigration enforcement, immigrant rights organizers play a crucial role in shaping and supporting these efforts. For instance, when organizers issue alerts about sightings of immigration officers, young adults can quickly inform their parents, enabling families to take necessary precautions. Likewise, through Know Your Rights workshops, families gain vital information about their legal options and pathways for immigration relief. There exists an interplay between these two levels of action, that is, between family-based and community-based sanctuary making efforts. Family efforts to protect loved ones can give rise to political activism, while organizing efforts provide families with the tools, knowledge, and community support needed to sustain sanctuary making at the family level. Understanding these connections highlights the importance of both intimate, everyday acts of resistance and the broader movement to challenge the geographies of deportability.

Beyond legal and logistical support, immigrant rights organizers also help foster relationships of trust and care in an environment where such connections are increasingly difficult to maintain. Within the geographies of deportability, nearly any social actor can become part of the pseudo-migra at a moment's notice. Many young adults have witnessed or personally experienced betrayal by neighbors, estranged partners, landlords, or employers who have taken on the role of informal immigration enforcers. In this context, immigrant rights organizers counteract widespread distrust and hypervigilance by cultivating networks of solidarity, mutual care, and collective resilience.

At the same time, just as families struggle to sustain sanctuary making amid dwindling resources, organizers also face significant challenges and limitations that must be acknowledged and addressed. In both cases, the constant demands of resistance and crisis response deplete resources—whether emotional, financial, or logistical—making it even more critical to mobilize greater support for grassroots organizations working to uphold these efforts. This includes addressing issues of insufficient funding, a lack of volunteers and resources, concerns about personal safety, gaps in knowledge about immigration officers' evolving tactics, and worries about their own families' vulnerability stemming from forms of disclosure by proxy. Ultimately, the story of immigrant rights organizing in San Diego is one of solidarity and agency, as much as it is one rife with barriers and tensions. Stronger efforts are needed across policy, research, and practice to address these challenges and better support immigrant rights organizations and the families they serve.

Future Directions in Research, Policy, and Practice

IN MANY WAYS, the day of the 2020 U.S. presidential election brought a renewed sense of hope. The previous four years under the first Trump administration had been marked by growing anti-immigrant sentiment, constant threats of mass deportation, and acute levels of fear and anxiety among members of undocumented and mixed-status families.[1] For many immigrant families and organizers alike, the hope was that a Biden administration would bring comprehensive immigration reform proposals back to the table and even see them come to fruition.

However, in San Diego County, interior enforcement operations soon returned to business as usual. The advocacy organization UdB reported sightings of immigration officers inside an apartment complex in Escondido only a few days after the Biden administration was inaugurated. In a YouTube video titled "Redadas de ICE siguen bajo la administración de Biden, hostigando a trabajadores Mexicanos" (ICE raids continue under the Biden administration, harassing Mexican workers), recorded on February 2, 2021, organizers documented two vehicles that belonged to ICE and were patrolling predominantly Latino neighborhoods at dawn.[2] In keeping with the era of enforcement in the shadows, the ICE officers were seen driving unmarked SUVs. At first glance, the vehicles blended into the backdrop of a bustling parking lot as residents of a large apartment complex departed for work. However, upon closer inspection, organizers identified the vehicles as belonging to ICE, noting the sirens and *rejillas* (bars) on the inside, and began alerting residents to their presence. UdB organizers reported several other sightings of immigration officers in North County San Diego in the following months.[3]

Later that spring, it became clear that on matters of immigration, the Biden administration would not be much different than Trump's. This was especially the case when it came to its treatment of asylum seekers, unaccompanied children, and recent arrivals (individuals who migrated less than a year before). For example, in 2020 the Trump administration began implementing Title 42—a practice that allows immigration officials at the U.S. land borders to exclude noncitizens under the premise of public health concerns,[4] and the Biden administration continued this practice.[5] By the time this policy came to an end in the spring of 2023, immigration officials had already expelled 2.8 million migrants.[6] Regardless of the political party in power, policies enacted by both Republicans and Democrats have aided in the exclusion and criminalization of immigrants under the era of enforcement in the shadows. Such efforts have, in turn, contributed to the further entrenchment of the geographies of deportability and their widespread impact on individuals, families, and communities.

This bipartisan reality is not lost on young adults. Many recognize that the Obama administration, even as it implemented meaningful changes like DACA, also deported a record number of people. In fact, many of the young adults whose parents were deported recounted that many of those arrests took place between 2009 and 2016. To this day, young adults and their families are struggling with the effects of Obama-era policies either in the U.S. (upon their loved one returning without authorization) or across borders (if their loved one remained in their country of birth following deportation). The nature of interior enforcement operations under the era of enforcement in the shadows is not limited to a particular political party. Regardless of the administration in power, immigration officers increasingly employ tactics such as patrolling specific apartment complexes while undercover, questioning individuals they "suspect" of being undocumented when they are most vulnerable (either alone or in front of young children), and collaborating with the pseudo-migra to access databases and facilitate arrests.

Although both Democrats and Republicans share responsibility for ushering in an era of enforcement in the shadows, the geographies of deportability may evolve in scope and intensity depending on the political climate and the presidential administration in power. Under openly hostile and anti-immigrant administrations, like President Trump's, these geographies are trending toward rapid intensification and expansion—extending further into the interior of the country and reaching deeper into families' daily lives.

How do we make sense of ongoing changes in immigration policy and enforcement practices across time and space? How are the geographies of deportability and families' sanctuary making efforts fluctuating, and at what cost? Relatedly, what are the short- and long-term consequences of this environment on the lives of young adults and their families? What can be done at the level of policy and institutional practice to counteract the era of enforcement in the shadows and its ensuing geographies of deportability? In what follows, I synthesize the scholarly impacts of this research and offer suggestions for how scholars might employ the theoretical tools utilized in this book to address these and related questions. I conclude with a set of recommendations for both policymakers and service providers geared toward better supporting young adults and their families.

THEORETICAL CONTRIBUTIONS AND PRACTICAL APPLICATIONS

I began this book by situating the lives of immigrant families like the Aguilars in the context of what I call the era of enforcement in the shadows. This term emphasizes the covert and ubiquitous means by which immigration authorities infiltrate all aspects of everyday life within immigrant families across the country. While changes in U.S. immigration policy and practices since the late 20th century initially gave rise to the era of enforcement in the shadows, conditions have worsened, to the point that officers' stealth is becoming an increasingly integral feature of their operations on the ground. This raises significant concerns about the lack of transparency and accountability in officers' actions and the pervasive impact of interior enforcement on a substantial segment of the population.

The concept of the "era of enforcement in the shadows" synthesizes research from crimmigration, immigration federalism, and the rise of the immigration surveillance state,[7] to elucidate enforcement practices at the ground level. While addressing distinct aspects of immigration control, these forces increasingly intersect, revealing underlying patterns that influence enforcement activities. Scholars have previously identified and explored these phenomena. However, they have typically analyzed them in isolation. For instance, studies on immigration federalism may examine the discretionary power of police officers to profile drivers they suspect of being undocumented. However, these studies often do not connect such practices to the broader efforts of collecting vast amounts of data on both noncitizens and citizens, a central focus of the immigration surveillance literature.

In both theory and practice, immigration federalism, crimmigration, and immigration surveillance have become increasingly intertwined. Immigration federalism refers to the devolution of immigration enforcement from federal authorities to state and local actors.[8] Proposed legislation like Senate Bill 4 (TX) and Senate Bill 1718 (FL) exemplify this by seeking to require employers, hospital staff, and police officers to play a role in immigration enforcement, effectively deputizing them as pseudo-migra. At the same time, if implemented, these laws would contribute to crimmigration, which refers to the growing overlap between the criminal and immigration system.[9] By mandating that these nonfederal actors report undocumented individuals, such policies increase the criminalization of immigration status and facilitate deportation. These policies also feed into immigration surveillance by encouraging nonfederal agents to share data across agencies, connecting hospitals, businesses, and law enforcement with immigration authorities. This integration extends the reach of immigration officers through technological and bureaucratic means.[10] Together, these mechanisms sustain the era of enforcement in the shadows, where immigration control is no longer solely the domain of federal action, but instead operates through a decentralized system of devolution, criminalization, and surveillance.

In the era of enforcement in the shadows, the reach of immigration officers is both expanding and deepening. To capture this phenomenon, I introduced the concept of geographies of deportability, which refers to the cumulative set of specific spaces and settings that immigrant families come to associate with immigration enforcement and the heightened risk of deportation. Traditional and nontraditional hot spots—whether immigration federal checkpoints, ports of entry, workplaces, grocery stores, public streets, or apartment complexes—become marked by fear and vigilance, reshaping the daily lives of those navigating these landscapes.

Through a geographies of deportability lens, we gain a deeper understanding of the lives of immigrant families. This framework reveals how families become acutely aware of the dynamics that sustain an environment of vulnerability and surveillance. They recognize the ease with which otherwise mundane settings could transform into hot spots for immigration enforcement. Families also understand the role of various actors who function as pseudo-migra. Moreover, families are acutely aware of the risks associated with information sharing, as data collected by one agency can readily be accessed and used by others, thereby expanding the reach of immigration enforcement. These insights underscore the pervasive and insidious nature of deportability, in which spaces and relationships that might otherwise foster safety and trust instead become fraught with potential danger.

The era of enforcement in the shadows as I have outlined it captures the distinct shift of enforcement from the border to nontraditional sites of the interior. Geographies of deportability, as a conceptual framework, provide a structured and systematic lens through which to map the interactions among policies, actors, and practices—illuminating their far-reaching effects on families. While previous studies have documented shifts in enforcement and detention rates from the border to the interior,[11] this book broadens the scope by shifting the emphasis to the impact that immigration enforcement has on local communities on the ground rather than keeping most of the focus on the U.S.-Mexico physical border or the federal apparatus of border control. This includes unearthing the array of tactics (camouflage, discretion, cross-data sharing), actors (immigration and police officers, employers, neighbors), and settings (the workplace, ethnic grocery stores, public roads, homes) implicated in the process. In doing so, we can trace the extent to which these geographies are shifting, including whether hot spots are increasing or decreasing in their potency. We can also identify the set of policies, practices, and actors that intensify or weaken the geographies of deportability.

This framework encourages us to map where the threat of deportation is localized as it is shaped by both formal and informal shifts in policy and enforcement practices. At the time of data collection for this book, San Diego was not considered a sanctuary city, despite California's statewide sanctuary policies. However, as of December 2024, San Diego officially became a sanctuary city. Sanctuary policies generally aim to prevent collaboration between police and immigration officers. Early in Trump's second presidential administration, however, reports surfaced that immigration officers were departing from the Escondido Police Department early to patrol neighborhoods and conduct targeted arrests. This suggests some level of informal collaboration. Another form of implicit cooperation often associated with sanctuary policies involves police officers turning a blind eye. For instance, during targeted immigration arrests, officers—often armed, in plain clothes, and operating with an intensity resembling a kidnapping—use deceit and force. Despite this, local police frequently choose to look the other way. Ultimately, it is crucial to monitor changes in policy and enforcement practices, both those that are highly visible and formalized and those that are more subtle and implicit.

As the geographies of deportability deepen and expand, families are compelled to partake in what I have been referring to as sanctuary making—a socioemotional process whereby individual members constantly restructure their daily routines, roles, and responsibilities to create environments of safety, belonging, and protection. By centering young adults' efforts in their family's sanctuary making, we see their distinct yet interconnected roles as backup parents, emotional anchors, and legal brokers. These roles demand significant time and energy, often sustained over many years, forcing young adults to prioritize their family's needs and well-being above their own. Young adults sometimes distribute responsibilities among siblings based on factors such as age, gender, birth order, and immigration status. While this approach may lessen the burden on any individual child, it can also create tensions within the family. These insights expose the underbelly of sanctuary making—where its protective intentions can mask the limitations and emotional consequences that often go unnoticed and underappreciated. To this end, by gaining a deeper understanding of the systemic pressures faced by young adults due to the geographies of deportability and the associated burdens of sanctuary making, school personnel and others can devise ways to alleviate the significant hardships these young people endure.

Unique to this study is its qualitative focus on families, and especially the young 1.5- and 2nd-generation adults who anchor them. This emphasis allowed me to reveal how young adults and their families both perceive and respond to changes in policy, practices, and ultimately the spaces they inhabit. They possess both acute awareness—understanding how the threat of deportation is continually manifested in their communities—and agency, as they engage in dynamic socioemotional processes to foster a sense of belonging and safety in their communities. Their efforts reveal that sanctuary is not something that is given by the state or institutions but rather must be created from the ground up. Policymakers, social service providers, and immigrant rights organizers, too, can play a critical role in bolstering families' sanctuary making efforts.

By situating the lives of young 1.5- and 2nd-generation adults within the framework of the geographies of deportability and sanctuary making, this book uncovers the often hidden emotional and material tolls of enforcement. It highlights the pervasive anxieties and fears that arise from the mere possibility that a loved one might encounter a hot spot or interact with the pseudo-migra. These fears manifest as an unrelenting cycle of preoccupation, requiring young adults to constantly anticipate and prepare for worst-case scenarios. This vigilance takes an emotional toll, as young adults grapple with anguish when loved ones leave for work or become unaccounted for and with the lingering trauma tied to objects and sounds reminiscent of an arrest—like orange cones, sirens, or loud knocks at the door. Beyond the emotional strain, enforcement produces material consequences: self-evictions, missed opportunities, delays in accessing legal benefits, and acts of communal erasure that fracture family bonds. At a deeper level, the constant state of alertness deprives young adults of the ability to truly rest. Many endure years of recurrent immigration-related nightmares, sudden emotional breakdowns, and overwhelming stress. These conditions reveal how enforcement extends its reach far beyond legal systems, embedding itself in the daily lives and inner worlds of those navigating the geographies of deportability.

Notably, this book reveals that the consequences of enforcement are felt across generations (including the 1st, 1.5, and 2nd generations) and immigration statuses (including those who identify as undocumented, have DACA or TPS, and green card holders or U.S. citizens whose loved ones are undocumented). They are also felt across the spectrum of enforcement (including the alert, confinement, expulsion, and reentry phases), and spaces of everyday life (encompassing both the public and private realms). Relatedly, even those who are deported or who have adjusted their immigration status (who theoretically should be exempt from the fear of deportation) continue to endure the toll of enforcement for years. These insights highlight the wide-ranging, profound, and ever-lasting spillover effects of U.S. immigration policies and enforcement practices on families and indeed a large segment of the U.S. population.

There are also shared elements in legal consciousness across generations. Initially, fear was thought to primarily affect undocumented adults. However, I find that fear operates alongside stigma and a sense of responsibility and vigilance shaping the lives of children and young adults. Indeed, making distinctions between who is a child and who is a young adult becomes complicated by an immigration regime whose violence compels protective actions from young people starting at an early age.

Scholars may find the geographies of deportability framework useful for examining how deportability is mapped onto evolving social and physical geographies across different regions of the country. To this end, it is important to pay attention to the social and spatial dynamics surrounding sightings of immigration officers, news of immigration raids, immigration-related arrests. This includes examining the role of the pseudo-migra. Arguably, border communities more closely resemble some of the hot spots I have described here. In the Rio Grande Valley (RGV) in Texas, for example, immigrant families are similarly physically bounded by the presence of federal immigration checkpoints found to the north and ports of entry located to the south along the U.S.-Mexico border. Notably, the checkpoints in the RGV are always active. This means that undocumented immigrants are always prevented from safely and legally driving north of the area, which poses significant challenges when it comes to their ability to access medical services and employment and educational opportunities.[12] To circumvent this hot spot in this context may require greater coordinated resources. Young adults may need to rely on their extended networks with more frequency to secure opportunities in the RGV to avoid driving through the checkpoint. Alternatively, they may consider traveling at greater financial and environmental cost by airplane to access opportunities outside of the RGV.[13]

Nationwide, many deportations occur following encounters with law enforcement, who transform public roads and specific intersections, such as those monitored by DUI checkpoints, into these hot spots. Scholars can map and analyze these and other coordinates to understand the nature and impact of hot spots, tailored to the specifics of each locale. Although certain hot spots recur across cities and states, their characteristics, dynamics, and effects can differ. Additionally, as policies and practices evolve, new hot spots emerge, while existing ones are contested. Consequently, the nature of families' sanctuary making efforts also varies.

Scholars can utilize the geographies of deportability framework in various ways to explore distinct phenomena. For instance, they might interview other key groups within the immigrant population, such as unaccompanied minors and asylum seekers, to uncover the places they associate with immigration enforcement from their unique perspectives. Moreover, while examining these perceptions across different cities and states, significant variations are likely based on factors such as individuals' legal status, duration of residence in the U.S., age upon arrival, and other relevant characteristics. Recently arrived migrants, for example, may experience ports of entry and processing centers as key hot spots that feature most prominently in their lives. In contrast, undocumented immigrants who have lived in the U.S. for longer periods, like those featured in this study, may identify federal immigration and DUI checkpoints in the interior as central hot spots regulating their lives.

Other approaches to studying the geographies of deportability include the use of observations, interviews with immigration officials or immigrant rights organizers, and Freedom of Information Act (FOIA) requests about the physical locations where CBP or ICE have arrested or monitored undocumented immigrants.[14] Robust, multifaceted approaches are essential for tracing the geographies of deportability across time and space, especially in the era of enforcement in the shadows. Such data can provide a comprehensive understanding about the impact of immigration enforcement on various segments of the immigrant population. It can also shed light on patterns of deportation across the country that are not immediately visible, such as the ways certain neighborhoods are disproportionately targeted.

Notably, organizations in other parts of the country have undertaken efforts to map the geographical distribution of immigration enforcement activities. In New York, the Immigrant Defense Project (IDP) and the Center for Constitutional Rights created an interactive "ICEwatch" map that features information about more than 1,300 immigration enforcement activities in the area.[15] This includes information about where an arrest or sighting of immigration officers took place and the tactics that immigration officers employed. By recording the settings where enforcement activities are taking place, sanctuary making efforts at the community level such as these are essential to creating digital archives that serve as alternative means of documentation. From these digital archives we can learn about broader patterns of racialized policing and work toward addressing them. When residents in Arivaca, Arizona, for example, decided to monitor the federal immigration checkpoint themselves, they found that a Latino-occupied vehicle was *"more than 26 times more likely* to be required to show identification than a white-occupied vehicle. And Latino-occupied vehicles were *nearly 20 times more likely* to be ordered to secondary inspection."* Their findings, as reported by the ACLU, stemmed from more than 100 hours of observation that spanned several months.[16]

Alongside documenting the geographies of deportability and families' efforts at sanctuary making, it is crucial to explore ongoing immigrant rights organizing on the ground. Such examinations can shed light on how the state manipulates spaces, based on insights from immigrant rights organizers. They also illuminate how the meanings of these spaces are contested and by whom. This approach offers a more dynamic understanding of space, which considers the various actors involved and in turn provides us with a rich portrait of the geographies of deportability and sanctuary making across the individual, family, and community levels.

I would also be remiss if I did not mention that we cannot assume that every family works in unison or is free from tension. A handful of the young adults I interviewed had strained relationships with their parents at one point or another. Facing financial pressures and limited resources, there were frequent arguments between parents and their children. Some recalled instances when their parents became angry, distant, or hurtful, such as when learning about their children's sexual orientations.[17] In some cases, their parents were no longer in their lives—they had either passed away or had lost contact with them. Thus, while the concept of sanctuary making is valuable for understanding the dynamics within the nuclear family that help individuals mitigate or cope with the effects of the geographies of deportability, it is also critical to recognize and explore the harms, injuries, and tensions inherent in these relationships.[18] I find it useful to think of sanctuary making as a dynamic and relational process undertaken by more than two people within the same household or family unit, with its own set of benefits, opportunities, forms of support, tensions, and limitations. It is also important to note that sanctuary making can extend beyond the family unit. Organizers, extended relatives, partners, trusted friends, and others can be involved in the process, too. Indeed, a key implication of this book's emphasis on the extensive pressures that immigrant families already face is that extended networks of nonfamily member advocates may have important new roles to play in the remaking of sanctuary.

By developing the theoretical framework of the geographies of deportability and sanctuary making, I hope to enable others to study its manifestations while considering the specifics of the locales—both geographic and disciplinary—where they are found. This framework aims to provide a theoretical toolkit for researchers to examine both existing and emerging hot spots and the responses of young adults and their families. Over time, this work may aggregate to enhance our understanding of meta-structures of enforcement in the shadows and sanctuary making processes, not only across the U.S. but also transnationally in the context of global migration control.

RECOMMENDATIONS FOR POLICYMAKERS,
EDUCATORS, COUNSELORS, AND OTHERS
WORKING CLOSELY WITH YOUNG ADULTS

Over the years, in both my research and personal experience, I have grappled with what it means for young adults to lead their lives in the face of expanding enforcement measures. I am also reminded of the many young adults I have met who became green card holders or U.S. citizens, yet were never-theless still contending with the "remnants" or "afterlife" of growing up un-documented.[19] Surely it is essential that undocumented immigrants be able to adjust their immigration status. It is an important stepping stone, a mean-ingful turning point over the course of their lives. In the context of the era of enforcement in the shadows and its resulting geographies of deportability, the suffering faced by young adults and their families is both profound and far-reaching. This suffering penetrates family dynamics and the intimacies of daily life, affecting multiple generations and differing citizenship and docu-mentation statuses. Policymakers, educators, counselors, and others in the fields of immigration and social services can employ various strategies to sup-port young adults and their families during this challenging time.

First, in response to the structural violence inflicted by the state on both migrants and immigrants through the threat of deportation, a necessary so-lution would be to broaden pathways to U.S. citizenship. These pathways should inclusively accommodate undocumented immigrants with estab-lished ties in the country, asylum seekers, unaccompanied children, and re-cent arrivals.

The conclusions drawn in this book suggest the importance of pursuing certain concrete changes to the immigration system and practices. I argue that there is a need to allow families to petition for an adjustment of status as a unit rather than as individuals. The immigration system is such that only individuals who meet certain eligibility requirements may apply for an adjustment of status. Under current U.S. immigration law, U.S. citizens, whether by birth or naturalization, may petition for their spouses. (This is by no means easy or straightforward, as couples must contend with the fi-nancial and emotional costs embedded in the process.)[20] Yet even when one individual member can adjust their immigration status, the entire family continues to feel the effects of enforcement by virtue of having at least one member who remains undocumented and therefore subject to deportability. Therefore, it is not enough to solely rely on solutions for individuals. Com-prehensive support is necessary for the whole family, which must encompass assistance for members who are prohibited from legally rejoining their fami-lies in the U.S. following a deportation. This is an issue I return to later in this chapter, as many of the families I have spoken to over the years are con-tending with some kind of bar to entry or reentry that prevents them from legally adjusting their immigration status despite close ties to a U.S. citizen parent, spouse, or sibling who could otherwise petition for them.

Second, this book provides useful insights into how various actors can work to challenge the era of enforcement in the shadows and its expanding geographies of deportability, which are implemented through public policies and institutional employees, and in public places.

In chapter 1, I demonstrated how changes in U.S. immigration policy and practice are facilitating the era of enforcement in the shadows. This includes immigration officers' growing reliance on the pseudo-migra, as well as their monitoring of a growing share of noncitizens and citizens alike using databases and deceitful tactics to hide in plain sight. Policymakers, I argue, can impose greater accountability for officers' actions on the ground. This might entail introducing bills that limit the range and type of information that immigration officers can collect and use for enforcement purposes. Policymakers can also impose boundaries on the cross-sharing of data between agencies (like ICE and the DMV or law enforcement).

In chapter 2, I argued that in the era of enforcement in the shadows, the geographies of deportability are penetrating more deeply into the everyday lives of undocumented and mixed-status families, causing greater disruption. Central to the expansion of the geographies of deportability is a dynamic process whereby various social actors are contesting the use of space in ways that ultimately prioritize certain meanings over others. Take for example the case of public roads, where there are competing interests and uses. From residents' perspective, public roads primarily serve as a means to fulfill their responsibilities, enabling travel between home, work, and school. These sites, however, are increasingly being transformed into hot spots by the state using immigration or DUI checkpoints. There are also efforts underway by immigrant rights organizers to reclaim the use of these sites by exposing immigration officers' tactics to police public space and alerting families of such hot spots. Policymakers also play a role in this process by implementing legislation that can either expand or restrict the ability of law enforcement to work with immigration. To this end, efforts can be made to contest hot spots by restricting the state's ability to rely on the pseudo-migra (short of preventing it altogether). Citizens can participate in this process by contesting policing in public spaces, showing support and solidarity for immigrant families, and documenting the tactics of immigration officers on the ground.

Third, social service providers, educators, and counselors can apply new insights about the effects of enforcement to design meaningful interventions that ease the burdens young adults face.

In chapter 3, I explored the emotionally and materially labor-intensive roles young adults assume as backup parents, emotional anchors, and legal brokers, navigating and contesting the geographies of deportability. By recognizing these challenges, social service providers, educators, and counselors can play a pivotal role in alleviating the pressures on young adults and supporting their well-being. For example, school personnel can collaborate with grassroots organizations to host events aimed at helping young adults understand the range of tactics typically employed by immigration officers. These efforts can help young adults understand the range of risks that are embedded in their daily routines, including the ability to discern between risks that are arguably more hypothetical in nature and how these risks are evolving over time. Immigration lawyers can also create videos tailored to young adults and their parents in which they discuss recent changes in U.S. immigration policy and address common concerns and fears.

Educators and counselors can compile information about local and institutional resources that are open to undocumented students and their families. This includes information on medical services, scholarship opportunities, emergency housing and transportation, legal rights, and community building events. The key is to identify resources that are trustworthy, accessible, and preferably up to date. Staff members can become familiar with applicable laws and best practices aimed at protecting undocumented students' privacy and confidentiality. Students may hesitate to disclose information about their parents on various school forms or fear immigration enforcement actions near campus. Staff members can attend an "UndocuAlly" training, which typically features information about the set of policies that help protect students' information and rights. Equipped with this knowledge, staff members can reassure students about their safety, answer critical questions, and acknowledge the set of worries and fears they are contending with.

With respect to young adults' role as legal brokers, schools and organizations can partner to offer workshops that invite families to understand their options for immigration relief. At these events, immigration lawyers can speak with the entire family about their immigration case. Organizers may be especially mindful of the fact that young adults are often tasked with mediating information between their families and the state, and therefore may equip young adults with the language and tools to take on such tasks at home. This includes developing pamphlets that explain in simple terms some common legal terms, procedures, or laws. Relatedly, educators, counselors, and administrators can work together to share important information about changes in U.S. immigration policy and enforcement with students and their parents.

Across roles, I find that DACA plays a significant role in shaping young adults' ability to contribute to their families' sanctuary making efforts. Consequently, it is imperative for policymakers, organizers, and others to advocate for the continuation of the DACA program and for the expansion of its parameters to include youth who have been previously excluded. The same is true for similar initiatives such as Deferred Action for Parents of Americans, Advance Parole, and Parole in Place. Leaders of schools and organizations can help bridge the gap between those who work with students and those who work on advocating for policies like DACA. Taken together, these efforts can create communities of sanctuary that effectively address the emotional, legal, and educational needs of young adults in tandem.

For some of the young adults in this study, school personnel and immigrant rights organizers were an important source of emotional support, encouragement, and resources. Luna, who received support from school personnel and community leaders, explained, "Eventually, I realized that I needed to stay in school because it was keeping me sane. It was giving me the strength to fight back, to be the strong person that I needed to be for my siblings, for my mom and for my dad." When sanctuary making extends to the community level, young adults' legal consciousness can be a source of motivation, determination, and strength in ways that motivate them to become politically active or civically engaged.

There are important efforts underway to provide direct services and support to undocumented immigrants and their families across schools and cities. School personnel can support undocumented-led organizations and immigrant rights grassroots organizations. These collectives, particularly those that are grassroots and student led, are often understaffed and underfunded. Educators, staff members, and others can help by volunteering their time, donating money, and spreading the word about their efforts.

Next, it is imperative for scholars and others to gain a deeper understanding of how immigration law and enforcement impact young adults across time and space.

In chapter 4, I discussed the emotional and material tolls of enforcement. I found that young adults are often contending with sudden emotional breakdowns, recurrent immigration-related nightmares, and overwhelming stress. There are also several material consequences in the form of missed educational opportunities, derailed trajectories, legal lags, and communal erasures. Based on these insights, it is important for researchers, policymakers, and practitioners alike to recognize the lingering and often hidden effects of growing up undocumented and dealing with enforcement. While scholars have utilized photo-elicitation interviews and art as effective means of inquiry and discussion about the emotional world of children in undocumented and mixed-status families,[21] longitudinal studies that trace the effects of the geographies of deportability alongside trauma-informed interviews between parents and children are also needed.

Relatedly, this book reveals that even young adults who are U.S.-born citizens develop their own kind of legal consciousness in ways that parallel those of their undocumented counterparts. In my conversations with school personnel over the years, many expressed the need to serve this growing segment of the immigrant population while at the same time recognizing that doing so entailed a unique set of barriers and challenges. Among these is the fact that many schools do not keep track of the number of U.S.-born citizens whose parents are undocumented, for various reasons, including issues of privacy and safety. It is difficult to know the size of this population across campuses, which may limit the allocation of resources. Another challenge has to do with the fact that U.S.-born citizens whose parents are undocumented may often refrain from accessing resources that are otherwise available to them, because of concern about how their undocumented peers may perceive them. U.S.-born citizen students might feel that their needs pale in comparison to those of their undocumented peers and as such may not want to use up resources. In other instances, U.S.-born students largely opt to conceal information about their parents' immigration status to avoid the risk of detection. These circumstances can make it challenging for school personnel to adequately serve the immigrant student population, which includes both undocumented and U.S.-born citizens whose parents are undocumented. By recognizing these complexities, efforts can be made to raise awareness about the experiences of students in mixed-status families, including their needs and concerns, in ways that are mindful of the experiences of students who are underprivileged by virtue of their status as DACA recipients or undocumented immigrants. School personnel can also create programming that is specific to U.S.-born citizens whose parents are undocumented, such as safe spaces where youths can discuss the sense of privilege, responsibility, and guilt that are common among this group.[22] Immigration lawyers may facilitate workshops geared toward demystifying the process of children helping their parents adjust their immigration status once they reach the age of 21 (a process that is not available to all but is nevertheless central to young adults' legal consciousness).

What is especially important when undertaking this type of work is for policymakers and practitioners alike to be attuned to the ways young adults are managing their identities and roles in the context of evolving geographies. This includes a recognition of the multiple responsibilities young adults are managing across school, work, and home. It also entails an acknowledgement of the set of common concerns and fears that young adults may experience in the process.

As this book reveals, interior enforcement practices are overburdening the lives of young adults, who are often at the center of their families' sanctuary making efforts. Individuals who are sympathetic to the plight of young adults and their families can help bolster their sanctuary making efforts by volunteering their time or donating to an immigrant rights organization. The public can also stay up to date with changes in U.S. immigration policy and enforcement, and in the process, critically analyze and question such changes. Relatedly, it is imperative to continue spreading awareness about the lives of young adults and their families under the era of enforcement in the shadows. This book invites readers across the country to reimagine landscapes based on communal definitions of resistance and solidarity.

ADDRESSING THE ADDITIONAL CHALLENGES FACING INDIVIDUALS WITH (RE)ENTRY BARS

Over the years I have met many families who are contending with what is commonly referred to as *el castigo,* or (re)entry bars. Under the Immigration and Nationality Act, there are three different types of bars that noncitizens may be subjected to depending on the length of their unlawful presence in the U.S. The first of these, the 3-year bar, applies to those who "seek admission within three years of departing the United States, after having accrued more than 180 days but less than one year of unlawful presence during a single stay and before removal proceedings begin."[23] For example, an undocumented mother who entered the U.S. with a Border Crossing Card (BCC), remained here for 10 months, then departed to attend a loved one's funeral, and shortly afterward reentered the U.S. with her BCC, may be subjected to the 3-year bar. This means that even if she had a U.S. citizen child over the age of 21 who could otherwise petition her for an adjustment of status based on family-based preferences, she might nevertheless be deemed inadmissible until three years have passed. In contrast, the 10-year bar applies to those who accrued a longer period of unlawful presence (one year or more) and subsequently departed. Last, the permanent bar is issued to those who "reenter or try to reenter the United States without being admitted or paroled after having accrued more than one year of unlawful presence in the aggregate during one or more stays in the United States."[24] This bar severely impacts the well-being of families in which a member has undergone multiple deportations, as it prevents them from legally and safely reuniting in the U.S.

Determining whether an individual has accumulated unlawful presence and triggered one of these bars is often the first step undertaken by immigration lawyers during their assessment of a person's eligibility for an adjustment of status. Yet it can be difficult to calculate an individual's unlawful presence, especially when there are multiple entries and exits. Over the course of time, people may forget their specific dates of entry and departure, which would prevent lawyers from assessing how much time has elapsed between entries. This is further complicated by the fact that CBP officers often do not carefully explain their procedures, so people do not entirely know the details of their entries and exits.[25] While a person may be able to obtain their travel records from CBP through an FOIA request, the process can be lengthy, with some waiting months for a response. Many individuals will consult different immigration lawyers before proceeding with their potential cases but often find that CBP's records are either partial or incomplete, and at times are even nonexistent, despite the memory of having interacted with CBP.

Based on my conversations with both families who are seeking some form of relief and immigration lawyers (or interns) who assist families with the process over the years, I have learned that this is an area that demands significant attention and adequate support. There are many undocumented individuals in mixed-status families who meet all other eligibility requirements but are unable to adjust their immigration status because they are subjected to one of these bars. There are also family units in which one member may be able to adjust their status, but another is unable to because of the bars. In these circumstances, families often hesitate to proceed with the adjustment of status process for the qualifying member, fearing exposure of the entire family or perceiving the process as unfair. Consequently, they may choose to forgo this opportunity, holding out hope until a time when both parents can adjust their immigration statuses.

There have been efforts to address the detrimental and lasting impacts of the 3- and 10-year bars in policy circles. As part of his presidential campaign in 2020, former U.S. secretary of housing and urban development Julian Castro proposed to lead efforts to reform the country's immigration system in part by ending the 3- and 10-year bars. Following court litigation brought forth by the Northwest Immigrant Rights Project, USCIS issued new guidance on the interpretation of the 3- and 10-year bars in 2023.[26] Under a policy update, USCIS clarified that individuals facing a 3- or 10-year bar no longer need to leave the U.S. to fulfill the requirement—they can remain in the country during that time. While other forms of inadmissibility may still apply, this was an important step that allowed some individuals to apply for an adjustment of status if their bar had already expired.

These efforts generally do not address the permanent bar. In fact, there has been very little conversation about or support for ending the permanent bar. This comes at a significant cost to individuals whose only option to reunite with their families is often to attempt to reenter the U.S. without authorization after deportation. It likely impacts a growing number of families, especially considering the wave of mass deportations that the U.S. is still experiencing. For those subjected to any of these bars, the chances of adjusting their immigration status are slim. It is also particularly concerning that recent years have been marked by policymakers' attempts to further criminalize unauthorized (re)entries, at both the federal and state levels.

ENFORCEMENT IN THE SHADOWS UNDER TRUMP'S SECOND TERM

In many ways, the 2024 U.S. presidential election cycle resembled that of 2016, in which young adults and their families found themselves increasingly fearful and worried as it became apparent that Donald J. Trump would be the next president of the U.S.[27] For years Trump campaigned on a promise of stricter immigration policies, heightened enforcement, and increased deportations. We know from his first term as president that the anti-immigrant rhetoric fueled by his administration penetrated classroom walls, affecting the educational experiences and well-being of immigrant students, particularly those who identify as undocumented or who are U.S. citizens from mixed-status families.[28]

During his 2024 campaign, Trump repeatedly called for "mass deportations," which he said he would authorize the military and law enforcement to carry out alongside immigration officers. It is difficult to predict the extent to which the new Trump administration will be able to carry out such plans, particularly given that immigration agencies have never had at their disposal the personnel necessary to conduct arrests on a mass scale.[29] However, there is widespread fear in immigrant communities, where information about raids, checkpoints, and sightings of police or immigration officers travels quickly. As the geographies of deportability expand and deepen, it becomes increasingly difficult for immigrant families to know where they can feel safe and whom to trust. This adds stress and pressure, particularly on young adults, who are often tasked with distinguishing between tangible and hypothetical risks. As the stakes rise, young adults and their families may forgo opportunities that would otherwise be available to them, out of an abundance of caution.

There are also growing fears and worries, many of which are difficult to pin down and counteract. Take for example the growing uncertainty surrounding the future of DACA. Should the program come to an end, young adults are worried that their family's information could be used for immigration enforcement purposes. On the one hand, practitioners have been able to reassure young adults that while USCIS collects highly sensitive and personal information, it typically does not utilize it for enforcement purposes. On the other hand, for young adults and practitioners alike, much remains unknown and within the realm of possibility when it comes to President Trump's intention to carry out mass deportations, part of which, some have speculated, may target DACA recipients and their families.

Although the future of DACA rests with the courts and the sitting presidential administration, President Trump's ongoing and escalating attacks on various segments of the immigration population highlight the vulnerability of even those with some type of legal protection. Indeed, within days of his second presidential term, DHS Secretary Kristi Noem announced that TPS protections for approximately 600,000 Venezuelans would come to an end as of September 10, 2025.[30] It is likely that the Trump administration will discontinue TPS for other countries and attack similar programs. This will have devastating consequences for the recipients of these programs and their families, many of whom have greatly benefited from the opportunity to work legally and feel safe from deportation.[31]

The opening salvo of Trump's second presidential administration vividly demonstrates how the infrastructure behind the era of enforcement in the shadows can be rapidly mobilized and further entrenched. This mobilization aims to intensify and expand the geographies of deportability, facilitating arrests and sowing greater chaos across immigrant communities. Within days of Trump's 2025 inauguration, and following a series of executive orders, the DHS and the Department of Justice (DOJ) issued separate memos outlining significant changes in the interpretation of certain protections and the implementation of enforcement practices. For instance, in one memo, acting DHS Secretary Benjamine Huffman authorized immigration officers to carry out arrests in sensitive locations such as schools, churches, and hospitals—spaces that were previously considered off-limits to immigration enforcement.[32] Shortly thereafter, rumors began to circulate in different parts of the country warning people about sightings of immigration officers outside schools and hospitals. The rumors were often unconfirmed yet spread quickly, as people feared encountering immigration officers. What is particularly concerning is that even when these rumors are false, they have a detrimental effect on undocumented immigrants and their loved ones, who learn to be on edge and navigate their surroundings with extra caution. For example, parents may become fearful of dropping off or picking up their children following rumors about sightings of immigration officers outside of a school. This can lead to a significant drop in school attendance.[33]

President Trump's call to expand expedited removal, 287g programs, and even to prosecute state and local officials who do not cooperate with the enforcement of immigration laws, also illustrates the tension that is inherent in the expansion of the geographies of deportability across all levels of government. In response, some city officials, like the mayor of Chicago, publicly reasserted their commitment to protect immigrant families in alignment with state-level policies. In other parts of the country, state and local officials remained silent or voiced support for President Trump's efforts. In Huntington Beach, California, for instance, the city council passed a resolution declaring itself a "non-sanctuary city" just days after President Trump's second inauguration, marking a sharp contrast to California's stance as a sanctuary state. Three weeks later, the city council of El Cajon, in San Diego, did the same. As tensions escalate across all levels of government over immigration enforcement, more states and cities are likely to distance themselves from the now highly politicized term "sanctuary," both symbolically and in practice. As sanctuary designations and protections disappear across states, cities, hospitals, churches, and schools, families will face greater burdens, challenges, and stress. Young adults will take on increasing responsibilities: tracking changing regulations, making sense of them, and helping their families navigate growing vulnerabilities.

In other parts of the country, efforts are underway to expand the social geographies of deportability by transforming a wide range of actors into extensions of the pseudo-migra. For example, in the state of Florida, legislators passed Senate Bill 1718, which in part requires a greater number of businesses to verify their employees' immigration status.[34] It also mandates that individuals working in hospitals ask patients about their immigration status. Although parts of this policy have not yet been implemented and are pending court litigation, efforts like this nevertheless turn hospitals and worksites into hot spots by introducing the heightened risk of arrest in these settings. In the process, figures such as employers and hospital workers—whose primary roles are to provide employment opportunities and medical services, respectively—are transformed into potential agents of immigration enforcement.

Similarly, in the state of Texas, Governor Greg Abbott signed Senate Bill 4, which would authorize police officers to enforce matters of immigration law. (As of this writing, SB 4 is not in effect, pending court litigation.) House Representative Ryan Guillen (TX) also introduced a bill that would in part allow civilians to arrest and detain individuals they suspect to be undocumented as part of a new "Border Protection Unit."[35] In Mississippi, similar efforts were underway under House Bill 1484, which if enacted would have created a state-funded bounty hunter program aimed at compensating civilians with $1,000 for each undocumented person they reported.[36]

Under Trump's second presidential administration, a race has emerged within the Republican Party to adopt extreme anti-immigrant policies and practices at all levels. What is particularly troubling about these policies is that even if they do not pass or are struck down by the courts, they still foster a hyperxenophobic climate that can shape public opinion about immigrants and influence day-to-day interactions between strangers. In this environment, the concern is that individuals may feel emboldened to take action and participate in the pseudo-migra by reporting those they "suspect" to be undocumented, likely based on problematic misconceptions about individuals' race, ethnicity, and country of birth.[37] We are seeing proof of this on campuses like Arizona State University, where the student-run Republican Club held an on-campus event encouraging students to report their classmates to ICE.[38]

Among young adults and their families, this environment fosters a sense of exclusion and deep distrust in others. Of primary concern are past disclosures and the extent to which estranged partners and peers might feel compelled to report them to immigration authorities if circumstances change. Young adults are more likely to distance themselves from others and avoid developing intimate relationships. They may hesitate to be fully open about their status and related concerns, which creates a barrier to building networks of care and solidarity, while also preventing them from receiving adequate and timely emotional support.

Families' sanctuary making efforts are becoming even more pressing in this context. There is an impetus on the part of young adults to stay up to date with the latest news on immigration policy, identify trustworthy resources, and protect their families from the possibility of detection. They are called into action almost instantly after rumors begin to circulate about an upcoming immigration raid or sightings of immigration officers. Upon receiving a notification from their peers or social media, young adults are tasked with promptly verifying the source and information. To do this, they may rely on insights from their friends, community organizers, or news media reports. Additional information is often scant, and it is difficult to confirm the validity of these rumors. Young adults may opt to alert their parents, siblings, and friends in an abundance of caution. As rumors tend to spread and intensify in the lead-up to presidential elections, shortly after an inauguration, and steadily during particularly anti-immigrant political climates, young adults can become consumed by news of deportations and their roles as backup parents, emotional anchors, and legal brokers. Consequently, it becomes imperative for school personnel, social service providers, and immigrant rights organizers, among others, to assist in families' sanctuary making efforts and lessen the burden that young adults are under.

Yet fear and worry are growing even among individuals who are empathetic to the plight of undocumented students and their families, in ways that hinder collective efforts of support. I have had a chance to track and observe much of this through a separate project that examines the basic needs of immigrant college students and the experiences of school personnel working with them.[39] For instance, under certain circumstances, school personnel become hesitant to share with staff from other campuses how they are supporting undocumented students through alternate programs and routes. Leadership at some campuses refrain from issuing statements of support for undocumented students to avoid drawing attention from conservative groups, leaving these students feeling isolated and unsupported within their own campus communities.

Considering the era of enforcement in the shadows and its expanding geographies of deportability, it appears that one of the biggest challenges in the years to come is to reclaim the narrative around immigration. Even among Democratic policymakers, long gone are the days when they stood at the helm of CIR proposals (though these have their own shortcomings).[40] There were glimpses of them during former President Biden's final year with the "Keeping Families Together" proposal, but such efforts are now short-lived, often brought to a halt or prevented from being considered in the first place. Potential routes to political transformation thus themselves have become cast into the shadows.

At a time when millions are being forced to migrate due to political turmoil, climate change, war, and economic instability, questions about the enforcement apparatus are central to understanding the lived experiences of migrants and immigrants in both the U.S. and other parts of the world—as individuals, families, *and* communities. My hope is that the theoretical tools and empirical insights offered in this book can better equip communities to understand the mechanisms through which the state makes use of social and physical geographies to negatively impact young adults and their families, and in the process to dream up new possibilities for a greater collective remaking of sanctuary at all levels.

APPENDIX

Methodological Considerations

Over the years, I have worked closely with undocumented students, their families, and allies through my research, teaching, and service. This includes my work as the founder of *My Undocumented Life*—an online platform that provides up-to-date information to immigrant families—and as a former member of undocumented youth-led organizations. In what follows, I offer an account of the research process behind this book project.

RESEARCH QUESTIONS AND DESIGN

When I initially conceived of the idea for this project, I was interested in examining the educational experiences and political activism of young adults in undocumented and mixed-status families. I conducted preliminary interviews with young adults in which I asked about their reasons for pursuing higher education or becoming politically involved, including how they navigated the college application process, the challenges they encountered during their educational journeys, and the factors that compelled them to join immigrant rights organizing efforts. These interviews were instrumental in shaping the direction of my project, including who I would go on to interview and what type of questions I asked.

The young adults with whom I initially spoke described the constant threat and reality of deportation that they had endured for years. Some of them had a loved one who was previously deported—a father, mother, or sibling. What is more, they all knew of others in their neighborhood—coworkers, friends of family members, and neighbors—who were deported. Enforcement, it became apparent, was a central feature of daily life within undocumented and mixed-status families. It subsequently shaped young adults' well-being; aspirations; and participation at home, school, and work.

I also learned early on that enforcement has both direct and indirect impacts, which are often felt at the family level. This compelled me to recruit young adults whose parents lived with the threat of deportation but had never been arrested and those who had a parent who had been arrested, detained, or deported. I also expanded my sample to include not only young adults but also their relatives. Whenever possible, I interviewed young adults' parents, spouse, or siblings to gain a deeper understanding of the consequences of enforcement for young adults and their families.

Once interviews were underway, participants mentioned specific settings that they had come to associate with enforcement. This included specific neighborhoods, ethnic grocery stores, the local swap meet, and local parks. In these settings young adults and their families saw immigration officers or heard rumors about an immigration raid. However transient these events were, they left a powerful imprint on young adults' perceptions of enforcement. These settings represented sites they had to navigate with extra caution or avoid altogether. Over time, young adults became keenly attuned to their surroundings. They were tasked with discerning between immediate or potential threats of deportation, often at a moment's notice. This encouraged me to ask questions about young adults' perceptions, mindsets, and behaviors in ways that centered the spatial contexts they were embedded in.

From this initial set of interviews, I formulated my central question: What happens to our understanding of the lived experiences of young adults when we center enforcement? I also developed more specific, and related, empirical research questions: What are the specific places and social actors that young adults and their families have learned to associate with enforcement and subsequently a heightened threat of deportation? What are the strategies that young adults employ to navigate this landscape of enforcement? What are the psychosocial consequences of this reality for young adults' participation across various social institutions, such as the household, work, and school, as well as for their well-being, mindset, and aspirations? To address these questions, I interviewed members of undocumented and mixed-status families—many of them young adults—with various immigration statuses and positions along the spectrum of enforcement.

I spoke with individuals who met the following eligibility requirements: they had to (1) be age 18 years or older; (2) physically reside in San Diego County, California, or have grown up there; and (3) have an immediate family member who was undocumented or had been detained or deported from the U.S. at any point. During the recruitment process, I reached out to my network. This included acquaintances, educators, counselors, immigrant rights organizers, and lawyers whom I have gotten to know over the years through my research and advocacy efforts in San Diego. I also recruited participants through snowball sampling methods. At the end of each interview, I asked participants if they knew anyone who might be interested in sharing their experiences and perspectives with me. I encouraged them to share the flyer and my contact information with their family and friends so that anyone who was interested in learning more about the project could reach out to me with questions or to schedule an interview.

At the start of each interview, I reviewed the purpose of the study and the procedures, and encouraged participants to express any questions or concerns they had about the study or my work in this field. I asked participants to complete a short intake sheet to capture key demographic information. I obtained verbal assent from participants before beginning the interview. During the interview, I used a semistructured interview guide to discuss themes related to participants' migration journey, family life, immigration policy, enforcement practices, and aspirations. I recorded interviews for transcription purposes only. Every participant received $20 in compensation for their time. I also created a packet of resources that I shared with participants at the end of each interview.

Given the political climate at the time of data collection and the sensitive nature of the topic, I created a robust data security plan to safeguard participants' privacy and confidentiality. During the data collection process itself, I did not store participants' contact information on my phone. Instead, I kept each one's last message to send a reminder about the interview the night before or that morning, which I deleted once we met. I also instructed participants to refrain from sharing any names of relatives, friends, worksites, or schools. During presentations and publications, I replaced all names with pseudonyms and omitted details that are not central to the story or argument, such as the exact date of our interview or when a member was arrested. I also obtained a certificate of confidentiality (CoC) through the National Institutes of Health. This certificate allows me "to legally refuse to disclose information that may identify [a participant] in any federal, state, or local civil, criminal, administrative, legislative, or other proceedings, for example, if there is a court subpoena." I informed participants about the steps I would take to protect their privacy and confidentiality. I also encouraged them to ask me any questions about the data security procedures.

I was also mindful of the emotional terrain of conducting interviews on a sensitive and difficult topic with individuals who are directly affected. During each interview, I let participants guide the conversation, sharing as much or as little as they felt comfortable with. I memorized and practiced my interview guide multiple times, allowing the discussion to flow more organically. This enabled me to ask impromptu follow-up questions to explore the experiences participants wanted to emphasize. Because I was familiar with my guide, I could keep track of the themes and questions covered without needing to follow a strict order. I also reminded participants that we could pause or discontinue the interview if at any point they felt uncomfortable. They also had the opportunity to reschedule the interview or skip any questions they did not want to answer. I prefaced the especially sensitive and difficult questions with, "remember, you could skip this question or share as much or as little as you feel comfortable with." Overall, I found that participants generally appreciated the interview because it was one of their first opportunities to sit down and process much of the harm they had sustained over the years.

Over the next few years, I kept in touch with some of the families I had interviewed. I also supervised an additional set of interviews with immigrant rights organizers and volunteers. To recruit participants, I created a recruitment flyer and distributed it with grassroots organizations and nonprofits in San Diego. Three research assistants who had close ties to some of these organizations helped with the recruitment and data collection process. Allies represented different positions within these organizations, including volunteer, organizer, program manager, and executive director. Participants spoke about the goals of the organization(s) they belonged to, the nature and range of services and resources they provided to immigrant families, and the challenges they faced in doing this work. They also described the type of enforcement activities they had observed or heard of in San Diego; many of them had witnessed sightings of immigration officers, DUI checkpoints, and actual arrests. Interviews ranged from 30 minutes to 1.5 hours.[1] Allies received $40 in compensation for their time and participation in an interview. (Their compensation was double that of family members because by the time I supervised interviews with immigrant rights organizers I had secured substantial funding for my research.)

MY PERSONAL EXPERIENCE
IMMIGRATING TO SAN DIEGO

This project is deeply personal to me. I identify as a sociologist and education scholar who grew up undocumented in San Diego. I was born in Mexicali, Baja California, and I lived there until I was 12 years old. I have fond memories of growing up in Mexicali. I remember walking to the corner store with my cousins to run quick errands and play arcade games. There were also late summer nights when I would play *futbeis* (a combination of soccer and baseball) outdoors with my older sister and friends. There is also the Fiesta del Sol, the first fair I ever went to and which I returned to for many years with my family for delicious food, shopping, concerts, and games. I also remember the hot summers when the temperature would reach over 100 degrees, and we would have no other option but to spend the day inside the only room in the house that had air conditioning. I will never forget the joy I felt during New Year's Eve when we spent time visiting both sides of my parents' families and ate *pozole*, *menudo*, *tamales*, and *buñuelos*, while counting down to midnight with the sound of fireworks and Ramón Ayala (a popular Mexican singer of Norteño music) in the background.

At 12 years old, it was difficult for me to describe or fully comprehend what it meant for our family to uproot our entire lives—leaving behind our house, friendships, and familiar places—in search of better opportunities. Nevertheless, I was old enough to recognize the hardships my parents endured in Mexico as they tried to provide for us, their three children. My father worked long days and was barely making ends meet. Sometimes, several days would pass before we would see him. My mother also cared for us; she ensured we did well in school, prepared us meals, and made sure that we always had a clean and safe home to return to from school. My sister and I were doing well in school at the time, but my parents foresaw the uphill battle we would face to pursue a college education in Mexico. It was financially out of reach. There was also no guarantee that there would be a well-paying job at the end. In fact, at the time no one on either side of the family had graduated from college. For these and a few other reasons, we immigrated to San Diego in 2001.

Having grown up undocumented in San Diego, I developed a passion for conducting research on immigration. Yet while I had studied the topic of immigration as an undergraduate and then graduate student, I focused on more uplifting aspects of this experience, namely, undocumented youths' sense of agency, civic engagement, political activism, and educational pursuits.[2] As a scholar in training, I immersed myself in the literature and recognized that while research in sociology and education increasingly captured the experiences of undocumented young adults like myself, a key aspect of our daily lives—the constant threat and reality of deportation—had yet to be fully explored. This realization motivated me to contribute to a more nuanced and comprehensive perspective, highlighting how this fear shapes our experiences in profound ways.

At around the same time, in 2016, I conducted preliminary interviews with undocumented young adults in what I thought would be a study about their educational trajectories and political activism. It was through those conversations that I realized my academic intervention would come from confronting the palpable fear of deportation that respondents, and I, too, were grappling with. This is a fear that is manufactured by larger sociopolitical forces and is deeply embedded in the spaces in which undocumented young adults and their families carry out their lives. It is also a fear that for many is realized (when a loved one is arrested), compounded (when multiple relatives are arrested), or amplified (when a loved one returns to the U.S. without legal authorization postdeportation and must contend with the fear of incarceration and deportation). This set of interviews crystallized my interest in conducting a qualitative study of the enforcement apparatus through the lens of those directly impacted.

NOTES

CHAPTER 1. ENFORCEMENT IN THE SHADOWS

1. I have replaced all names of individuals and schools with pseudonyms to protect participants' identities and confidentiality.

2. Under Assembly Bill 60, Gabriel was able to obtain a driver's license in the state of California.

3. I had separate interviews with Monica and Damián. I did not interview Julián because institutional review board restrictions precluded me from interviewing minors. However, I came to learn more about Julián's experiences at school, aspirations, and well-being through informal conversations with him whenever I stopped by to visit his family and through my conversations with his mother and older brother.

4. De Leon 2015.

5. DACA provides eligible undocumented young adults with access to a work permit and relief from deportation on a two-year renewable basis.

6. See also Patler and Gonzalez 2021.

7. This includes 11.3 million U.S. citizens who are members of mixed-status families, as well as 2.4 million green card or visa holders in these households and the estimated 10.1 undocumented individuals. Fwd.Us, "New Data Analysis Shows 28 Million People, Including Nearly 20 Million Latinos, Are at Risk of Family Separation in 2025," October 24, 2024, https://www.fwd.us/news/mixed-status -families-oct/.

8. Becerra et al. 2012.

9. Kerwin and Warren 2020; Pandey, Parreñas, and Sabio 2021.

10. Abrego 2011; Gonzales 2011, 2015; Rumbaut 2006; Kasinitz et al. 2008; Waters and Pineau 2015. Scholars have also made important distinctions among undocumented young adults who arrive between the ages of 13 and 17, referred to as the 1.25 generation (Diaz-Strong 2021), and those who arrive without their parents (Canizales 2024). Young adults' age at arrival and household context both shape their participation across various social institutions (Canizales 2023; Diaz-Strong and Ybarra 2016).

11. Gonzales 2015; see also, for example, Abrego 2006; Gleeson 2010; Gleeson and Gonzales 2012.

12. Sociologists Cecilia Menjívar and Leisy Abrego (2012) introduced the concept of legal violence to draw attention to the often normalized but injurious effects of the law that have the potential to derail immigrants' incorporation trajectories in the United States.

13. Chacón 2012; Kalhan 2013; Muñiz 2022; Stumpf 2012.

14. Motomura 2014.

15. Armenta 2012; Varsanyi 2010.

16. Gulasekaram and Ramakrishnan 2015; Motomura 1999; Spiro 1997.

17. Varsanyi et al. 2012.

18. Coleman 2012; Coleman and Kocher 2011; Varsanyi 2008. See also the work of Moinester (2018).

19. The official government website for E-Verify is https://www.e-verify.gov/.

20. Stumpf 2012.

21. Marc R. Rosenblum, "E-Verify: Strengths, Weaknesses, and Proposals for Reform," Migration Policy Institute, February 2011, https://www.migrationpolicy .org/research/e-verify-strengths-weaknesses-and-proposals-reform..

22. At the time of this writing, the official E-Verify government website yields approximately 828,426 entries when searching for hiring site locations across the country that currently use the program; see "E-Verify Employer Search," accessed May 12, 2025, https://www.e-verify.gov/about-e-verify/e-verify-data/how-to-find -participating-employers.

23. Goldstein and Alonso-Bejarano 2017; Gomberg-Muñoz and Nussbaum-Barberena 2011; Valdivia 2019a.

24. Stumpf 2012.

25. See, for example, Armenta 2017; Coleman 2012; Garcia 2019; Provine and Varsanyi 2012; Varsanyi et al. 2012.

26. Ayón et al. 2011; García 2018; Gleeson 2010; Gleeson and Gonzales 2012; Valdivia 2019a.

27. These are part of my early findings which appeared in Valdivia (2019a).

28. The term "la migra" is commonly used in Latinx immigrant communities to refer to immigration agents (Hernández 2010). I add the prefix "pseudo" to highlight social actors whose main roles do not involve enforcing immigration law, yet who act like immigration officers—either actively, by checking immigration status and reporting individuals, or passively, by collecting and storing personal data that may be accessed by immigration authorities. See also, for example, the work of Menjívar (2014) on the "poli-migra" (the multiple "migras") and that of immigrant rights organizations, which typically employ the term "polimigra" to refer to police officers who now collaborate with immigration authorities. Migrant Justice, "Vermont Sheriff on Collaboration with Deportation Agents: 'We Don't Need Further Restrictions on What We're Already Doing,'" February 4, 2024, https://migrantjustice .net/no-polimigra-2-7-24.

29. See also Armenta 2012; Coleman 2012; Del Real 2019; Walsh 2014.

30. Del Real 2019; Zatz and Rodriguez 2015.

31. Pham 2008.

32. For a list of current 287(g) agreements, see U.S. Immigration and Customs Enforcement, Delegation of Immigration Authority Section 287(g) Immigration and Nationality Act, accessed May 12, 2025, https://www.ice.gov/identify-and-arrest/287g.

33. American Immigration Council, "The 287(g) Program: An Overview," January 20, 2025, https://www.americanimmigrationcouncil.org/research/287g-program-immigration.

34. Beckett and Evans 2015; Golash-Boza 2015; Guillermo Cantor, Mark Noferi, and Daniel E. Martínez, 2015. "Enforcement Overdrive: A Comprehensive Assessment of ICE's Criminal Alien Program," American Immigration Council, 2015, www.americanimmigrationcouncil.org/sites/default/files/research/enforcement_overdrive_a_comprehensive_assessment_of_ices_criminal_alien_program_final.pdf.

35. Morales and Curry 2021; Wong et al. 2021.

36. Pham 2008; Walsh 2014. See also, for example, Chacón (2017) on the growing privatization of immigration law and enforcement.

37. Esbenshade et al. 2010.

38. Kalhan 2013; Nevins 2002.

39. Brian A. Reaves and Timothy C. Hart, "Federal Law Enforcement Officers, 2000," *Bureau of Justice Statistics Bulletin*, July 2001, https://bjs.ojp.gov/content/pub/pdf/fleoo.pdf.

40. Justin Doubleday, "USCIS Workforce Bounces Back, but Agency Faces Murky Funding Future," Federal News Network, December 9, 2024, https://federalnewsnetwork.com/budget/2024/12/uscis-workforce-bounces-back-but-agency-faces-murky-funding-future/.

41. U.S. Customs and Border Protection, "About CBP," accessed May 12, 2025, www.cbp.gov/about.; U.S. Immigration and Customs Enforcement, "Who We Are," accessed May 12, 2025, https://www.ice.gov/about-ice#:~:text=ICE%20now%20has%20more%20than,States%20and%20around%20the%20world.

42. American Immigration Council, "The Cost of Immigration Enforcement and Border Security," August 14, 2024, https://www.americanimmigrationcouncil.org/research/the-cost-of-immigration-enforcement-and-border-security.

43. Andreas 2022; Dunn 1996, 2001.

44. Natasha Bertrand, Priscilla Alvarez, Haley Britzky, Oren Liebermann, and Katie Bo Lillis, "US Military Ordering Thousands More Troops to Sourthern Border," *CNN*, January 22, 2025, https://www.cnn.com/2025/01/22/politics/us-military-troops-southern-border/index.html.

45. Jeff Mason, Idrees Ali, and Ted Hesson, "Trump to Prepare Facility at Guantanamo for 30,000 Migrants," *Reuters*, January 29, 2025, https://www.reuters.com/world/us/trump-says-he-will-instruct-homeland-security-pentagon-prepare-migrant-facility-2025-01-29/.

46. Goldstein and Alonso-Bejarano 2017; Martinez-Aranda 2022; Muñiz 2022.

47. Brayne 2021.

48. Wang et al. 2022.

49. U.S. Department of Homeland Security, "DHS/OBIM/PIA–001 Automated Biometric Identification System," accessed May 12, 2025, https://www.dhs.gov/publication/dhsnppdpia-002-automated-biometric-identification-system.

50. As of December 2021, the system consisted of more than 320 million unique identifiers. U.S. Department of Homeland Security, "Biometrics," accessed May 12, 2025, https://www.dhs.gov/biometrics.

51. Kalhan 2013; Joan Friedland, "How ICE Uses Databases and Information-Sharing to Deport Immigrants," National Immigration Law Center, 2018, https://www.nilc.org/2018/01/25/how-ice-uses-databases-and-information-sharing-to-deport-immigrants/. See also, for example, Drew Harwell, "ICE Investigators Used a Private Utility Database Covering Millions to Pursue Immigration Violations," *Washington Post*, February 26, 2021, https://www.washingtonpost.com/technology/2021/02/26/ice-private-utility-data/.

52. Muñiz 2020, 2022.

53. Joel Rubin, "It's Legal for an Immigration Agent to Pretend to Be a Police Officer Outside Someone's Door: But Should It Be?," *Los Angeles Times*, February 20, 2017, https://www.latimes.com/local/lanow/la-me-immigration-deportation-ruses-20170219-story.html.

54. De Genova 2013, 1181.

55. De Genova 2002, 2004.

56. Alex Ward, "How the World Is Reacting to Trump's Family Separation Policy," *Vox*, June 20, 2018, https://www.vox.com/world/2018/6/20/17483738/trump-family-separation-border-trudeau-may-reaction.

57. Vega 2018.

58. De Genova 2002.

59. Muñiz 2022.

60. Chavez 2012; Suárez-Orozco et al. 2011.

61. Since the 1960s and reaching a particularly high peak in the late 1970s, there has been a steady rise of negative portrayals about immigration, and immigrants more specifically, on media coverage (Chavez 2013). Many of these narratives paint immigrants as prone to crime even though research on this has yielded null or negative associations (Ousey and Kubrin 2018).

62. Abrego 2014; Chavez 2007; Coutin 2005; De Genova 2002; Dreby 2015; Garcia 2019; Gonzales 2011, 2015; Menjívar and Kanstroom 2013; Ngai 2004; Willen 2007.

63. De Genova 2002, 2004. See also Harrison and Lloyd 2012.

64. Asad 2020a, 2023; Abrego 2011; Canizales 2024; Cebulko 2021; Ellis, Offidani-Bertrand, and Ferrera 2022; Garcia 2019; Golash-Boza and Valdez 2018; Schmalzbauer 2014; Silver 2018; Simmons, Menjívar, and Valdez 2021.

65. This includes contexts that are "nested" (Golash-Boza and Valdez 2018). See also the work of Ellis, Gonzales, and García (2018), Flores and Chapa (2009), Garcia (2019), and Silver (2018).

66. Central to a dynamic view of space is Henri Lefebvre's (1991) conceptualization of the "spaces of material practice" (space as it is experienced through our senses), "representations of space" (space as conceived through maps, designs, pictures, words), and "spaces of representation" (space as it is lived through our ideas, fears, imaginations), as well as David Harvey's (2009) interpretation of space as absolute, relative, and relational.

67. Delaney 2015; Davidson and Milligan 2007; Flores, Escudero, and Burciaga 2019.

68. Harvey 2009.

69. Lipsitz 2011.

70. Soja 1996.

71. Harvey 2009.

72. I first introduced the concept of "geographies of deportability" in Valdivia (2019a) to denote "the social, political, and physical sites produced by the law where immigration enforcement is localized, thereby heightening undocumented immigrants' vulnerability to deportation" (104).

73. Sociologist C. Wright Mills (1959) originated the concept of the "sociological imagination" to denote the relationship between individuals' biographies and broader structural and historical contexts. Geographer David Harvey (2005) elaborated on Mills's concept with the idea of a "geographic imagination," to emphasize that individuals also recognize the central role of space in their own biographies in ways that allow them to make sense of the relevance of events in their neighborhoods and other places and to creatively make use of space.

74. Sanctuary policies have their roots in organizing efforts to aid Central American refugees during the 1980s (see, e.g., Coutin 1993; Soltz Chinchilla, Hamilton, and Loucky 2009).

75. While there is ongoing debate over what constitutes a sanctuary jurisdiction (Martinez-Schuldt and Martinez 2017), some attribute the official designation of California as a sanctuary state to the passage of Senate Bill 54 in 2017 (Kubrin and Bartos 2020; Villazor and Godinez-Navarro 2019).

76. Green 2019; Serrano et al. 2018.

77. Abrego 2014; Bryceson 2019; Menjívar, Abrego, and Schmalzbauer 2016; Suárez-Orozco, Suárez-Orozco, and Todorova 2008; Van Hook and Glick 2020.

78. Asad 2023; García 2019; Dreby 2015; Ramirez 2023; Yoshikawa 2011.

79. Cebulko 2018; Cho 2021; Clark-Ibáñez 2015; Gonzales 2015; Patler 2018.

80. Brayne 2014; Haskins and Jacobsen 2017; Patler and Gonzalez 2021; Valdivia 2021.

81. I introduced the concept of "emotional anchoring" in Valdivia (2021) to describe "the process of learning how a family member is feeling and coping (whether through a conversation or personal reflection about changes in their demeanor) and subsequently adopting responsibilities to support them" (70).

82. Delgado (2020) introduced the term "legal brokering" to describe how young adults share legal resources with their undocumented parents (see also, e.g., Garcia Valdivia 2022). I extend this concept by situating legal brokering as a key form

of sanctuary making, that is often done in tandem with—but also distinct from—backup parenting or emotional anchoring. I also argue that legal brokering is not solely about managing risk but is part of a broader effort to reclaim safety, security, and belonging in the city amid the era of enforcement in the shadows and its geographies of deportability.

83. Chua and Engel 2019; Ewick and Silbey 1998; Merry 1990.

84. Abrego 2011; Gonzales 2015; Gonzales and Chavez 2012.

85. Abrego 2019; Delgado 2022; Gonzalez 2023.

86. Menjívar and Abrego 2012. The concept itself is grounded on theories of structural and symbolic violence.

87. Villegas 2019; Stuesse 2018.

88. Abrego and Menjívar 2011; Martinez-Aranda 2020.

89. There are efforts underway to understand the role of institutional and local contexts in shaping legal violence (see, e.g., Gómez Cervantes and Menjívar 2020).

90. De Genova 2002.

91. I write more extensively in the appendix about my personal experience and the type of methodological considerations I made over the course of this project as someone who identifies as formerly undocumented.

92. Given the political climate during my interviews, I implemented a robust data security system—including obtaining a certificate of confidentiality through the National Institutes of Health, omitting names of apartment complexes and worksites, and withholding specific details of individuals' arrests.

93. Ayón et al. 2023; Chen 2020; Flores Morales 2021; Hing 2018; Menjívar and Abrego 2012.

94. This was through the Immigration Reform and Control Act of 1986. Betsy Cooper and Kevin O'Neil, "Lessons from the Immigration Reform and Control Act of 1986." Migration Policy Institute, 2005, https://www.migrationpolicy.org /research/lessons-immigration-reform-and-control-act-1986.

95. Asad 2020b; Chen 2020.

96. Valdivia 2025.

97. Brabeck and Xu 2010; Martinez-Aranda 2020; Patler and Gonzalez 2021; Rojas-Flores et al. 2017; Valdivia 2021; Zayas 2015.

98. Valdivia 2020.

99. Andrews 2023; Golash-Boza 2015.

100. Andrews and Khayar-Cámara 2022; Boehm 2016.

101. Brabeck and Xu 2010; Dreby 2015; Golash-Boza 2019; Valdivia 2021.

102. Under the Immigration and Nationality Act 212(a)(9)(B)(i)(I) and (II) and the INA 212(a)(9)(C)(i)(I), there are three types of unlawful presence bars for which a noncitizen may be found inadmissible unless an exception applies: the 3-year bar, the 10-year bar, and the permanent bar.

103. Valdivia 2025.

104. Valdivia 2025; Valdivia and Monreal 2025. See also, for example, Ryo (2017) on the issue of detainees internalizing notions of criminality.

105. Dreby 2015; Valdivia 2025; Zayas 2015.

106. This is in conversation with recent efforts to expand conceptualizations of deportation as a system consisting of multiple phases (Patler and Jones 2025), a corridor encompassing different sites and actors (Drotbohm and Hasselberg 2015), or a pyramid (Dreby 2012). In the case of detention, Ryo and Peacock (2019) similarly frame it within a broader social ecology, emphasizing how detainees' experiences are influenced not just by what happens within detention centers, but also by the surrounding community in which the center is located. The concept of the spectrum of enforcement is also in conversation with attempts to broaden our understanding of citizenship beyond the undocumented/documented binary in ways that recognize the spillover effects of enforcement (Chen 2020; Menjívar 2006).

107. Abrego 2014; Castañeda 2019; Dreby 2015; León 2020; López 2021; Menjívar, Abrego, and Schmalzbauer 2016; Schmalzbauer 2014; Rodriguez 2023.

108. Valdivia 2020.

109. This set of interviews is featured most prominently in chapter 5 of this book.

110. While the evolution of immigrant rights organizing in San Diego is outside of the scope of this book, other scholars have examined it in greater detail (see Patiño 2017).

111. Migration Policy Institute, "Profile of the Unauthorized Population: San Diego County, CA," accessed May 12, 2025. https://www.migrationpolicy.org/data/unauthorized-immigrant-population/county/6073.

112. Boyce (2024) provides a helpful historical analysis of the creation of this 100-mile border zone.

113. Trump's second presidential administration extended the use of expediated removal to apply to individuals *anywhere* in the country who have been here for less than two years. Camilo Montoya-Galvez, "U.S. Expands Expedited Deportations beyond Border Areas as Part of Trump Crackdown," *CBS News*, January 21, 2025, https://www.cbsnews.com/news/u-s-expands-expedited-deportations-beyond-border-areas-trump-crackdown/.

114. SBCC, "100-Mile Border Enforcement Zone," accessed May 12, 2025, https://www.southernborder.org/100_mile_border_enforcement_zone#:~:text=Their%20jurisdiction%20they%20claim%20spans,%2C%20Boston%20MA%2C%20%26%20more.

115. Chavez (2012).

116. Proposition 187 was eventually ruled unconstitutional. For a history of the passage and symbolic function of Prop 187 see Calavita (1996).

117. Esbenshade et al. 2010.

118. ACLU, "Escondido, CA Backs Down from Anti-immigrant Ordinance," December 14, 2006, https://www.aclu.org/press-releases/escondido-ca-backs-down-anti-immigrant-ordinance.

119. Among these are Assembly Bill 540 and 130/131, which expand undocumented students' access to in-state tuition rates and financial aid, respectively, in the state of California.

120. California Senate Bill 24, "Law Enforcement: Sharing Data," accessed May 12, 2025, https://leginfo.legislature.ca.gov/faces/billNavClient.xhtml?bill_id= 201720180SB54.

121. "78 Immigrants Detained by Border Patrol throughout the Central Valley, Officials Say," *ABC30 News*, January 12, 2025, https://www.youtube.com/watch?v= 56Lfw3kDjKQ.

122. "California Governor Newsom Vows 'Sanctuary to All Who Seek It' in Inauguration Speech," *KCAL News,* January 9, 2019, https://www.cbsnews.com /losangeles/news/gavin-newsom-california-governor-2/.

123. Edhat Staff, "Local Nonprofit Alerts Residents of ICE Operations in Santa Barbara and Goleta," *Ed Hat,* January 27, 2025, https://www.edhat.com/news/local -nonprofit-alerts-residents-of-ice-operations-in-santa-barbara-and-goleta/; Caitlin Dickerson, Nick Corasaniti, and Edgar Sandoval, "ICE Launches Raids Targeting Migrant Families," *New York Times*, July 14, 2019, https://www.nytimes.com/2019 /07/14/us/ice-immigration-raids.html; McKenzie Funk, "How ICE Picks Its Targets in the Surveillance Age," *New York Times Magazine*, October 2, 2019, https:// www.nytimes.com/2019/10/02/magazine/ice-surveillance-deportation.html.

124. Nevins 2002.

CHAPTER 2. GEOGRAPHIES OF DEPORTABILITY

1. Julia Ainsley and Andrew Blankstein, "Homeland Security Cancels Massive Roundups of Undocumented Immigrants," *NBC News*, September 7, 2017, https://www.nbcnews.com/news/us-news/ice-plans-mega-largest-immigration-raid -operation-its-kind-n799691.

2. Adam Edelman, "Trump Ends DACA Program, No New Applications Accepted," *NBC News*, September 5, 2017, https://www.nbcnews.com/politics /immigration/trump-dreamers-daca-immigration-announcement-n798686.

3. I published part of these early findings in Valdivia (2019a) and elaborated on them in Valdivia, Clark-Ibáñez, and Carreon (2022).

4. By employing the term "traditional" I do not suggest that these hot spots are justified or permanent. Rather, I aim to highlight the state's capacity to assert control over space through sustained, often violent tactics. Over time, such practices— once absent—become normalized and even accepted, making them difficult, though not impossible, to contest.

5. U.S. Customs and Border Protection, "Theodore L. Newton, Jr. and George F. Azrak Station," modified January 22, 2020, https://www.cbp.gov/border-security /along-us-borders/border-patrol-sectors/san-diego-sector-california/murrieta -station.

6. This is not true of all checkpoints along the U.S.-Mexico borderlands; some, like the one north of the Rio Grande Valley, operate around the clock (Castañeda and Melo 2019).

7. U.S. Department of Homeland Security. *Privacy Impact Assessment for the CBP License Plate Reader Technology*, December 2017, https://www.dhs.gov/sites /default/files/publications/privacy-pia-cbp049-cbplprtechnology-december2017.pdf.

8. Garcia (2019) introduced the concept of "legal passing" to capture the set of risk management strategies that undocumented immigrants employ to avoid detection. Cebulko (2018, 2021) introduced the notion of "blending in" to note that immigrants with lighter skin tones and other characteristics that resemble whites may be able to conceal their immigration status from others.

9. Alluding to undocumented residents' inability to safely travel through these checkpoints, scholars have described this area, and others like it along the U.S.-Mexico border, as a form of "spatial containment" (Castañeda and Melo 2019), "entrapment" (Nuñez and Heyman 2007), or "internal border zone" (Valdivia, Clark-Ibáñez, and Carreon 2022).

10. Coleman 2009, 2012; Moinester 2018; Provine et al. 2016; Varsanyi et al. 2012.

11. This changed to some extent in 2015 after the passage of Assembly Bill (AB) 60, which provides eligible undocumented immigrants with access to a driver's license.

12. Ellipses enclosed within brackets indicate that a portion of the original quotation has been deliberately omitted to improve the clarity, conciseness, or narrative flow of the text. Ellipses presented without brackets denote a significant pause or moment of hesitation on the part of the speaker during the recorded interview.

13. There are occasional exceptions to this of course, as immigration policies and enforcement practices attempt to portray a non-site-specific and "color-blind" approach.

14. Coleman and Kocher 2011.

15. Boyles 2015; Goffman 2014; Jones 2019; Muñiz 2022; Rios 2011.

16. In some instances, children may learn about family members' immigration status and its implications through direct conversations. However, even when parents avoid discussing their legal status, children may still pick up on their parents' fears—such as during interactions in public spaces (e.g., upon seeing a police officer) or while watching news coverage about immigration (see, e.g., Abrego 2019; Dreby 2015).

17. Although I did not originally include questions about nightmares in my interview guide, one of my first respondents described a nightmare following her father's deportation. This led me to explore whether others were experiencing similar immigration-related dreams.

18. Lopez 2019; Zayas 2015.

19. This is based on data from the 2023 American Community Survey about residents' race and ethnicity, which is made available to the public online on https://www .census.gov/programs-surveys/acs/data.html and can be broken down by zip code.

20. "Advocates Cite Increase in Illegal Immigrant Sweeps," *San Diego Union Tribune*, August 28, 2016, https://www.sandiegouniontribune.com/sdut-advocates -cite-increase-in-illegal-immigrant-2004may12-story.html.

21. The video is accessible only to group members, requiring an account on the specific social media platform and permission to join. (To protect the group's privacy, I do not name the platform or group.) It shows two uniformed officers engaging with an individual in a Special Supplemental Nutrition Program for Women, Infants, and Children (WIC) office parking lot. After a bystander states they are recording, the officers reveal they are undercover ICE agents and quickly leave in an unmarked Ford vehicle.

22. The coordinates are drawn from reports by immigrant rights organizers, volunteers, and community members via posts or comments on organization-moderated social media pages. While organizers verified several reports, not all have been fully vetted.

23. Despite having DACA, some young adults fear arrest—shaped by media reports of detained recipients, concerns over lapses in protection, and ongoing uncertainty about the program.

24. Immigration officers did not disclose their identities or intentions when questioning people near Maribel's home about her father's appearance and whereabouts. As a result, any information provided was likely shared unknowingly.

25. Desmond and Tolbert Kimbro 2015; Hoke and Boen 2021.

26. CA DMV, "DMV Surpasses 1 Million Driver Licenses under AB 60," April 4, 2018, https://www.dmv.ca.gov/portal/news-and-media/dmv-surpasses-1-million-driver-licenses-under-ab-60/.

27. This reorientation is critical to the production of a vulnerable and exploitable workforce (De Genova 2002, 2004; Harrison and Lloyd 2012; Golash-Boza 2015).

28. Clark-Ibáñez 2004; Rodriguez Vega 2023.

29. Menjívar and Lakhani 2016.

30. Davidson and Milligan 2007; Lipsitz 2011.

31. See also De Genova 2002, 2004; Menjivar et al. 2018; Menjívar 2021; Romero 2006.

CHAPTER 3. SANCTUARY MAKING AND YOUNG ADULTS

1. For example, on March 8, 2018, ABC 7 news reported the arrest of an undocumented mother who lived in San Diego with her children. The reporting includes a video of the arrest taken by one of the children. The report and video can be accessed at "ICE Agents Arrest Undocumented Mom in Front of Children in San Diego," *ABC 7*, March 9, 2018, https://abc7.com/undocumented-woman-arrest-immigrant-san-diego-mom-arrested-ice-agents/3196448/.

2. UdB is a grassroots immigrant rights organization in San Diego County.

3. Scholars have documented the risk-management and coping strategies that undocumented immigrants and their families use under the threat of deportation (Asad 2023; Castañeda 2019; Delgado 2022; Dreby 2015; García 2019; Prieto 2018; Ramirez 2023; Rodriguez 2023). However, much of this literature emphasizes physical safety

and survival. In contrast, sanctuary making highlights how families claim space by cultivating emotional security, solidarity, belonging, and stability. This framework reveals the depth of families' efforts not just to endure, but to assert their presence in the places they call home. Sanctuary making emerges in direct response to the geographies of deportability, which shape and compel these efforts—while families' practices, in turn, influence how they experience and navigate those geographies.

4. Children are active agents and participants within their families and communities (Faulstich Orellana 2009; Rodriguez Vega 2023; see also, e.g., the work of Uprichard 2008 on children as "being and becoming").

5. Rodriguez Vega 2023; Suárez-Orozco et al. 2011.

6. Dreby 2012, 2015, 47.

7. See also Ayón and Philbin (2017).

8. See also Smith et al. (2021).

9. De Genova 2002, 2004.

10. De facto deportation refers to children who, though not formally deported, are compelled to leave the U.S. to reunite with a deported parent (Kanstroom 2010).

11. Valdivia 2025.

12. See also Abrego (2019) on young adults' legal relational consciousness.

13. For more than a decade, Alianza Comunitaria has responded to checkpoint reports in San Diego through a text and social media alert system that notifies subscribers of DUI checkpoint locations and times. Similarly, Unión del Barrio shares updates on immigration activity via social media.

14. See also Estrada (2019).

15. Dreby 2015.

16. See also Gonzalez and Patler (2021).

17. I first published these findings on Valdivia (2021).

18. Boszormenyi-Nagy and Spark 1973; Chase 1999; Jurkovic, Thirkield, and Morrell 2001.

19. Immigrant rights organizations regularly share Know Your Rights materials in formats like pamphlets and "red cards"—brightly colored cards that explain how to assert one's rights during encounters with police or immigration officers.

20. Randy Capps, Michael Fix, and Jie Zong, "The Education and Work Profiles of the DACA Population," Migration Policy Institute, 2017, www.migrationpolicy .org/research/education-and-work-profiles-daca-population..

21. Abrego 2019; Aranda, Vaquera, and Castañeda 2020; Cebulko and Silver 2016; Gonzales, Terriquez, and Ruszczyk 2014; Patler and Cabrera 2015; Roth 2019; Tom K. Wong and Carolina Valdivia, "In Their Own Words: A Nationwide Survey of Undocumented Millennials," Center for Comparative Immigration Studies, 2014, https://ccis.ucsd.edu/_files/wp191.pdf. .

22. I discussed these early findings in Valdivia (2021).

23. Abrego 2014; Andrews 2018; Dreby and Adkins 2010; Foner and Dreby 2011; Levitt 2001; Oliveira 2018; Silver 2014; Smith 2006; Suárez-Orozco and Suárez-Orozco 2013; Van Hook and Glick 2020.

24. Abrego 2014; Boehm 2016; Levitt and Waters 2002; López 2021; Menjívar, Abrego, and Schmalzbauer 2016; Schmalzbauer 2006.

25. Boehm 2016.

26. See, for example, Valdivia 2025.

27. Abrego 2011.

28. Abrego 2019.

CHAPTER 4. THE EMOTIONAL AND MATERIAL TOLLS OF ENFORCEMENT

1. Kanstroom 2010, 2012.

2. Glenn-Levin Rodriguez 2017; Zatz and Rodriguez 2015.

3. See also Castañeda (2019) and Garcia Valdivia (2022).

4. Abrego 2018; Aranda, Vaquera, and Castañeda 2020; Delgado 2022; Gonzales et al. 2018; Roth 2019.

5. As a point of comparison, the Pew Research Center reports that the median household income of undocumented immigrants was approximately $36,000 in 2007, compared with $50,000 for individuals born in the U.S. "A Portrait of Unauthorized Immigrants in the United States," Pew Research Center, 2009, https://www.pewresearch.org/hispanic/2009/04/14/a-portrait-of-unauthorized -immigrants-in-the-united-states/. Relatedly, Alif, Battiwala, and Yoshikawa (2024) find that households with unauthorized or mixed-status children are more likely to experience poverty than those with fully documented children.

6. To be eligible for DACA, applicants must have arrived in the U.S. before reaching their 16th birthday. Having arrived just a few months after turning 16, Maricela was left out of DACA.

7. Abrego 2008; Cebulko and Silver 2016; Clark-Ibáñez 2015; Flores 2016; Gonzales 2015.

8. See also Lauby (2018).

9. See, for example, the cases of Xiu Qing You and Antonio de Jesus Martinez from New York, who were both detained at a USCIS office when they showed up for their interviews. New York Civil Liberties Union, "Court Stays Deportation of Father Arrested at Immigration Interview," *NYCLU,* March 2, 2018, https://www .nyclu.org/en/press-releases/court-stays-deportation-father-arrested-immigration -interview.

10. Abrego 2018; Cebulko and Silver 2016; Gonzales, Terriquez, and Ruszczyk 2014; Patler and Cabrera 2015; Roth 2019; Tom K. Wong and Carolina Valdivia, "In Their Own Words: A Nationwide Survey of Undocumented Millennials," Center for Comparative Immigration Studies, 2014, https://ccis.ucsd.edu/_files/wp191.pdf. .

11. Phillimore and Cheung 2021.

12. This is a significant fee compared to other lawyers charging around $400–$500 and immigrant rights organizations offering similar services at low or no cost.

13. See also Patler and Gonzalez (2021) on families' system avoidance in the aftermath of detention.

14. See also Valdivia and Monreal (2025).

15. Abrego 2008; Negrón-Gonzales 2014; Patler 2018; Unzueta Carrasco and Seif 2014.

16. See also Clark-Ibáñez and Swan (2019), who frame the plight of undocumented immigrants and their families as a matter of human rights, respect, and dignity.

17. I use the terms "subconsciousness" and "unconscious" interchangeably to describe mental context beneath conscious awareness—an arena in which fears, worries, and other preoccupations reside.

18. Carlos Cabrera-Lomeli, "If You're a Mixed-Status Student Still Struggling with FAFSA, You Have Options," *KQED,* April 12, 2024, https://www.kqed.org/news/11979367/fafsa-2024-the-big-error-affecting-mixed-status-families-and-what-to-do-if-youre-an-affected-student.

19. This became most apparent to me through the UndocuBasic Needs project I have led since 2023.

CHAPTER 5. RECLAIMING THE CITY

1. Unión del Barrio, "Border Patrol Raids Home in Sherman Heights," Facebook, August 26, 2020, https://www.facebook.com/100064587283523/videos/987411341680883.

2. Ramakrishnan and Bloemraad 2008; Voss and Bloemraad 2011.

3. Barberena, Jiménez, and Michael P. Young 2014; Bloemraad and Trost 2008; Gonzales 2013; Pallares and Flores-Gonzalez 2010; Zepeda-Millán 2017.

4. De Graauw 2016; Gleeson 2008; Milkman 2011, 2018.

5. Coutin 1993; Soltz Chinchilla, Hamilton, and Loucky 2009.

6. Nicholls 2013.

7. See also Abrego and Negrón-Gonzalez (2020) and Heredia (2015).

8. Nicholls, Uitermark, and van Haperen 2016.

9. Colbern and Ramakrishn an 2018; Ramakrishnan and Bloemraad 2008.

10. Patler 2010.

11. Terriquez and Lin 2019; Wong, García, and Valdivia 2019.

12. Corrunker 2012; Nicholls 2013; Nicholls and Fiorito 2015; Seif 2011; Terriquez, Brenes, and Lopez 2018.

13. Since 2001, various versions of the DREAM Act have been introduced, but none have been passed into law.

14. Escudero 2020; Nicholls 2013; Valdivia 2019b.

15. Enriquez and Saguy 2016; Galindo 2012; Zimmerman 2011.

16. Patty Arteaga, Nancy Bercaw, Jose Centeno-Melendez, Alex Hanesworth, and Delia Beristain Noreiga, "Making History Happen: Reflecting on DACA and

Its Impact," National Museum of American History, 2022, https://americanhistory
.si.edu/blog/reflecting-on-daca-and-its-impact.

17. Negrón-Gonzales 2014; Terriquez 2017; Wong, García, and Valdivia 2019.

18. Escudero 2020; Flores 2021; Martínez 2024; Nicholls 2013.

19. Abrego and Negrón-Gonzales 2020; Escudero 2020; Fiorito and Nicholls
2023; Martínez 2024; Terriquez and Milkman 2021; Terriquez, Brenes, and Lopez
2018.

20. Burciaga and Martinez 2017; Nicholls 2020.

21. Nicholls 2013.

22. Galvez 2017; Unzueta Carrasco and Seif 2014.

23. Abrego and Negrón-Gonzales 2020; Unzueta Carrasco and Seif 2014.

24. Patler 2018; Unzueta, Mora Villalpando, and Cházaro 2018.

25. Nicholls, Uitermark, and van Haperen 2016.

26. Kocher 2017; Gleeson and Sampat 2017.

27. Burciaga and Martinez 2017; Escudero 2020; Lauby 2021; Negrón-Gonzales
2013; Nicholls 2013; Swerts 2015; Terriquez 2017; Unzueta Carrasco and Seif 2014.

28. Cuevas 2021; Neinhusser and Oshio 2018; Schwab 2019; Valdivia 2020.

29. Zepeda-Millan and Wallace 2018.

30. Kocher 2017; Gleeson and Sampat 2017.

31. Universidad Popular, "About Alianza Comunitaria," accessed May 8, 2025,
https://www.unipopular.org/rapidresponseconference.

32. Alianza 760, Facebook page, accessed May 8, 2025, https://www.facebook
.com/Alianza760/,

33. Alianza Comunitaria, Instagram page, accessed May 8, 2025, https://www
.instagram.com/alianzacomunitaria/?hl=en.

34. Police departments sometimes issue public notices about upcoming DUI
checkpoints without disclosing exact locations. Organizers use this information to
warn undocumented residents.

35. Adrian Florido, "Escondido Settles Lawsuit over Checkpoint Monitors,"
KPBS, October 26, 2012, https://www.kpbs.org/news/public-safety/2012/10/26
/escondido-settles-lawsuit-over-checkpoint-monitors; Ruxandra Guidi, "Clashes
over Police Checkpoints and Deportations Increasing in Escondido," *KJZZ Phoenix*, November 1, 2010, https://www.kjzz.org/2010-11-01/content-8522-clashes-over
-police-checkpoints-and-deportations-increasing-escondido.

36. Unión del Barrio, Facebook page, accessed May 8, 2025, https://uniondel
barrio.org/main/4-2/about-udb/.

37. In several videos shared by Unión del Barrio, immigration officers are seen
leaving a neighborhood upon realizing organizers are following and recording them.

38. SD Rapid Response, official website, accessed May 8, 2025, https://rapid
responsesd.org/.

39. Camilo et al. 2024.

40. Abrego 2018; Aranda, Vaquera, and Castañeda 2020; Roth 2019.

41. Martínez 2024.

1. Campos 2021; Muñoz et al. 2018; Valdivia 2020; Valdivia et al. 2021a; Valdivia et al. 2021b.

2. Unión Del Barrio, "Redadas de ICE siguen bajo la administración de Biden, hostigando a trabajadores Mexicanos," YouTube, February 2021, https://www.youtube.com/watch?v=zfsPMWtMRB0.

3. Unión Del Barrio reported such sightings through its public Facebook page and YouTube channel.

4. Sherman-Stokes 2021.

5. "Real America with Jorge Ramos: The Invisible Border Wall," *Univision News*, June 7, 2021, https://www.univision.com/univision-news/immigration/real-america-with-jorge-ramos-the-invisible-border-wall.

6. Muzaffar Chishti, Kathleen Bush-Joseph, and Julian Montalvo, "Title 42 Post-modern: U.S. Pandemic-Era Expulsions Policy Did Not Shut Down the Border," Migration Policy Institute, 2024, https://migrationpolicy.org/article/title-42-autopsy.

7. Asad 2023; García Hernández 2018; Gulasekaram and Ramakrishnan 2015; Kalhan 2014; Stumpf 2006.

8. Motomura 2014; Spiro 1997; Varsanyi et al. 2012.

9. Stumpf 2006.

10. Kalhan 2014.

11. Coleman 2012; Moinester 2018; Motomura 2011; Nguyen and Gill 2016; Provine and Varsanyi 2012.

12. Castañeda 2019; Castañeda and Melo 2019.

13. The airport may function as a hot spot in part because Transportation Security Administration agents could inquire about a person's immigration status and subject them to detainment.

14. For guidance on interviewing immigration officers, I recommend the work of Vega (2025), and for insights into researching immigration agencies via FOIA requests, see Muñiz (2022).

15. Immigrant Defense Project, "ICEwatch: ICE Raids Tactics Map," last modified April 2022, https://www.immigrantdefenseproject.org/icewatch/.

16. Chris Rickerd, "A Dangerous Precedent: Why Allow Racial Profiling at or Near the Border," *ACLU News & Commentary*, December 8, 2014, https://www.aclu.org/news/immigrants-rights/dangerous-precedent-why-allow-racial-profiling-or-near-border (emphasis in original).

17. See also the work of Maldonado Dominguez (2020) on the internal and external threats that families navigate in the context of illegality, xenophobia, and homophobia.

18. See chapter 4 of this book. See also the work of Del Real (2019), Maldonado Dominguez (2020), Menjívar (2000), and Rosales (2020).

19. See also the work of Andrews (2023) on the "afterlife" of deportation and that of Robles (2024) on the "remnants" of illegality.

20. See also the work of Enriquez (2020), Gomberg-Muñoz (2016), León (2020), and López (2021) for detailed accounts of how mixed-status families navigate these processes.

21. Clark-Ibáñez 2004; Rodriguez Vega (2023).

22. See also Abrego (2019).

23. U.S. Citizenship and immigration Services, "Unlawful Presence and Inadmissibility," accessed October 2, 2025, https://www.uscis.gov/laws-and-policy/other-resources/unlawful-presence-and-inadmissibility.

24. U.S. Citizenship and immigration Services, "Unlawful Presence and Inadmissibility."

25. See also Gomberg-Muñoz (2016).

26. Ariel Brown, "USCIS & BIA Affirm Three- and Ten-Year Unlawful Presence Bars Can Run in the U.S.," Immigrant Legal Resource Center, 2023, https://www.ilrc.org/sites/default/files/2023-08/USCIS%20%26%20BIA%20Affirm%20Three-%20and%20Ten-Year%20Unlawful%20Presence%20Bars%20Can%20Run%20in%20the%20US.pdf.

27. Aranda et al. 2023; Valdez, Wagner, and Minero 2021; Valdivia 2020.

28. Valdivia et al. 2021b; see also Pérez Huber and Muñoz 2021.

29. De Genova 2002; Golash-Boza 2015.

30. Suzanne Gamboa, "Trump Administration Strips Venezuelans of Latest Protection from Deportation," *NBC News*, January 29, 2025, https://www.nbcnews.com/news/latino/tps-canceled-venezuelans-trump-noem-rcna189840.

31. Gleeson and Griffith 2022. Although to be sure, TPS is a form of "liminal legality" (Menjívar 2006) and as such is associated with significant limitations and vulnerabilities for its recipients.

32. U.S. Department of Homeland Security, "Statement from a DHS Spokesperson on Directives Expanding Law Enforcement and Ending the Abuse of Humanitarian Parole," January 21, 2025, https://www.dhs.gov/news/2025/01/21/statement-dhs-spokesperson-directives-expanding-law-enforcement-and-ending-abuse.

33. Gándara and Ee 2021; Kirksey and Sattin-Bajaj 2023; Kirksey et al. 2020.

34. Gary Fineout, "Florida GOP Passes Sweeping Anti-Immigration Bill That Gives DeSantis $12 Million for Migrant Transports," *Politico*, May 2, 2023, https://www.politico.com/news/2023/05/02/desantis-anti-immigration-florida-00095012.

35. Karen Brooks Harper, "Texas House Passes Sweeping Border Funding Bill, Guts Proposed Policing Unit," *Texas Tribune*, May 10, 2023, https://www.texastribune.org/2023/05/10/texas-legislature-border-funding/.

36. Michael McEwen, "Immigrants' Rights Advocates Alarmed at Proposed State Enforcement Changes," *MPB*, January 29, 2025, https://www.mpbonline.org/blogs/news/immigrants-rights-advocates-alarmed-at-proposed-state-enforcement-changes/.

37. See also the work of Flores and Schachter (2018) on the social construction of illegality.

38. Helen Rummel, "Hundreds of Protesters at ASU Drown Out GOP Student Event Seeking to Report Classmates to ICE," *AZ Central*, January 31, 2025, https://

www.azcentral.com/story/news/politics/arizona/2025/01/31/asu-republican-group
-ice-protest/78090821007/.

39. The UndocuBasic Needs project seeks to better understand and help address the basic needs of students who identify as undocumented or from mixed-status families (www.UndocuBasicNeeds.org).

40. Jorge Ramos, "Op-Ed: From 'Yes We Can', to 'No We Could Not' (Democrat's Unmet Promises)," *Univision News*, April 16, 2022, https://www.univision .com/univision-news/opinion/oped-jorge-ramos-on-democrats-unmet-promises.

APPENDIX

1. A couple of participants opted instead for an off-the-record conversation, with succinct answers submitted in a separate Word document.

2. Valdivia 2015, 2019b; Wong, Garcia, and Valdivia 2019; Tom K. Wong and Carolina Valdivia, "In Their Own Words: A Nationwide Survey of Undocumented Millennials," Center for Comparative Immigration Studies, 2014, https://ccis.ucsd .edu/_files/wp191.pdf.

REFERENCES

Abrego, Leisy J. 2006. "'I Can't Go to College Because I Don't Have Papers': Incorporation Patterns of Latino Undocumented Youth." *Latino Studies* 4:212–231. [CMS 15.48]

———. 2008. "Legitimacy, Social Identity, and the Mobilization of Law: The Effects of Assembly Bill 540 on Undocumented Students in California." *Law & Social Inquiry* 33 (3): 709–734.

———. 2011. "Legal Consciousness of Undocumented Latinos: Fear and Stigma as Barriers to Claims-Making for First- and 1.5-Generation Immigrants: Legal Consciousness of Undocumented Latinos." *Law & Society Review* 45 (2): 337–370.

———. 2014. *Sacrificing Families: Navigating Laws, Labor, and Love across Borders.* Redwood City, CA: Stanford University Press.

———. 2018. "Renewed Optimism and Spatial Mobility: Legal Consciousness of Latino Deferred Action for Childhood Arrivals Recipients and Their Families in Los Angeles." *Ethnicities* 18 (2): 192–207.

———. 2019. "Relational Legal Consciousness of U.S. Citizenship: Privilege, Responsibility, Guilt, and Love in Latino Mixed-Status Families." *Law & Society Review* 5 (3): 641–670.

Abrego, Leisy J., and Cecilia Menjívar. 2011. "Immigrant Latina Mothers as Targets of Legal Violence." *International Journal of Sociology of the Family* 37 (1): 9–26.

Abrego, Leisy J., and Genevieve Negrón-Gonzales. 2020. *We Are Not Dreamers: Undocumented Scholars Theorize Undocumented Life in the United States.* Durham, NC: Duke University Press.

Alif, Ahmed, Tanya Battiwala, and Hirokazu Yoshikawa. 2024. "The Influence of Children's Immigration Status on Households with Unauthorized Parents." *Children and Youth Services* 165:107887.

Andreas, Peter. 2022. *Border Games: The Politics of Policing the U.S.-Mexico Divide.* Ithaca, NY: Cornell University Press.

Andrews, Abigail. 2018. *Undocumented Politics: Place, Gender, and the Pathways of Mexican Migrants.* Oakland: University of California Press.

———. 2023. *Banished Men: How Migrants Endure the Violence of Deportation*. Oakland: University of California Press.

Andrews, Abigail, and Fátima Khayar-Cámara. 2022. "Forced Out of Fatherhood: How Men Strive to Parent Post-Deportation." *Social Problems* 69 (3): 699–716.

Aranda, Elizabeth, Elizabeth Vaquera, and Heide Castañeda. 2020. "Shifting Roles in Families of Deferred Action for Childhood Arrivals (DACA) Recipients and Implications for the Transition to Adulthood." *Journal of Family Issues* 42 (9): 2111–2132.

Aranda, Elizabeth, Elizabeth Vaquera, Heide Castañeda, and Girsea Martinez Rosas. 2023. "Undocumented Again? DACA Rescission, Emotions, and Incorporation Outcomes among Young Adults." *Social Forces* 101 (3): 1321–1342.

Armenta, Amada. 2012. "From Sheriff's Deputies to Immigration Officers: Screening Immigrant Status in a Tennessee Jail." *Law & Policy* 34 (2): 191–210.

———. 2017. *Protect, Serve, and Deport: The Rise of Policing as Immigration Enforcement*. Oakland: University of California Press.

Asad, Asad L. 2020a. "On the Radar: System Embeddedness and Latin American Immigrants' Perceived Risk of Deportation." *Law & Society Review* 54 (1): 133–167.

———. 2020b. "Latinos' Deportation Fears by Citizenship and Legal Status, 2007 to 2018." *Proceedings of the National Academy of Sciences* 117 (16): 8836–8844.

———. 2023. *Engage and Evade: How Latino Immigrant Families Manage Surveillance in Everyday Life*. Princeton, NJ: Princeton University Press.

Ayón, Cecilia, Mirella Deniz-Zaragoza, Gillian Marshall, and Javier Hernandez. 2023. "Retirement Is Not an Option for the Undocumented: Undocumented Latinx Older Adults' Perceptions of Financial (In)security in the United States." *Social Work Research* 47 (1): 18–33.

Ayón, Cecilia, Maria Gurrola, Lorraine Moya Salas, David Androff, and Judy Krysik. 2011. "Intended and Unintended Consequences of the Employer Sanction Law on Latino Families." *Qualitative Social Work* 11 (6): 587–603.

Ayón, Cecilia, and Sandy P. Philbin. 2017. "Tú No Eres de Aquí': Latino Children's Experiences of Institutional and Interpersonal Discrimination and Microaggressions." *Social Work Research* 41 (1): 19–30.

Barberena, Laura, Hortencia Jiménez, and Michael P. Young. 2014. "'It Just Happened': Telescoping Anxiety, Defiance, and Emergent Collective Behavior in the Student Walkouts of 2006." *Social Problems* 61 (1): 42–60.

Becerra, David, David K. Androff, Cecilia Ayón, and Jason T. Castillo. 2012. "Fear vs. Facts: Examining the Economic Impact of Undocumented Immigrants in the US." *Journal of Sociology and Social Welfare* 39 (4): 111–136.

Beckett, Katherine, and Heather Evans. 2015. "Crimmigration at the Local Level: Criminal Justice Processes in the Shadow of Deportation." *Law & Society Review* 49 (1): 241–277.

Bloemraad, Irene, and Christine Trost. 2008. "It's a Family Affair: Intergenerational Mobilization in the Spring 2006 Protests." *American Behavioral Scientist* 52 (4): 507–532.

Boehm, Deborah A. 2016. *Returned: Going and Coming in an Age of Deportation.* Oakland: University of California Press.

———. 2018. "Separated Families: Barriers to Family Reunification after Deportation." *Journal on Migration and Human Security* 5 (2): 401–416.

Boszormenyi-Nagy, Ivan, and Geraldine M. Spark. 1973. *Invisible Loyalties: Reciprocity in Intergenerational Family Therapy.* New York: Harper & Row.

Boyce, Geoff. 2024. "Mass Deportation and the Intensity of Policing in the United States' 100-Mile Border Zone: Complicating the 'Border'/'Interior' Enforcement Binary." *Law & Policy* 46 (2): 90–111.

Boyles, Andrea S. 2015. *Race, Place, and Suburban Policing: Too Close for Comfort.* Oakland: University of California Press.

Brabeck, Kalina, and Qingwen Xu. 2010. "The Impact of Detention and Deportation on Latino Immigrant Children and Families: A Quantitative Exploration." *Hispanic Journal of Behavioral Sciences* 32 (2): 341–361.

Brayne, Sarah. 2014. "Surveillance and System Avoidance: Criminal Justice Contact and Institutional Attachment." *American Sociological Review* 79 (3): 367–391.

———. 2021. *Predict and Surveil: Data, Discretion, and the Future of Policing.* Oxford: Oxford University Press.

Bryceson, Deborah Fahy. 2019. "Transnational Families Negotiating Migration and Care Life Cycles across Nation-State Borders." *Journal of Ethnic and Migration Studies* 45 (16): 3042–3064.

Burciaga, Edelina, and Lisa M. Martinez. 2017. "How Do Political Contexts Shape Undocumented Youth Movements? Evidence from Three Immigrant Destinations." *Mobilization: An International Quarterly* 22 (4): 451–471.

Calavita, Kitty. 1996. "The New Politics of Immigration: 'Balanced-Budget Conservatism' and the Symbolism of Proposition 187." *Social Problems* 43 (3): 284–305.

Camilo, Diana, Keisha Chin Goosby, Josefina Espino, Michelle Ramos Pellicia, Marisol Clark- Ibáñez, and Carolina Valdivia. 2024. "Map for Change: Rising in Support of Undocumented Students." In *Promoting Equitable Classroom Practices in Higher Education: Approaches Beyond Curriculum,* edited by Melanie Burdick, Heidi Hallman and Valerie Mendoza, 118–138. Charlotte, NC: Information Age Publishing.

Campos, Liliana. 2021. "Mental Health Outcomes of Various Types of Fear among University Students Who Have an Undocumented Legal Status during the Donald Trump Presidency." PhD diss., University of San Francisco.

Canizales, Stephanie L. 2023. "Work Primacy and the Social Incorporation of Unaccompanied, Undocumented Latinx Youth in the United States." *Social Forces* 101 (3): 1372–1395.

———. 2024. *Sin Padres, Ni Papeles: Unaccompanied Migrant Youth Coming of Age in the United States.* Oakland: University of California Press.

Castañeda, Heidi. 2019. *Borders of Belonging: Struggle and Solidarity in Mixed-Status Families.* Redwood City, CA: Stanford University Press.

Castañeda, Heidi, and Milena Melo. 2019. "Geographies of Confinement for Immigrant Youth: Checkpoints and Immobilities along the US/Mexico Border." *Law & Policy* 41 (1): 80–102.

Cebulko, Kara. 2018. "Privilege without Papers: Intersecting Inequalities among 1.5-Generation Brazilians in Massachusetts." *Ethnicities* 18 (2): 225–241.

———. 2021. "Becoming White in a White Supremacist State: The Public and Psychological Wages of Whiteness for Undocumented 1.5-Generation Brazilians." *Social Sciences* 10 (5): 184.

Cebulko, Kara, and Alexis Silver. 2016. "Navigating DACA in Hospitable and Hostile States: State Responses and Access to Membership in the Wake of Deferred Action for Childhood Arrivals." *American Behavioral Scientist* 60 (13): 1553–1574.

Ceciliano-Navarro, Yajaira, and Tanya Maria Golash-Boza. 2021. "'Trauma Makes You Grow Up Quicker': The Financial & Emotional Burdens of Deportation & Incarceration." *Daedalus* 150 (2): 165–179.

Chacón, Jennifer. 2012. "Overcriminalizing Immigration." *Journal of Criminal Law & Criminology* 102 (3): 613–652.

———. 2017. "Privatized Immigration Enforcement." *Harvard Civil Rights-Civil Liberties Law Review* 52 (1): 1–46.

Chase, Nancy. 1999. *Burdened Children: Theory, Research, and Treatment of Parentification*. Edited by Nancy D. Chase. Thousand Oaks, CA: Sage Publications.

Chavez, Leo R. 2007. "The Condition of Illegality." *International Migration* 45 (3): 192–196.

———. 2012. *Shadowed Lives: Undocumented Immigrants in American Society*. 3rd ed. Fort Worth, TX: Harcourt Brace College Publishers.

———. 2013. *The Latino Threat: Constructing Immigrants, Citizens, and the Nation*. 2nd ed. Redwood City, CA: Stanford University Press.

Chen, Ming Hsu. 2020. *Pursuing Citizenship in the Enforcement Era*. Redwood City, CA: Stanford University Press.

Cho, Esther Yoona. 2021. "Selective Disclosure as a Self-Protective Process: Navigating Friendships as Asian and Latino Undocumented Young Adults." *Social Forces* 100 (2): 540–563.

Chua, Lynette J., and David M. Engel. 2019. "Legal Consciousness Reconsidered." *Annual Review of Law and Social Science* 15 (1): 335–353.

Clark-Ibáñez, Marisol. 2004. "Framing the Social World with Photo-Elicitation Interviews." *American Behavioral Scientist* 47 (12): 1507–1527.

———. 2015. *Undocumented Latino Youth: Navigating Their Worlds*. Boulder, CO: Lynne Rienner.

Clark-Ibáñez, Marisol, and Richelle Swan. 2019. *Unauthorized: Portraits of Latino Immigrants*. Lanham, MD: Rowman & Littlefield.

Colbern, Allan, and S. Karthick Ramakrishnan. 2018. "Citizens of California: How the Golden State Went from Worst to First on Immigrant Rights." *New Political Science* 2 (40): 353–367.

Coleman, Mathew. 2009. "What Counts as the Politics and Practice of Security, and Where? Devolution and Immigrant Insecurity after 9/11." *Annals of the Association of American Geographers* 99 (5): 904–913.

———. 2012. "The 'Local' Migration State: The Site-Specific Devolution of Immigration Enforcement in the U.S. South." *Law & Policy* 34 (2): 159–190.

Coleman, Mathew, and Austin Kocher. 2011. "Detention, Deportation, Devolution and Immigrant Incapacitation in the US, Post 9/11." *Geographical Journal* 177 (3): 228–237.

Corrunker, Laura. 2012. "Coming Out of the Shadows: DREAM Act Activism in the Context of Global Anti-deportation Activism." *Indiana Journal of Global Legal Studies* 19 (1): 143–168.

Coutin, Susan Bibler. 1993. *The Culture of Protest: Religious Activism and the U.S. Sanctuary Movement.* Boulder, CO: Westview Press.

———. 2005. "Being en Route." *American Anthropologist* 107 (2): 195–206.

Cuevas, Stephany. 2021. "Ever-Present 'Illegality:' How Political Climate Impacts Undocumented Latinx Parents' Engagement in Students' Postsecondary Access and Success." *Journal of College Access* 6 (2): 44–64.

Davidson, Joyce, and Christine Milligan. 2007. "Embodying Emotion Sending Space: Introducing Emotional Geographies." *Social & Cultural Geography* 5 (4): 523–532.

De Genova, Nicholas. 2002. "Migrant 'Illegality' and Deportability in Everyday Life." *Annual Review of Anthropology* 31: 419–447.

———. 2004. "The Legal Production of Mexican/Migrant 'Illegality.'" *Latino Studies* 2:160–185.

———. 2013. "Spectacles of Migrant 'Illegality': The Scene of Exclusion, the Obscene of Inclusion." *Ethnic and Racial Studies* 36 (7): 1180–1198.

De Graauw, Els. 2016. *Making Immigrant Rights Real: Nonprofits and the Politics of Integration in San Francisco.* Ithaca, NY: Cornell University Press.

De Leon, Jason. 2015. *Land of Open Graves: Living and Dying on the Migrant Trail.* Oakland: University of California Press.

Del Real, Deisy. 2019. "Toxic Ties: The Reproduction of Legal Violence within Mixed-Status Intimate Partners, Relatives, and Friends." *International Migration Review* 53 (2): 548–570.

Delaney, David. 2015. "Legal Geography I: Constitutivities, Complexities, and Contingencies." *Progress in Human Geography* 39 (1): 96–102.

Delgado, Vanessa. 2020. "'They Think I'm a Lawyer': Undocumented College Students as Legal Brokers for Their Undocumented Parents." *Law & Policy* 42 (3): 261–283.

———. 2022. "Leveraging Protections, Navigating Punishments: How Adult Children of Undocumented Immigrants Mediate Illegality in Latinx Families." *Journal of Marriage and Family* 84:1427–1445.

Desmond, Matthew, and Rachel Tolbert Kimbro. 2015. "Eviction's Fallout: Housing, Hardship, and Health." *Social Forces* 94 (1): 295–324.

Diaz-Strong, Daysi X. 2021. "Why We Could Not Study:' The Gendered Enrollment Barriers of 1.25 Generation Immigrants." *Children and Youth Services Review*, no. 122.

Diaz-Strong, Daysi X., and Marci A. Ybarra. 2016. "Disparities in High School Completion among Latinos: The Role of the Age-at-Arrival and Immigration Status." *Children and Youth Services Review* 71:282–289.

Dreby, Joanna. 2012. "The Burden of Deportation on Children in Mexican Immigrant Families." *Journal of Marriage and Family* 74 (4): 829–845.

———. 2015. *Everyday Illegal: When Policies Undermine Immigrant Families*. Oakland: University of California Press.

Dreby, Joanna, and Timothy Adkins. 2010. "Inequalities in Transnational Families." *Sociology Compass* 4 (8): 673–689.

Drotbohm, Heike, and Ines Hasselberg. 2015. "Deportation, Anxiety, Justice: New Ethnographic Perspectives." *Journal of Ethnic and Migration Studies* 41 (4): 551–562.

Dunn, Timothy J. 1996. *The Militarization of the U.S.-Mexico Border, 1978–1992: Low-Intensity Conflict Doctrine Comes Home*. Austin: CMAS Books, University of Texas.

———. 2001. "Border Militarization via Drug and Immigration Enforcement: Human Rights Implications." *Social Justice* 28 (2): 7–30.

Ellis, Basia D., Roberto G. Gonzales, and Sarah A. Rendón García. 2018. "The Power of Inclusion: Theorizing 'Abjectivity' and Agency under DACA." *Cultural Studies ßà Critical Methodologies* 19 (3): 161–172.

Ellis, Basia D., Carly Offidani-Bertrand, and Maria Joy Ferrera. 2022. "'No Way! Like Only Hispanics Are Illegal': Examining the Racialized Psychosocial Development of Migrant 'Illegality' across Immigrant Groups in the United States." *Journal of Adolescent Research* 38 (3): 528–561.

Enriquez, Laura E. 2020. *Of Love and Papers: How Immigration Policy Affects Romance and Family*. Oakland: University of California Press.

Esbenshade, Jill, Benjamin Wright, Paul Cortopassi, Arthur Reed, and Jerry Flores. 2010. "The 'Law and Order' Foundation of Local Ordinances: A Four Locale Study of Hazleton, Pennsylvania; Escondido, California; Farmers Branch, Texas; and Prince William County, Virginia." In *Taking Local Control: Immigration Policy Activism in U.S. Cities and States*, edited by Monica W. Varsanyi, 255–274. Redwood City, CA: Stanford University Press.

Escudero, Kevin. 2020. *Organizing while Undocumented: Immigrant Youth's Political Activism under the Law*. New York: New York University Press.

Estrada, Emir. 2019. *Kids at Work: Latinx Families Selling Food on the Streets of Los Angeles*. New York: New York University Press.

Ewick, Patricia, and Susan S. Silbey. 1998. *The Common Place of Law: Stories from Everyday Life*. Chicago: University of Chicago Press.

Faulstich Orellana, Marjorie. 2009. *Translating Childhoods: Immigrant Youth, Language, and Culture*. New Brunswick, NJ: Rutgers University Press.

Fiorito, Tara, and Walter J. Nicholls. 2023. "Representational Hierarchies in Social Movements: A Case Study of the Undocumented Immigrant Youth Movement." *American Journal of Sociology* 129 (2): 485–529.

Flores, Andrea. 2016. "Forms of Exclusion: Undocumented Students Navigating Financial Aid and Inclusion in the United States." *American Ethnologist* 43 (3): 540–554.

———. 2021. *The Succeeders: How Immigrant Youth Are Transforming What It Means to Belong in America*. Oakland: University of California Press.

Flores, René D., and Ariela Schachter. 2018. "Who Are the 'Illegals'? The Social Construction of Illegality in the United States." *American Sociological Review* 83 (5): 839–868.

Flores, Stella M., and Jorge Chapa. 2009. "Latino Immigrant Access to Higher Education in a Bipolar Context of Reception." *Journal of Hispanic Higher Education* 8 (1): 90–109.

Flores Morales, Josefina. 2021. "Aging and Undocumented: The Sociology of Aging Meets Immigration Status." *Sociology Compass* 15 (4): 1–13.

Flores, Andrea, Kevin Escudero, and Edelina Burciaga. 2019. "Legal-Spatial Consciousness: A Legal Geography Framework for Examining Migrant Illegality." *Law & Policy* 41 (1): 12–33.

Foner, Nancy, and Joanna Dreby. 2011. "Relations between the Generations in Immigrant Families." *Annual Review of Sociology* 37 (1): 545–564.

Galindo, René. 2012. "Undocumented & Unafraid: The DREAM Act 5 and the Public Disclosure of Undocumented Status as a Political Act." *Urban Review* 44 (5): 589–611.

Gálvez, Alyshia. 2017. "Unafraid and Unapologetic, Still: Three Cofounders of the Lehman College DREAM Team in New York City on the Past, Present, and Future of Undocumented Youth Organizing." *NACLA Report on the Americas* 49 (2): 198–205.

Gándara, Patricia, and Jongyeon Ee. 2021. *Schools under Siege: The Impact of Immigration Enforcement on Educational Equity.* Cambridge, MA: Harvard University Press.

Garcia, Angela S. 2019. *Legal Passing: Navigating Undocumented Life and Local Immigration Law.* Oakland: University of California Press.

García, San Juanita. 2018. "Living a Deportation Threat: Anticipatory Stressors Confronted by Undocumented Mexican Immigrant Women." *Race and Social Problems* 10:221–234.

García Hernández, César Cuauhtémoc. 2018. "Deconstructing Crimmigration." *UC Davis Law Review* 52 (1): 197–253.

García Valdivia, Isabel. 2022. "Legal Power in Action: How Latinx Adult Children Mitigate the Effects of Parents' Legal Status through Brokering." *Social Problems* 69 (2): 335–355.

Gashi, Liridona, Willy Pedersen, and Thomas Ugelvik. 2021. "The Pains of Detainment: Experience of Time and Coping Strategies at Immigration Detention Centres." *Theoretical Criminology* 25 (1): 88–106.

Gleeson, Shannon. 2008. "Organizing for Immigrant Labor Rights: Latino Immigrants in San Jose and Houston." In *Civic Hopes and Political Realities: Immigrants, Community Organizations, and Political Engagement,* edited by S. Karthick Ramakrishnan and Irene Bloemraad, 107–133. New York: Russell Sage Foundation.

———. 2010. "Labor Rights for All? The Role of Undocumented Immigrant Status for Worker Claims Making." *Law & Social Inquiry* 35 (3): 561–602.

———. 2016. *Precarious Claims.* Oakland: University of California Press.

Gleeson, Shannon, and Roberto G. Gonzales. 2012. "When Do Papers Matter? An Institutional Analysis of Undocumented Life in the United States." *International Migration* 50 (4): 1–19.

Gleeson, Shannon, and Kati L. Griffith. 2022. "Workers with Temporary Protected Status: The Value and Limits of Delinking Immigration and Employment Status." In *Race, Gender and Contemporary International Labor Migration Regimes*, edited by Leticia Saucedo and Robyn Magalit Rodriguez, 112–125. Northampton, MA: Edward Elgar Publishing.

Gleeson, Shannon, and Prerna Sampat. 2017. "Immigrant Resistance in the Age of Trump." *New Labor Forum* 27 (1): 86–95.

Glenn-Levin Rodriguez, Naomi. 2017. *Fragile Families: Foster Care, Immigration, and Citizenship*. Philadelphia: University of Pennsylvania Press.

Goffman, Alice. 2014. *On the Run: Fugitive Life in an American City*. Chicago: University of Chicago Press.

Golash-Boza, Tanya M. 2015 *Deported: Immigrant Policing, Disposable Labor, and Global Capitalism*. New York: New York University Press.

———. 2019. "Punishment beyond the Deportee: The Collateral Consequences of Deportation." *American Behavioral Scientist* 63 (9): 1331–1349.

Golash-Boza, Tanya M., and Zulema Valdez. 2018. "Nested Contexts of Reception: Undocumented Students at the University of California, Central." *Sociological Perspectives* 61 (4): 535–552.

Goldstein, Daniel M., and Carolina Alonso-Bejarano. 2017. "E-Terrify: Securitized Immigration and Biometric Surveillance in the Workplace." *Human Organization* 76 (1): 1–14.

Gomberg-Muñoz, Ruth. 2016. *Becoming Legal: Immigration Law and Mixed-Status Families*. Oxford: Oxford University Press.

Gomberg-Muñoz, Ruth, and Laura Nussbaum-Barberena. 2011. "Is Immigration Policy Labor Policy? Immigration Enforcement, Undocumented Workers, and the State." *Human Organization* 70 (4): 366–375.

Gómez Cervantes, Andrea, and Cecilia Menjívar. 2020. "Legal Violence, Health, and Access to Care: Latina Immigrants in Rural and Urban Kansas." *Journal of Health and Social Behavior* 61 (3): 307–323.

Gonzales, Alfonso. 2013. *Reform without Justice: Latino Migrant Politics and the Homeland Security State*. Oxford: Oxford University Press.

Gonzales, Roberto G. 2011. "Learning to Be Illegal: Undocumented Youth and Shifting Legal Contexts in the Transition to Adulthood." *American Sociological Review* 76 (4): 602–619.

———. 2015. *Lives in Limbo: Undocumented and Coming of Age in America*. Oakland: University of California Press.

Gonzales, Roberto G., Basia Ellis, Sarah A. Rendón-García, and Kristina Brant. 2018. "(Un)authorized Transitions: Illegality, DACA, and the Life Course." *Research in Human Development* 15 (3–4): 345–359.

Gonzales, Roberto G., and Leo Chavez. 2012. "'Awakening to a Nightmare': Abjectivity and Illegality in the Lives of Undocumented 1.5-Generation Latino Immigrants in the United States." *Current Anthropology* 53 (3): 255–281.

Gonzales, Roberto G., Carola Suárez-Orozco, and Maria Cecilia Dedios-Sanguineti. 2013. "No Place to Belong: Contextualizing Concepts of Mental Health among

Undocumented Immigrant Youth in the United States." *American Behavioral Scientist* 57 (8): 1174–1199.

Gonzales, Roberto G., Veronica Terriquez, and Stephen P. Ruszczyk. 2014. "Becoming DACAmented: Assessing the Short-Term Benefits of Deferred Action for Childhood Arrivals (DACA)." *American Behavioral Scientist* 58 (14): 1852–1872.

Gonzalez, Gabriela. 2023. "Undocumented Consciousness: Citizenship and Illegality in the Lives of US Citizen Youth." *Law & Policy* 45 (1): 45–65.

Gonzalez, Gabriela, and Caitlin Patler. 2021. "The Educational Consequences of Parental Immigration Detention." *Sociological Perspectives* 64 (2): 301–320.

Green, Kristen. 2019. "Sanctuary Campuses: The University's Role in Protecting Undocumented Students from Changing Immigration Policies." *UCLA Law Review* 66:1030.

Gulasekaram, Pratheepan, and S. Karthick Ramakrishnan. 2015. *The New Immigration Federalism*. Cambridge: Cambridge University Press.

Harrison, Jill Lindsey, and Sarah E. Lloyd. 2012. "Illegality at Work: Deportability and the Productive New Era of Immigration Enforcement." *Antipode* 44 (2): 365–385.

Harvey, David. 2005. "The Sociological and Geographical Imaginations." *International Journal of Politics, Culture, and Society* 18 (3/4): 211–255.

———. 2009. *Cosmopolitanism and the Geographies of Freedom*. New York City: Columbia University Press.

Haskins, Anna R., and Wade C. Jacobsen. 2017. "Schools as Surveilling Institutions? Paternal Incarceration, System Avoidance, and Parental Involvement in Schooling." *American Sociological Review* 82 (4): 657–684.

Heredia, Luisa Laura. 2015. "Of Radicals and DREAMers: Harnessing Exceptionality to Challenge Immigration Control." *Association of Mexican American Educators Journal* 9 (3): 74–85.

Hernández, Kelly Lytle. 2010. *Migra! A History of the U.S. Border Patrol*. Berkeley: University of California Press.

Hing, Bill. 2018. "Entering the Trump Ice Age: Contextualizing the New Immigration Enforcement Regime." *Texas A&M Law Review* 5 (2): 254–321.

Hoke, Morgan K., and Courtney E. Boen. 2021. "The Health Impacts of Eviction: Evidence from the National Longitudinal Study of Adolescent to Adult Health." *Social Science & Medicine* 273:113742.

Jones, Jennifer A. 2019. *The Browning of the New South*. Chicago: University of Chicago Press.

Jurkovic, Gregory J., Alison Thirkield, and Richard Morrell. 2001. "Parentification of Adult Children of Divorce: A Multidimensional Analysis." *Journal of Youth and Adolescence* 30:245–257.

Kalhan, Anil. 2013. "Immigration Policing and Federalism through the Lens of Technology, Surveillance, and Privacy." *Ohio State Law Journal* 74:1105–1165.

———. 2014. "Immigration Surveillance." *Maryland Law Review* 74 (1): 1–78.

Kanstroom, Daniel. 2010. *Deportation Nation: Outsiders in American History*. Cambridge, MA: Harvard University Press.

———. 2012. *Aftermath: Deportation Law and the New American Diaspora*. Oxford: Oxford University Press.

Kasinitz, Philip, Mary C. Waters, John H. Mollenkopf, and Jennifer Holdaway. 2008. *Inheriting the City: The Children of Immigrants Come of Age*. Cambridge, MA: Harvard University Press.

Kerwin, Donald, and Robert Warren. 2020. "US Foreign-Born Workers in the Global Pandemic: Essential and Marginalized." *Journal on Migration and Human Security* 8 (3): 282–300.

Kirksey, J. Jacob, and Carolyn Sattin-Bajaj. 2023. "Immigration and Customs Enforcement Raids the Pillar of a Community: Student Achievement, Absenteeism, and Mobility Following a Large Worksite Enforcement Operation in North Texas." *American Behavioral Scientist* (November). https://doi.org/10.1177/00027642231215992.

Kirksey, J. Jacob, Carolyn Sattin-Bajaj, Michael A. Gottfried, Jennifer Freeman, and Christopher S. Ozuna. 2020. "Deportations Near the Schoolyard: Examining Immigration Enforcement and Racial/Ethnic Gaps in Educational Outcomes." *AERA Open* 6 (1): 1–18.

Kocher, Austin. 2017. "The New Resistance: Immigrant Rights Mobilization in an Era of Trump." *Journal of Latin American Geography* 16 (2): 165–171.

Kubrin, Charis E., and Bradley J. Bartos. 2020. "Sanctuary Status and Crime in California: What's the Connection?" *Justice Evaluation Journal* 3 (2): 115–133.

Lauby, Fanny. 2018. "DACA Applications and Anxiety among Undocumented Youths." *International Journal of Migration, Health and Social Care* 14 (3): 318–331.

———. 2021. "The Leadership Challenge: Undocumented Youths in Social Movement Coalitions in the United States." *Social Movement Studies* 20 (5): 549–566.

Lefebvre, Henri. 1991. *The Production of Space*. Cambridge, MA: Blackwell.

León, Lucía. 2020. "Legalization through Marriage: When Love and Papers Converge." In *We Are Not Dreamers: Undocumented Scholars Theorize Undocumented Life in the United States*, edited by Leisy J. Abrego and Genevieve Negrón-Gonzales, 190–210. Durham, NC: Duke University Press.

Levitt, Peggy. 2001. *The Transnational Villagers*. Berkeley: University of California Press.

Levitt, Peggy, and Mary C. Waters. 2002. *The Changing Face of Home: The Transnational Lives of the Second Generation*. New York: Russell Sage Foundation.

Lipsitz, George. 2011. *How Racism Takes Place*. Philadelphia: Temple University Press.

López, Jane Lilly. 2021. *Unauthorized Love: Mixed-Citizenship Couples Negotiating Intimacy, Immigration, and the State*. Redwood City, CA: Stanford University Press.

Lopez, William D. 2019. *Separated: Family and Community in the Aftermath of an Immigration Raid*. Baltimore, MD: Johns Hopkins University Press.

Lovato, Kristina. 2019. "Forced Separations: A Qualitative Examining of How Latino/a Adolescents cope with Parental Deportation." *Children and Youth Services Review* 98: 42–50.

Maldonado Dominguez, Katy Joseline. 2020. "Undocumented Queer Parenting: Navigating External and Internal Threats to Family." In *We Are Not Dreamers: Undocumented Scholars Theorize Undocumented Life in the United States*, edited by Leisy J. Abrego and Genevieve Negrón-Gonzales, 211–234. Durham, NC: Duke University Press.

Martínez, Rafael A. 2024. *Illegalized: Undocumented Youth Movements in the United States*. Tucson: University of Arizona Press.

Martinez-Aranda, Mirian G. 2020. "Collective Liminality: The Spillover Effects of Indeterminate Detention on Immigrant Families." *Law & Society Review* 54 (4): 755–787.

———. 2022. "Extended Punishment: Criminalising Immigrants through Surveillance Technology." *Journal of Ethnic and Migration Studies* 48 (1): 74–91.

Martínez-Schuldt, Ricardo D., and Daniel E. Martínez. 2017. "Sanctuary Policies and City-Level Incidents of Violence, 1990 to 2010." *Justice Quarterly* 36 (4): 567–593.

Menjívar, Cecilia. 2000. *Fragmented Ties: Salvadoran Immigrant Networks in America*. Berkeley: University of California Press.

———. 2006. "Liminal Legality: Salvadoran and Guatemalan Immigrants' Lives in the United States." *American Journal of Sociology* 111 (4): 999–1037.

———. 2014. "The 'Poli-Migra': Multilayered Legislation, Enforcement Practices, and What We Can Learn About and from Today's Approaches." *American Behavioral Scientist* 58 (13): 1805–1819.

———. 2021. "The Racialization of 'Illegality.'" *Daedalus* 150 (2): 91–105.

Menjívar, Cecilia, and Leisy J. Abrego. 2012. "Legal Violence: Immigration Law and the Lives of Central American Immigrants." *American Journal of Sociology* 117 (5): 1380–1421.

Menjívar, Cecilia, Leisy J. Abrego, and Leah C. Schmalzbauer. 2016. *Immigrant Families*. Cambridge, UK: Polity Press.

Menjívar, Cecilia, and Daniel Kanstroom, eds. 2013. *Constructing Immigrant "Illegality": Critiques, Experiences, and Responses*. Cambridge: Cambridge University Press.

Menjívar, Cecilia, and Sarah M. Lakhani. 2016. "Transformative Effects of Immigration Law: Immigrants' Personal and Social Metamorphoses through Regularization." *American Journal of Sociology* 121 (6): 1818–1855.

Menjívar, Cecilia, William Paul Simmons, Daniel Alvord, and Elizabeth Salerno Valdez. 2018. "Immigration Enforcement, the Racialization of Legal Status, and Perceptions of the Police." *Du Bois Review: Social Science Research on Race* 15 (1): 107–128.

Merry, Sally Engel. 1990. *Getting Justice and Getting Even: Legal Consciousness among Working-Class Americans*. Chicago: University of Chicago Press.

Milkman, Ruth, ed. 2011. "Immigrant Workers, Precarious Work, and the US Labor Movement." *Globalizations* 8 (3): 361–372.

———. 2018. *Organizing Immigrants: The Challenge for Unions in Contemporary California*. Ithaca, NY: Cornell University Press.

Mills, C. Wright. 1959. *The Sociological Imagination*. Oxford: Oxford University Press.

Moinester, Margot. 2018. "Beyond the Border and into the Heartland: Spatial Patterning of U.S. Immigration Detention." *Demography* 55:1147–1193.

Morales, Maria Cristina, and Theodore R. Curry. 2021. "Citizenship Profiling and Diminishing Procedural Justice: Local Immigration Enforcement and the Reduction of Police Legitimacy among Individuals and in Latina/o Neighbourhoods." *Ethnic and Racial Studies* 44 (1): 134–153.

Motomura, Hiroshi. 1999. "Federalism, International Human Rights, and Immigration Exceptionalism." *University of Colorado Law Review* 70 (4): 1361–1394.

———. 2011. "The Discretion That Matters: Federal Immigration Enforcement, State and Local Arrests, and the Civil-Criminal Line." *UCLA Law Review* 58:1819–1858.

———. 2014. *Immigration Outside the Law*. Oxford: Oxford University Press.

Muñiz, Ana. 2020. "Secondary Ensnarement: Surveillance Systems in the Service of Punitive Immigration Enforcement." *Punishment & Society* 22 (4): 461–482.

———. 2022. *Borderland Circuitry: Immigration Surveillance in the United States and Beyond*. Oakland: University of California Press.

Muñoz, Susana M., Darsella Vigil, Elizabeth Jach, and Marisela Rodriguez-Gutierrez. 2018. "Unpacking Resilience and Trauma: Examining the 'Trump Effect' in Higher Education for Undocumented Latinx College Students." *Association of Mexican American Educators Journal* 12 (3): 33–52.

Negrón-Gonzales, Genevieve. 2013. "Navigating 'Illegality': Undocumented Youth & Oppositional Consciousness." *Children and Youth Services Review* 35 (8): 1284–1290.

———. 2014. "Undocumented, Unafraid, and Unapologetic: Re-articulatory Practices and Migrant Youth 'Illegality.'" *Latino Studies* 12:259–278.

Nevins, Joseph. 2002. *Operation Gatekeeper: The Rise of the "Illegal Alien" and the Remaking of the U.S.-Mexico Boundary*. New York: Routledge.

Ngai, Mae. 2004. *Impossible Subjects: Illegal Aliens and the Making of Modern America*. Princeton, NJ: Princeton University Press.

Nguyen, Mai Thi, and Hannah Gill. 2016. "Interior Immigration Enforcement: The Impacts of Expanding Local Law Enforcement Authority." *Urban Studies* 53 (2): 302–323.

Nicholls, Walter J. 2013. *The DREAMers: How the Undocumented Youth Movement Transformed the Immigrant Rights Debate*. Redwood City, CA: Stanford University Press.

———. 2020. "The Uneven Geographies of Politicisation: The Case of the Undocumented Immigrant Youth Movement in the United States." *Antipode* 53 (2): 465–485.

Nicholls, Walter J., and Tara Fiorito. 2015. "Dreamers Unbound: Immigrant Youth Mobilizing." *New Labor Forum* 24 (1): 86–92.

Nicholls, Walter J., Justus Uitermark, and Sander van Haperen. 2016. "The Networked Grassroots: How Radicals Outflanked Reformists in the United States' Immigrant Rights Movement." *Journal of Ethnic and Migration Studies* 42 (6): 1036–1054.

Nienhusser, H. Kenny, and Toko Oshio. 2018. "Awakened Hatred and Heightened Fears: 'The Trump Effect' on the Lives of Mixed-Status Families." *Cultural Studies ßà Critical Methodologies* 19 (3): 173–183.

Nuñez, Guillermina Gina, and Josiah Heyman. 2007. "Entrapment Processes and Immigrant Communities in a Time of Heightened Border Vigilance." *Human Organization* 66 (4): 354–365.

Ojeda, Victoria D., Christopher Magana, Jose Luis Burgos, and Adriana Carolnia Vargas-Ojeda. 2020. "Deported Men's and Father's Perspective: The Impacts of Family Separation on Children and Families in the U.S." *Frontiers in Psychiatry* 11.

Oliveira, Gabrielle. 2018. *Motherhood across Borders: Immigrants and Their Children in Mexico and New York*. New York: New York University Press.

Ousey, Graham C., and Charis E. Kubrin. 2018. "Immigration and Crime: Assessing a Contentious Issue." *Annual Review of Criminology* 1:63–84.

Pallares, Amalia, and Nilda Flores-Gonzalez. 2010. *¡Marcha! Latino Chicago and the Immigrant Rights Movement*. Champaign: University of Illinois Press.

Pandey, Kritika, Rhacel Salazar Parreñas, and Gianne Sheena Sabio. 2021. "Essential and Expendable: Migrant Domestic Workers and the COVID-19 Pandemic." *American Behavioral Scientist* 65 (1): 1287–1301.

Patiño, Jimmy. 2017. *Raza Sí, Migra No: Chicano Movement Struggles for Immigrant Rights in San Diego*. Chapel Hill: University of North Carolina Press.

Patler, Caitlin. 2010. "Alliance-Building and Organizing for Immigrant Rights: The Case of the Coalition for Humane Immigrant Rights of Los Angeles." In *Working for Justice: The L.A. Model of Organizing and Advocacy*., edited by Ruth Milkman, Joshua Bloom, and Victor Narro, 71–88. Ithaca, NY: Cornell University Press.

———. 2018. "To Reveal or Conceal: How Diverse Undocumented Youth Navigate Legal Status Disclosure." *Sociological Perspectives* 61 (6): 857–873.

Patler, Caitlin, and Jorge A. Cabrera. 2015. "From Undocumented to DACAmented: Impacts of the Deferred Action for Childhood Arrivals (DACA) Program." Institute for Research on Labor and Employment. https://escholarship.org/uc/item /3060d4z3.

Patler, Caitlin, and Gabriela Gonzalez. 2021. "Compounded Vulnerability: The Consequences of Immigration Detention for Institutional Attachment and System Avoidance in Mixed-Immigration-Status Families." *Social Problems* 68 (4): 886–902.

Patler, Caitlin, and Bradford Jones. 2025. "The US Deportation System: History, Impacts, and New Empirical Research." *RSF: The Russell Sage Foundation Journal of the Social Sciences* 11 (4).

Pérez Huber, Lindsay, and Susana M. Muñoz. 2021. *Why They Hate Us: How Racist Rhetoric Impacts Education*. New York City: Teachers College Press.

Pham, Huyen. 2008. "The Private Enforcement of Immigration Laws." *Georgetown Law Journal* 96:777–826.

Phillimore, Jenny, and Sin Yi Cheung. 2021. "The Violence of Uncertainty: Empirical Evidence on How Asylum Waiting Time Undermines Refugee Health." *Social Science Medicine* 282.

Prieto, Greg. 2018. *Immigrants under Threat: Risk and Resistance in Deportation Nation.* New York: New York University Press.

Provine, Doris Marie, and Monica W. Varsanyi. 2012. "Scaled Down: Perspectives on State and Local Creation and Enforcement of Immigration Law; Introduction to the Special Issue of Law & Policy." *Law & Policy* 34 (2): 105.

Provine, Doris Marie, Monica W. Varsanyi, Paul G. Lewis, and Scott H. Decker. 2016. *Policing Immigrants: Local Law Enforcement on the Front Lines.* Chicago: University of Chicago Press.

Ramakrishnan, S. Karthick, and Irene Bloemraad, eds. 2008. *Civic Hopes and Political Realities: Immigrants, Community Organizations, and Political Engagement.* New York: Russell Sage Foundation.

Ramirez, Blanca A. 2023. "Anchoring Work: How Latinx Mixed-Status Families Respond to Interior Immigration Enforcement." *Journal of Ethnic and Migration Studies* 50 (4): 772–791.

Rios, Victor M. 2011. *Punished: Policing the Lives of Black and Latino Boys.* New York: New York University Press.

Robles, Jozef C. 2024. "Remnants of Illegality: DACA, Legal Status, and Unlearning Illegality." *Journal of Ethnic and Migration Studies* 51 (9): 2203–21.

Rodriguez, Cassaundra. 2023. *Contested Americans: Mixed-Status Families in Anti-Immigrant Times.* New York: New York University Press.

Rodriguez Vega, Silvia. 2023. *Drawing Deportation: Art and Resistance among Immigrant Children.* New York: New York University Press.

Rojas-Flores, Lisseth, Mari L. Clements, J. Hwang Koo, and Judy London. 2017. "Trauma and Psychological Distress in Latino Citizen Children Following Parental Detention and Deportation." *Psychological Trauma: Theory, Research, Practice and Policy* 9 (3): 352–361.

Romero, Mary. 2006. "Racial Profiling and Immigration Law Enforcement: Rounding Up of Usual Suspects in the Latino Community." *Critical Sociology* 32 (2–3): 447–473.

Rosales, Rocío. 2020. *Street Vending, Illegality, and Ethnic Community in Los Angeles.* Oakland: University of California Press.

Roth, Benjamin J. 2019. "The Double Bind of DACA: Exploring the Legal Violence of Liminal Status for Undocumented Youth." *Ethnic and Racial Studies* 42 (15): 2548–2565.

Rumbaut, Ruben. 2006. "Ages, Life Stages, and Generational Cohorts: Decomposing the Immigrant First and Second Generations in the United States." *International Migration Review* 38 (3): 1160–1205.

Ryo, Emily. 2017. "Fostering Legal Cynicism through Immigration Detention." *California Law Review* 90 (5): 999–1054.

Ryo, Emily, and Ian Peacock. 2019. "Beyond the Walls: The Importance of Community Contexts in Immigration Detention." *American Behavioral Scientist* 63 (9): 1250–1275.

Schmalzbauer, Leah. 2006. *Striving and Surviving: A Daily Life Analysis of Honduran Transnational Families.* New York: Routledge.

———. 2014. *The Last Best Place? Gender, Family, and Migration in the New West.* Redwood City, CA: Stanford University Press.

Schwab, William A. 2018. *Dreams Derailed: Undocumented Youths in the Trump Era.* Fayetteville: University of Arkansas Press.

Seif, Hinda. 2011. "Unapologetic and Unafraid: Immigrant Youth Come out from the Shadows." *New Directions for Child and Adolescent Development* 134:59–75.

Serrano, Uriel, Andrea Del Carmen Vazquez, Raul Meneses Samperio, and Allison Mattheis. 2018. "Symbolic Sanctuary and Discursive Dissonance: Limitations of Policy and Practice to Support Undocumented Students at Hispanic Serving Institutions." *AMAE* 12 (3): 169.

Sherman-Stokes, Sarah. 2021. "Public Health and the Power to Exclude: Immigrant Expulsions at the Border." *Georgetown Immigration Law Journal* 36 (1): 261–290.

Silver, Alexis. 2014. "Families across Borders: The Emotional Impacts of Migration on Origin Families." *International Migration* 52 (3): 194–220.

———. 2018. *Shifting Boundaries: Immigrant Youth, Negotiating National, State, and Small-Town Politics.* Redwood City, CA: Stanford University Press.

Simmons, William Paul, Cecilia Menjívar, and Elizabeth Salerno Valdez. 2021. "The Gendered Effects of Local Immigration Enforcement: Latinas' Social Isolation in Chicago, Houston, Los Angeles, and Phoenix." *International Migration Review* 55 (1): 108–134.

Smith, Robert C. 2006. *Mexican New York: Transnational Lives of New Immigrants.* Berkeley: University of California Press.

Smith, Robert Courtney, Andrés Besserer Rayas, Daisy Flores, Angelo Cabrera, Guillermo Yrizar Barbosa, Karina Weinstein, Maria Xique, Michelle Bialeck, and Eduardo Torres. 2021. "Disrupting the Traffic Stop-to-Deportation Pipeline: The New York State Greenlight Law's Intent and Implementation." *Journal on Migration and Human Security* 9 (2): 94–110.

Soja, Edward. 1996. *Thirdspace: Journeys to Los Angeles and Other Real-and-Imagined Places.* Cambridge, MA: Blackwell.

Soltz Chinchilla, Norma, Nora Hamilton, and James Loucky. 2009. "The Sanctuary Movement and Central American Activism in Los Angeles." *Latin American Perspectives* 36 (6): 101–126.

Spiro, Peter J. 1997. "Learning to Life with Immigration Federalism." *Connecticut Law Review* 29 (4): 1627–1646.

Stuesse, Angela. 2018. "When They're Done with You: Legal Violence and Structural Vulnerability among Injured Immigrant Poultry Workers." *Anthropology of Work Review* 39 (2): 79–93.

Stumpf, Juliet P. 2006. "The Crimmigration Crisis: Immigrants, Crime, and Sovereign Power." *American University Law Review* 56 (2): 368–419.

———. 2012. "Getting to Work: Why Nobody Cares about E-Verify (And Why They Should)." *UC Irvine Law Review* 2 (1): 381–414.

Suárez-Orozco, Carola, and Marcelo M. Suárez-Orozco. 2013. "Transnationalism of the Heart: Familyhood across Borders." In *What Is Parenthood: Contemporary*

Debates about the Family, edited by Linda C. McClain and Daniel Cere, 279–298. New York: New York University Press.

Suárez-Orozco, Carola, Marcelo M. Suárez-Orozco, and Irina Todorova. 2009. *Learning a New Land: Immigrant Students in American Society*. Cambridge, MA: Harvard University Press.

Suárez-Orozco, Carola, Hirokazu Yoshikawa, Robert R. Ternashi, and Marcelo M. Suárez-Orozco. 2011. "Growing Up in the Shadows: The Developmental Implications of Unauthorized Status." *Harvard Educational Review* 81 (3): 438–471.

Swerts, Thomas. 2015. "Gaining a Voice: Storytelling and Undocumented Youth Activism in Chicago." *Mobilization: An International Quarterly* 20 (3): 345–360.

Terriquez, Veronica. 2017. "Legal Status, Civic Organizations, and Political Participation among Latino Young Adults." *Sociological Quarterly* 58 (2): 315–336.

Terriquez, Veronica, Tizoc Brenes, and Abdiel Lopez. 2018. "Intersectionality as a Multipurpose Collective Action Frame: The Case of the Undocumented Youth Movement." *Ethnicities* 18 (2): 260–276.

Terriquez, Veronica, and May Lin. 2019. "Yesterday They Marched, Today They Mobilised the Vote: A Developmental Model for Civic Leadership among the Children of Immigrants." *Journal of Ethnic and Migration Studies* 46 (4): 747–769.

Terriquez, Veronica, and Ruth Milkman. 2021. "Immigrant and Refugee Youth Organizing in Solidarity with the Movement for Black Lives." *Gender & Society* 35 (4): 577–587.

Unzueta Carrasco, Tania A., and Hinda Seif. 2014. "Disrupting the Dream: Undocumented Youth Reframe Citizenship and Deportability through Anti-deportation Activism." *Latino Studies* 12 (2): 279–299.

Unzueta, Tania, Maru Mora Villalpando, and Angélica Cházaro. 2018. "We Fell in Love in a Hopeless Place: A Grassroots History from #Not1More to Abolish ICE." Medium. https://medium.com/@LaTania/we-fell-in-love-in-a-hopeless-place-a-grassroots-history-from-not1more-to-abolish-ice-23089cf21711.

Uprichard, Emma. 2008. "Children as 'Being and Becomings': Children, Childhood and Temporality." *Children & Society* 22 (4): 303–313.

Valdez, Carmen R., Kevin M. Wagner, and Laura P. Minero. 2021. "Emotional Reactions and Coping of Mexican Mixed-Status Immigrant Families in Anticipation of the 2016 Presidential Election." *Family Process* 60 (2): 623–638.

Valdivia, Carolina. 2015. "DREAMer Activism: Challenges and Opportunities." In *Undocumented Latino Youth: Navigating Their Worlds*, edited by Marisol Clark-Ibáñez, 163–178. Boulder, CO: Lynne Rienner.

———. 2019a. "Expanding Geographies of Deportability: How Immigration Enforcement at the Local Level Affects Undocumented and Mixed-Status Families: Expanding Geographies of Deportability." *Law & Policy* 41 (1): 103–119.

———. 2019b. "Youth Activism." In *Il/legal Encounters: Migration, Detention, and Deportation in the Lives of Young People*, edited by Deborah A. Boehm and Susan J. Terrio, 147–158. New York: New York University Press.

———. 2020. "Undocumented Young Adults' Heightened Vulnerability in the Trump Era." In *We Are Not Dreamers: Undocumented Scholars Theorize Undocumented Life in the United States*, edited by Leisy J. Abrego and Genevieve Negrón-Gonzales, 127–145. Durham, NC: Duke University Press.

———. 2021. "I Became a Mom Overnight: How Parental Detentions and Deportations Impact Young Adults' Role." *Harvard Educational Review* 91 (1): 62–82.

———. 2025. "Hyper-Illegality, Reentry, and Everyday Life in the United States Post-Deportation." *RSF: The Russell Sage Foundation Journal of the Social Sciences* 11 (4).

Valdivia, Carolina, Marisol Clark-Ibáñez, and Daniela Carreon. 2022. "'I'll Be Risking Myself Just to Get an Education': How Local-Level Immigration Enforcement Impacts undocumented Students' Pathways to College." *Journal of Ethnic and Migration Studies* 49 (5): 1154–1172.

Valdivia, Carolina, Marisol Clark-Ibáñez, Josefina Espino, and Carolina Lopez. 2021a. "'You Can't Learn If You Don't Feel Safe': Educators Working with Undocumented High School Students." In *Why They Hate Us: How Racist Rhetoric Impacts Education*, edited by Susana M. Muñoz and Lindsay Perez Huber, 93–119. New York: Teachers College Press.

Valdivia, Carolina, Marisol Clark-Ibáñez, Lucas Schacht, Juan Duran, and Sussana Mendoza. 2021b. "Heightened Uncertainty and Determination: The 'Trump Effect' and College Aspirations for Undocumented Students." *Journal of College Access* 6 (4): 28–43.

Valdivia, Carolina, and Angie B. Monreal. 2025. "Fear, Stigma, Hope, and *Desahogó*: Understanding the Role of Deportation History and Familial Ties on the Disclosure Process of Immigration-Related Experiences." *Journal of Ethnic and Migration Studies* 51 (11): 2873–2890.

Van Hook, Jennifer, and Jennifer E. Glick. 2020. "Spanning Borders, Cultures, and Generations: A Decade of Research on Immigrant Families." *Journal of Marriage and Family* 82 (1): 224–243.

Varsanyi, Monica W. 2008. "Immigration Policing through the Backdoor: City Ordinances, the 'Right to the City', and the Exclusion of Undocumented Day Laborers." *Urban Geography* 29 (1): 29–52.

———. 2010. *Taking Local Control: Immigration Policy Activism in U.S. Cities and States*. Redwood City, CA: Stanford University Press.

Varsanyi, Monica W., Paul G. Lewis, Doris Marie Provine, and Scott Decker. 2012. "A Multilayered Jurisdictional Patchwork: Immigration Federalism in the United States." *Law & Policy* 34 (2): 138–158.

Vega, Irene I. 2018. "Empathy, Morality, and Criminality: The Legitimation Narratives of U.S. Border Patrol Agents." *Journal of Ethnic and Migration Studies* 44 (15): 2544–2561.

———. 2025. *Bordering on Indifference: Race and Morality in Immigration Enforcement*. Princeton, NJ: Princeton University Press.

Villazor, Rose Cuison, and Alma Godinez-Navarro. 2019. "Sanctuary States." *Southwestern Law Review* 48:503–524.

Villegas, Paloma E. 2019. "I Made Myself Small Like a Cat and Ran Away': Workplace Sexual Harassment, Precarious Immigration Status and Legal Violence." *Journal of Gender Studies* 28 (6): 674–686.

von Werthern, Martha, Katy Robjant, Zoe Chui, Rachel Schon, Livia Ottisova, Claire Mason, and Cornelius Katona. 2018. "The Impact of Immigration Detention on Mental Health: A Systematic Review." *BMC Psychiatry* 18: 1–19.

Voss, Kim, and Irene Bloemraad, eds. 2011. *Rallying for Immigrant Rights: The Fight for Inclusion in 21st Century America*. Berkeley: University of California Press.

Walsh, James P. 2014. "Watchful Citizens: Immigration Control, Surveillance and Societal Participation." *Social & Legal Studies* 23 (2): 237–259.

Wang, Nina, Allison McDonald, Daniel Bateyko, and Emily Tucker. 2022. *American Dragnet: Data-Driven Deportation in the 21st Century*. Washington, DC: Center on Privacy & Technology at Georgetown Law.

Waters, Mary C., and Marisa Gerstein Pineau, eds. 2015. *The Integration of Immigrants into American Society (Report of the National Academy of Sciences Consensus Committee on Integrating Immigrants into American Society)*. Washington, DC: National Academies Press.

Willen, Sarah S. 2007. "Toward a Critical Phenomenology of 'Illegality': State Power, Criminalization, and Abjectivity among Undocumented Migrant Workers in Tel Aviv, Israel." *International Migration* 45 (3): 8–38.

Wong, Tom K., Angela S. Garcia, and Carolina Valdivia. 2019. "The Political Incorporation of Undocumented Youth." *Social Problems* 66 (3): 356–372.

Wong, Tom K., S. Deborah Kang, Carolina Valdivia, Josefina Espino, Michelle Gonzalez, and Ella Peralta. 2021. "How Interior Immigration Enforcement Affects Trust in Law Enforcement." *Perspectives on Politics* 19 (2): 357–370.

Yoshikawa, Hirokazu. 2011. *Immigrants Raising Citizens: Undocumented Parents and Their Children*. New York: Russell Sage Foundation.

Zatz, Marjorie S., and Nancy Rodriguez. 2015. *Dreams and Nightmares: Immigration Policy, Youth, and Families*. Oakland: University of California Press.

Zayas, Luis H. 2015. *Forgotten Citizens: Deportation, Children, and the Making of American Exiles and Orphans*. Oxford: Oxford University Press.

Zepeda-Millán, Chris. 2017. *Latino Mass Mobilization: Immigration, Racialization, and Activism*. Cambridge: Cambridge University Press.

Zepeda-Millán, Chris, and Sophia Wallace. 2018. "Mobilizing for Immigrant and Latino Rights under Trump." In *The Resistance: The Dawn of the Anti-Trump Opposition Movement*, edited by. David S. Meyer and Sidney Tarrow, 90–108. Oxford: Oxford University Press.

Zimmerman, Arely M. 2011. "A Dream Detained: Undocumented Latino Youth and the DREAM Movement." *NACLA Report on the Americas* 44 (6): 14–17.

INDEX

Italicized page numbers refer to figures

Camp Pendleton, *30,* 33
caretaking, 4, 19, 33, 73, 84–86, 100, 102–3.
    See also backup parents
Carlos (case study), 44, 63
Carlsbad, CA, 29, *30*
Carmen (case study), 50–51, 90–91, 110,
    111–12, 116
Cassandra (case study), 81
Castro, Julian, 172
Catalina (case study), 147
Catholic Charities of San Diego, 146
Cebulko, Kara, 193n8
Cecilia (case study), 125
Center for Constitutional Rights, 163
Center on Privacy and Technology, 13
Central America, 22, 189n74. *See also*
    individual countries
Central Valley, 32
Cervantes family (Natalia and Yuridia),
    40–41, 45, 53–54, 79–80
Chavez, Leo, 31
checkpoints, 74, 77, 80, 109, 116, 118, 138,
    144, 158, 162–63, 173, 193n9, 195n13;
    DUI, 21, 33, 45–49, 55, 63, 66, 75, 81, 120,
    134, 141–42, 145–46, 148, 166, 182,
    198n34; enforcement at, 20–21, 23; in/
    around San Diego County, 31, 39–49,
    55; mobile, 39; Rio Grande Valley,
    192n6; San Clemente, 39, 43; Temecula,
    39, 43, 117; as traditional enforcement
    site, 5, 16–17, 38, 64
Child Protective Services (CPS), 83
Chula Vista, CA, 29, *30,* 44
citizenship, 24, 134, 150, 191n106; birthright,
    131; and mixed-status families, 24, 80,
    103; pathways to, 26, 35, 136–37, 165;
    private, 11
Clara (case study), 89–90
Clark-Ibáñez, Marisol, 66
CLEAR, 13
Coalition for Humane Immigrant Rights
    (CHIRLA), 136
college, 42, 70–71, 81–82, 88, 91, 98–99,
    102, 108, 113, 116–19, 122–23, 130, 146–
    47, 176, 179; and disclosure, 18, 124–26,
    167. *See also* financial aid
Coming Out of the Shadows rallies, 136

comites de resistencia (self-defense patrols),
    142
communal erasure, 121–22, 168–69
community organizing, 44, 47, 144,
    147–52, 176
COMPASS program (formerly Dreamer
    Resource Office), 146
Comprehensive Immigration Reform
    (CIR), 137, 155, 177
confinement phase, *25, 26, 28,* 161
contexts of reception, 15
coping mechanisms, 19, 59, 71–72, 82,
    84–87, 100, 104, 115, 123–29, 194n3
Coronado, CA, 29, *30*
Cougar Care Network, 147
covert enforcement, 7–8, 157. *See also*
    enforcement in the shadows
COVID-19 pandemic, 150
Criminal Alien Program, 11
criminalization, 8, 90, 135, 137, 156, 158, 172,
    188n61
crimmigration, 157–58
Crystal (case study), 116
Customs and Border Protection (CBP), 3,
    44, 52, 54, 128. *See also* Border Patrol

Daria (case study), 98–99
databases, 8, 11–13, 156, 166
data exploitation, 8
de facto deportation, 76, 83, 195n10
Deferred Action for Childhood Arrivals
    (DACA), 3, *25,* 49, 50, 52–54, 65, 67,
    107–8, 124, 130, 134, 136, 140, 151, 156,
    161, 185n5; application requirements,
    196n6; attacks on, 36–37, 57, 103, 114–15,
    131, 173; and checkpoints, 40, 44, 49,
    63, 74; exclusions from, 113, 196n6;
    limits of, 119–21, 194n23; and mixed-
    status families, 20, 24–26, 75–77,
    80–81, 92–93, 100, 102–5, 111–12,
    168–69
Deferred Action for Parents of Americans,
    168
De Genova, Nicholas, 13, 15
Delgado, Vanessa, 189n82
Del Mar, CA, 29, *30,* 33, 54
Democratic Party, 26, 156, 177

Department of Homeland Security (DHS), 11, 13, 173–74
Department of Justice (DOJ), 174
Department of Motor Vehicles (DMV), 10, 13, 79, 166
deportability, definition of, 15
deportation: as a continuum, 27; consequences of, 2–4, 18–19, 27–28, *28*, 42, 58, 72, 75–76, 81–87, 90, 92, 95–99, 103, 106–8, 111–12, 122–27; dreams about, 52; as legal violence, 22; meaning of, 21–22, 75–76, 101, 109; types of, 26
depression, 26–27, *28,* 87, 96, 112–14, 127, 131, 139
detention, 4, 6, 11, 73, 92, 126, 138, 159, 180, 190n104, 197n13; at checkpoints, 41, 42, 45, 50, 64; by civilians, 175; and communal erasure, 122; and confinement stage, 26, *28;* of DACA recipients, 194n23; and deportation, 98; detention centers, 2, 9, 12, 14, 26, 38, 49, 88, 191n106; and familial responsibilities, 93; fear of, 18, 51, 107, 152; at hot spots, 49, 86, 199n13; and legal brokering, 72, 88–89, 94; as legal violence, 22; political organizing around, 140, 147, 149; at USCIS, 196n9; and workplace enforcement, 105
disclosure, 125, 140; of deportation history, 125–27; by proxy, 151–52, 154; to school personnel, 83, 98–99, 126; selective, 18
discount stores, 10; targeted as hot spots, 53–55
discrimination, 10, 42, 76, 124
DREAM Act, 135–37, 197n13
DREAMer narrative, 137
Dreamer Center, 146
dreams, 51–52, 71, 113, 116, 129, 177, 193n17
driver's licenses, 2, 17, 31, 45–46, 63, 72, 74, 79–80, 92, 102, 118, 120, 145, 185n2, 193n11
Durante, Rubén (case study), 107

Eastlake, CA, 44
El Cajon, CA, 29, *30,* 174
el castigo (re-entry bars), 170. *See also* bars to reentry/status adjustment
El Salvador, 18

Emiliano (case study), 106
Emily (case study), 139
emotional anchoring, 5, 19, 33–35, 73, 84–87, 90–94, 99–100, 104, 112, 140, 160, 167, 176, 189n82; definition of, 72, 189n81
emotional support, 5, 19, 34, 71, 85–86, 94, 123, 127, 168, 176
employers, 1, 37, 77, 89, 107–8, 122; as immigration enforcers, 5, 7–11, 50, 64, 67, 105, 153, 158–59. *See also* E-Verify
Encinitas, CA, 29, *30*
enforcement in the shadows, 1–35, 43, 47, 53, 63, 116, 133–34, 155–59, 163–66, 170; and backup parenting, 78, 99; and family separation, 96, 130; and fear, 37–38, 59, 70; and hot spots, 43; and legal brokering, 189n82; political organizing around, 140–41, 148, 152–53; in Trump's second term, 172–77
enforcement status: definition of, 6–7; familial, 6, 28–29, 35, 42, 49, 60, 65, 88, 91–101, 112, 119, 124, 140
English language, 43, 76, 88, 94, 141
Erika (case study), 138–39, 150
Ernesto (case study), 65
Escondido, CA, 29, *30,* 31, 33, 36, 43, 46, 53–55, *56,* 63, 142, 145, 155, 159
Escondido Police Department (EPD), 142, 159
ethnic grocery stores: targeted as hot spots, 5, 8, 10, 16, 33, 53–55, 67, 159, 180
E-Verify, 9–11, 50, 105, 186n22
evictions, 61, 161
expedited removal, 174, 191n113
expulsion phase, *25,* 26–27, *28,* 62, 161

Facebook, 36, 133, 141, 143, 145, 150
Fallbrook, CA, *30,* 31, 43
family enforcement status, 6, 28–29, 35, 42, 49, 60, 65, 88, 91–101, 112, 119, 124, 140
family reunification, 3–4, 73, 75, 109, 111, 122; after deportation, 6, 27, *28,* 95–96, 97, 125, 171–72, 195n10
Fatima (case study), 54, 126
feeling: of anxiety, 23, 26, *28,* 37, 51, 67, 77, 87, 91, 113–14, 121, 128, 131, 155; of being

Founded in 1893,
UNIVERSITY OF CALIFORNIA PRESS
publishes bold, progressive books and journals
on topics in the arts, humanities, social sciences,
and natural sciences—with a focus on social
justice issues—that inspire thought and action
among readers worldwide.

The UC PRESS FOUNDATION
raises funds to uphold the press's vital role
as an independent, nonprofit publisher, and
receives philanthropic support from a wide
range of individuals and institutions—and from
committed readers like you. To learn more, visit
ucpress.edu/supportus.

www.ingramcontent.com/pod-product-compliance
Lightning Source LLC
Chambersburg PA
CBHW032348280326
41935CB00008B/487